MARITAL CRUELTY IN ANTEBELLUM AMERICA

CONFLICTING WORLDS

New Dimensions of the American Civil War

T. Michael Parrish, *Series Editor*

MARITAL CRUELTY

IN

ANTEBELLUM

AMERICA

ROBIN C. SAGER

LOUISIANA STATE UNIVERSITY PRESS

BATON ROUGE

Published with the assistance of the V. Ray Cardozier Fund

Published by Louisiana State University Press
Copyright © 2016 by Louisiana State University Press
All rights reserved
Manufactured in the United States of America
First printing

DESIGNER: *Mandy McDonald Scallan*
TYPEFACE: *Sentinel*
PRINTER AND BINDER: *Maple Press (Digital)*

Library of Congress Cataloging-in-Publication Data
Names: Sager, Robin C., 1981– author.
Title: Marital cruelty in Antebellum America / Robin C. Sager.
Description: Baton Rouge : Louisiana State University Press, [2016] | Series:
   Conflicting worlds : new dimensions of the American Civil War | Includes
   bibliographical references and index.
Identifiers: LCCN 2015040209| ISBN 978-0-8071-6310-8 (cloth : alk. paper)
   | ISBN
   978-0-8071-6311-5 (pdf) | ISBN 978-0-8071-6312-2 (epub) | ISBN 978-0-
   8071-6313-9 (mobi)
Subjects: LCSH: Marriage—United States—History—19th century. | Spousal
   abuse—United States—History—19th century. | Marital violence—United
   States—History—19th century. | Divorce—United States—History—19th
   century. | United States—Social conditions—To 1865.
Classification: LCC HQ535 .S24 2016 | DDC 306.81097309/034—dc23
LC record available at http://lccn.loc.gov/2015040209

CONTENTS

ACKNOWLEDGMENTS

Throughout the process of creating this work I have benefited from the assistance of many individuals and organizations. As a result, this book serves as a witness of their efforts as much as it reflects my own. To being with, I would like to thank John Boles for combining insightful intellectual guidance with an always appreciated dose of good humor and humanity. It was a joy to work with and learn from him. From the project's start, Stephanie Camp and Rosemary Hennessy challenged me to maintain a critical approach to the material. Stephanie, we will miss you. Other Rice University scholars and friends, including Edward Cox, Rebecca Goetz, and Lynda Crist, bolstered my own enthusiasm with their unflagging support.

My thanks extend well beyond Rice. I would like to express my appreciation for Vern Woods, my second grade teacher, whom I cherish to this day. At Austin College, my undergraduate mentor Light Cummins ignited my passion for historical inquiry and taught me the value of public service. I also need to recognize the efforts of Gregg Cantrell, my master's thesis adviser at Texas Christian University, who has been involved in every step of my graduate career. My thanks go to Stephanie Cole, who took me under her wing and greatly expanded my knowledge of nineteenth-century women's history.

My colleagues in the Department of History at the University of Evansville were helpful and encouraging during the final stages of the project. In addition, it gives me great pleasure to acknowledge the generous financial support of the following individuals and institutions: Rice University Department of History, Humanities Research Center, and Center for the Study of Women, Gender, and Sexuality; Dolph Briscoe Center for American History at the University of Texas at Austin; the Western Association of Women's Historians; and the Friends of the Wisconsin Libraries. In addition, a Mellon Research Fellowship from the Virginia Historical Society gave me the time and resources needed to dig deep into the intimate writings of antebellum southerners.

I also wish to thank the archival staffs at the Texas State Library and Archives, Dallas Public Library, East Texas Research Center, Sam Houston Regional Library and Research Center, Victoria Regional History Center, Library of Virginia, University of Wisconsin's Area Research Centers, Wisconsin Historical Society, Albert H. Small Special Collections Library at the University of Virginia, Dolph Briscoe Center for American History at the University of Texas at Austin, Earl Gregg Swem Library at the College of William and Mary, Virginia Historical Society, and the Rare Book, Manuscript, and Special Collections Library at Duke University. Thanks are extended as well to the numerous court clerks who kindly provided me with access to countless boxes of legal records.

Additionally, earlier versions of this study were presented at various academic conferences, including the American Historical Association, the American Society for Legal History, the International Conference on the History of Alcohol and Drugs, and the Texas State Historical Association. I wish to recognize the efforts of those scholars who took the time to comment on my work. My thanks also go out to my series editor, T. Michael Parrish; to the Louisiana State University Press marketing team; to my editors at the Press, Rand Dotson and Neal Novak; and to Gary Von Euer for his meticulous, and much appreciated, copyediting. It has been a real pleasure to work with such respected and valued professionals. I would also like to extend my appreciation to the press manuscript reader for such astute comments and observations on the work.

Above all, this book is dedicated to my family and friends. I have been blessed with the gift of a fiercely loyal and loving "inner circle," a fact that I give thanks for every day. Mari Plikuhn inspired me with her positive attitude and her professional accomplishments. My siblings, Britt, Will, and Katie, offered continual support and refused to let me take myself too seriously. I would also like to thank my dad, Woody, who oversaw this book from afar and who passed along his love of a good story. My cherished friend and mom, Debbie, taught me the value of dedication and the importance of following one's passions. Her encouragement gave me the strength to take risks, learn from failures, and celebrate victories. Mark, you are okay too. And,

Cleopatra, thank you for deleting passages of problematic prose with feline efficiency. I owe a particular debt of gratitude to my husband John, who lived with this work from inception to completion. The solid foundation of our relationship made it possible for me to venture forth and explore the challenges faced by other couples throughout history. It takes a truly exceptional man to love and tolerate a woman who has conflict on the mind for years on end. For these reasons and many others, I will always hold dear his partnership and friendship. To Henry, thank you for timing your arrival to coincide with the completed manuscript and for being a wonderful illustration that family matters most.

MARITAL CRUELTY IN ANTEBELLUM AMERICA

Introduction

Mary Jane Lansing appeared before the Winnebago County, Wisconsin, Circuit Court in 1862. She sought a divorce from her husband of ten years, Andrew, on the grounds of cruelty. Within her bill of complaint and accompanying deposition, Mary related a tale of intense suffering at the hands of her husband. After only a single year of marriage, Andrew embarked on a spree of domestic terror in which he sought to break down his wife's mental and physical faculties. His preferred mode of attack involved striking her on the head with blunt instruments while simultaneously wishing aloud for her death. The disjointed nature of his ramblings only added to her terror. In May of 1859 he slammed her against the bedroom wall, proclaiming, "Dam you I ought to have killed you years ago God damn you I will kill you-you need not think I am afraid to kill you." On one occasion when Mary lay in bed recovering from an illness, Andrew crept in the room and whispered that "he hoped she would have a relapse & die." Even with intervals of recovery her health remained fragile as a result of her husband's continuous assaults. She asked the circuit judge to save her life by dissolving her marriage. The court granted her request.[1]

The final verdict in the Lansing case, unfortunately, obscures as much as it reveals. On the surface it appears as if Mary came before the court, satisfied the legal threshold for divorce, and won her case. While accurate, this brief overview of events fails to capture the ways in which the Lansing case pushed the court and community to engage in a discussion regarding the proper treatment of spousal partners. Mary's claims set off a chain reaction of contemplation and conversation. Neighbors, relatives, and boarders in the ever-growing county all came forward to present their own unique account of the Lansing union. Some argued that the couple's mismatched personalities doomed them from the start, while others saw the potential for an amicable reunion. Fraught with high emotion, the available evidence reveals average men and women struggling to make sense of a complex situation. Armed with minimal to no formal legal knowledge, court participants sketched the outlines of what marital dysfunction looked like in antebellum America. In doing so, they brought the generally hidden subject of domestic violence into the light and reflected upon its meaning.

Countless conversations of this nature took place across antebellum America, forcing society to examine the boundaries between acceptable and unacceptable marital behaviors. Focusing on the struggles of aggrieved spouses, this book explores a series of questions that address the nature of marriage, violence, and region in the pre–Civil War United States. It seeks to understand: What was *cruel* in the mid-nineteenth century? Specifically, what was cruel *in marriage*? Who was, or could be, cruel? Who could know about domestic cruelty? How did understandings of marital discord vary between regions? Did instances of marital cruelty in southern or frontier societies reflect a uniquely violent context, as we have heretofore thought? While clearly not the norm, marriages in crisis forced men and women to examine and affirm their core values in the face of failure. Unfortunately for historians, intimate conflicts of this sort generally stayed behind closed doors, except when they spilled out into the public arena and left their mark on the archive via divorce proceedings. To ascertain the nature of marital cruelty, this work analyzes over 1,500 divorce cases across Virginia, Texas, and Wisconsin from 1840 to 1860.

The institution of marriage has always been a lightning rod for public discussion. During the two decades leading up to the Civil War, the conversations and controversies regarding matrimony reached a fevered pitch. This era encompassed the principal years of the divorce debates, the formative period of the women's rights movement, as well as the beginning of campaigns against cruelty in the United States. It was also during this time that men and women across the country engaged in a struggle to determine what exactly it meant to be married. The stakes were high. Marriage helped to regulate everything from labor relations to emotional stability. Because of its foundational role in society, any perceived threats or changes to marital norms brought to the surface latent fears of social chaos. Sensationalistic newspaper reports highlighting alternative relationship forms and dramatic divorce trials only fed the growing anxiety felt by the general populace.[2]

In this period of competing marital norms, divorce offered a potential safety valve for unhappy spouses. As documented by Nancy Cott, the percentage of couples pursuing separations climbed in the years leading up to the Civil War, causing panic for those who viewed divorce as contributing to the overall downfall of marriage. Legal divorce in the nineteenth century was adversarial, requiring one spouse to find fault with the other. The general outcome of most cases fell into three categories: absolute divorce, *a vinculo matrimonii,* with permission to remarry; bed and board separations, *a mensa et thoro,* denying the right to remarry; or, no divorce granted, thus keeping the union legally intact. Men and women received divorces for a wide array of reasons, including adultery, impotence, and desertion. Out of all possible grounds, cruelty presented a particular problem in that it was difficult to define and measure. When discussing legal cruelty, the conversations focused on where exactly to draw the line separating cruelty from insensitivity or abrasiveness. For the first quarter of the nineteenth century the vast majority of American judges and legislators were content to reference the 1790 English case of *Evans v. Evans.* In this ruling, Lord Stowell stated that legal cruelty required "a reasonable apprehension of danger to life, limb, or health." Other forms of mental distress or "what merely wounds the feelings" were not admissible as cruelty. Stowell's remarks gave a wide berth for chastisement, while still expanding English doctrine to include threats of violence. By mid-century, however, American courts began to depart from this model. "Judges increasingly recognized that physical well-being could be injured by behavior far more subtle than physical blows." The presence of catchall indignities statutes, such as the one found in Texas, gave testament to the transitional nature of legal cruelty in antebellum America.[3]

This movement towards an acceptance of the variable nature of cruelty owed much to the efforts of reformers. A rights awareness stemming from republican ideology bolstered a new humanitarian sensibility that developed over the first half of the nineteenth century, bringing with it increased attention to the problem of pain. Men and women began to differentiate necessary from unnecessary pain.

Indeed, reformers hoped to restore bodily integrity to a wide-ranging group of sufferers. As a result, the treatment of the enslaved, prisoners, children, wives, and even animals was called into question. Cruelty reflected a human choice to reject civilizing influences and to head down the path of savagery, inflicting pain without a higher purpose. Henry Clarke Wright, for example, called into question a husband's right of ownership of a wife's body, thus opening the way for a conversation about marital rape. At the same time, the Grimké sisters compared marriage to a state of slavery and drew attention to the intersecting cruelties of both systems. In a divorce setting, these concerns manifested via a newfound interest in the question: at what point did "acceptable" chastisement in marriage shade into cruelty?[4] No easy answer presented itself, especially because marriage appeared to be transitioning from traditional patriarchal models to an emphasis on contractual relations. This new understanding threatened to upend domestic relations by diminishing the rights of husbands. Coverture, for example, started to disappear as a legal concept denoting a man's outright ownership of his wife's body. Affect was touted as the new hallmark of proper unions. Companionate marriage, described by Anya Jabour as a "loving partnership," became the ideal. Under the terms of companionate relationships, both spouses emphasized the primacy of emotion over duty.[5]

However, the historical community remains at odds regarding the extent to which these ideas made their way into the daily lives of men and women. Some scholars emphasize the ways in which antebellum relationships transformed to include a heightened recognition of feelings and the mutuality of enterprise. Assertions such as these have had the possibly unintended effect of lending credibility to the argument that all husbands and wives tried to implement companionate marriage wholesale.[6] This work reaches a different set of conclusions and finds that husbands and wives fought to keep duty, not affection, as the focal point of their relationships. Simply put, romantic emotions could be a liability when survival was the priority. With that in mind, marital cruelty was a violation of responsibility, not of love. But antebellum men and women did not abandon companionate notions entirely. Instead, they reshaped traditional understandings of duty to include an emphasis on mutuality and equality in labor roles. What mattered, in the end, was channeling emotion into productive processes. It is true that reformers advocated for marital affection, but they also cautioned spouses to maintain emotional control.[7]

The study of marital anxieties and family discord really blossomed in the 1970s with the "discovery" of family violence. In the decade following, historians such as Elizabeth Pleck and Linda Gordon came forward with their studies of marriages and families in crisis. Legal historians also entered into the fray as Robert Griswold published a series of articles exploring the judicial evolution of matrimonial cruelty in nineteenth-century America. In more recent years, scholars of marital discord have tried to refocus attention away from policy and appellate decisions and back onto local experiences, as exemplified by personal accounts of abuse. This attempt has been only partially successful. Indeed, many of the most useful descriptions of cruelty are still found within studies of divorce.[8]

Another limitation within the cruelty historiography is that the great majority of works treat violence or cruelty by women as trivial, rare, or defensive. For example, David Peterson del Mar created one of the only monographs examining domestic violence in the nineteenth-century United States, yet he chose to exclude any discussion of violence perpetrated by wives. He defended this decision on the basis of the rarity of husband abuse. The danger here lies in equating historical significance with representativeness. A person/place/thing does not have to be representative of the whole to be historically significant. Violence may have been, in the words of Drew Gilpin Faust, "gendered male," but that only makes it all the more important to study those women who went against social conventions. Utilizing a gendered approach to cruelty allows us to explore what happens when we take women's marital violence seriously. It also makes it possible to consider what it means for antebellum men to be victims of marital abuse. And we find that white women across the country were perfectly able, and often willing, to engage in cruel and violent acts, a point too often downplayed.[9]

The persistent presence of domestic violence in society across time and space might lend itself to an analysis emphasizing continuity and similarity at the expense of change and difference. A multistate comparative approach addresses this historical problem by highlighting how regional contexts shaped understandings of cruelty. In particular, by focusing on southern and frontier cultures, this work interrogates much of what historians have argued about the relationship between violence and region. What we think we know about the South in the eighteenth and nineteenth centuries is that it was extraordinarily violent. Debates as to why the South seemed particularly prone to discord have ranged widely and drawn upon countless theories. Some cite the area's traditionally high temperatures for sparking general ill will, or the presence of Scots-Irish values for emphasizing aggression for any slight. Others point to the persistence of slavery, the surplus of young and single men, the absence of effective government, the widespread practice of carrying firearms, or the influence of an honor-driven culture.[10]

Southern honor, as described by historians, both stimulated and regulated the practice of violence in the South. Honor dictated and guided how white men behaved when faced with the possibility of threat or insult. According to traditional interpretations, southerners of all classes participated in honor culture by serving as an audience to ongoing contests of manhood. As Ariela Gross contends, in the antebellum South, "to display or exercise honor is to have an honorable character." In his seminal work on this cultural guideline, Bertram Wyatt-Brown makes the claim that honor-driven violence in southern society differentiated the region from the rest of nineteenth-century America. This distinctiveness extended into marital relations, as domestic assaults perpetrated by southerners, according to Wyatt-Brown, "probably exceeded" similar incidents elsewhere in numerical terms and in their presence across social classes. Following in the footsteps of Wyatt-Brown, historians of the South have focused on how honor stimulated violence, paying less attention to its regulatory functions. However, antebellum court records reveal that southerners valued honor, in part, because it kept chaos at bay during a period of rapid societal change. It did not condone discord wholesale but carefully distinguished between acceptable and unacceptable practices. Southern patriarchs ruled under significant social pressures to channel aggression in appropriate ways, i.e., in ways that did not threaten the larger practice of legitimate mastery. It is possible that the growing influence of a southern middle class, perhaps more removed from the violent elements of honor and more attuned to "northern" values, added to this social pressure. On the whole, discussions of marital cruelty in southern courtrooms reveal the extent to which the use of violence in domestic settings posed a dilemma not as easily answered as heretofore believed. Mounting criticisms focusing on the treatment of enslaved dependents in the South made it all the more imperative that other dependents, white wives in this case, be protected from the exercise of improper mastery. Therefore, we should exercise caution when pointing to the cultural construct of honor as an indicator of southern excesses in all areas of violence and cruelty.[11]

No one place or location will ever perfectly represent the diversity of an entire region. With this cautionary note in mind, the selection of Virginia for inclusion in this work was due to its position in the historiography as the quintessential southern state. The Old Dominion in the antebellum period was where centuries-old tradition met reformist social change seeping down from the North. Unfortunately, my racial analysis is shaped by the limitations of Virginia's legal records. The South refused to legally recognize the legitimacy of enslaved unions and, as a result, these relationships do not appear within cruelty divorce proceedings. This absence in the documentary record diminishes the potential for commentary on the marriages of enslaved men and women. Much can still be learned about the southern racial order through an awareness of the ways in which Virginia's slave system coexisted alongside increasingly contractual understandings of domestic relations. Investigating the existence of multiple forms of violence and cruelty in the South does not diminish the impact that brutal enslavement had on the region. Instead, it reflects a need for scholars to move away from blanket generalizations about the nature of discord. Approaching the historical problem of violence in the South from a comparative perspective and with a fresh set of questions "reveals patterns of violence that have remained hidden until now." It shows that marriages in the South were not excessively cruel or uncommonly peaceful. This leads us to wonder if the same could be said about antebellum frontier marriages.[12]

In American scholarship and myth, the frontier is the South's primary rival for the notorious label of most violent. This reputation developed over time and built upon descriptions of ethnic clashes, environmental challenges, economic struggles, and demographic misbalances. A study of frontier divorce records reveals the extreme brutality of husbands and wives in Texas and especially Wisconsin.

A focus on Texas allows for the test of an altered southern model. By 1845 settlers hailing from the South had established a firm grip on the state, yet they still dealt daily with challenges stemming from frontier conditions. These pre–Civil War settlers were often southern transplants ready to establish a new Old South, with an active system of racial slavery, on Texas soil. This mission of manifest destiny came to only partial fruition.[13] Transplanted Texans proved unable to replicate the foundation of shared family and marital values found in traditional southern societies, as exemplified by Virginia. Frontier life heightened gender role instabilities to the point of creating alternate domestic arrangements. Being married proved to be an incalculable advantage in pioneer society, yet Texas husbands and wives felt uncertain as to what exactly that relation entailed. Faced with unforeseen environmental difficulties, Texas women often shouldered more of the labor burden while their husbands attempted to enforce older understandings of mastery. Not always the isolated and overwhelmed shrinking violets, women on the southern frontier could be the victims or aggressors in marital conflicts. The record of their actions presented in court demonstrates that gender role confusion clashed with a yearning for the traditional and resulted in an increase in cruelty in antebellum Texas homes. By the onset of the Civil War, a growing population pushed the state out of its pioneer period and ushered in a new set of domestic challenges.[14]

To more fully understand the nature of frontier discord and to address the concern, raised by Edward Ayers, that brutality in Texas during the antebellum period simply reflected "Southern violence transplanted," this study also examines marital relations in Wisconsin. Divorce records from the Midwest provide us with an indication as to what it meant to be cruel in a frontier society populated primarily by northerners and immigrants. Wisconsin in the 1840s and 1850s was a place characterized by ethnic clashes, harsh settlement conditions, constant inward/outward migrations, and developing legal cultures. For settlers hailing from New England, the Mid-Atlantic, and Europe, adaptation was an uncomfortable but necessary part of survival. The very process of settlement challenged the stability of gender roles, prompting much anxiety and violence. In light of these challenges, unhappy men and women struggled for mastery and its attendant ability to define the meaning and actual practice of duty in marriage. After all, Wisconsin men did not have a system of honor or the subordination of an enslaved people to bolster their domestic authority. And not all Wisconsin women believed that proper household relations required wives to assume positions of dependency and submission. The role confusion found in Wisconsin fostered a heightened degree of brutality on the part of both men and women that supports an interpretation of the frontier as a site of extreme and pervasive violence.[15]

The legal systems within the three states also developed in different directions. And as conversations about cruelty emerged in tandem with the pursuit of separations, it is important to understand the varied legal environments navigated by troubled spouses. To begin with, Virginia owed a great deal to its English legal heritage and, as a result, adhered to a relatively conservative divorce model throughout the antebellum period. The legislature retained primary authority over the issuance of divorces until 1851, when this power passed to the courts of chancery. This transition mirrored a process occurring across the country as the constitutionality of legislative divorces became the subject of intense debate. Governed by principles of equity and fairness, Virginia courts gradually expanded the possible causes of divorce to include impotency, idiocy, bigamy, adultery, cruelty, just cause of bodily fear, abandonment, desertion, pregnancy at marriage, and criminal conviction/confinement. By the onset of the Civil War the Old Dominion had "neither the most permissive nor the most restricted list of grounds."[16]

In antebellum Texas, Spanish civil law and English common law combined to create a uniquely Texas "subdialect of the American dialect of law." This hybrid system did not recognize separate procedures for equity and law, and instead gave the district courts jurisdiction over general and criminal matters. In 1845 Texas entered the Union as a state that embraced married women's property rights, community property procedures, and liberal divorce grounds. These advances owed a great deal to the area's cultural history; however, frontier concerns also weighed heavily on lawmakers. They were torn between the dual needs of regulating marriage and at the same time maintaining sufficient flexibility in dealing with spousal conflicts. As a result, Texas district courts granted divorces based upon a set of causes designed to encompass a wide variety of matrimonial wrongs.

Marriages were dissolved on the basis of adultery, abandonment, and "excesses, cruel treatment, or outrages." The open-to-interpretation "excesses" clause allowed judges and juries a great deal of leeway in determining the future of problem couples.[17]

Wisconsin joined the Union only three years after Texas, and by that time it had established a reputation as a territory with a liberal legal culture. Soon after statehood, the legislature passed a women's property law and legislators repeatedly, and unsuccessfully, attempted to introduce full women's suffrage. It was also during this period that divorce transitioned from being both a legislative and judicial process to one under the jurisdiction of the courts only. Circuit judges heard the majority of divorce cases, and they could dissolve a union on the basis of a wide variety of grounds. The Revised Statutes of 1849 allowed for absolute divorce in situations of adultery, impotency, imprisonment for three or more years, willful desertion of at least a year, cruelty, or habitual drunkenness. Wisconsin lawmakers viewed marriage as a civil agreement, open to many possible violations. Adding to the mix, settlers to the state often brought with them contractual understandings of marriage made even more fluid by the influence of harsh living conditions.[18]

Because marital discord was a taboo subject, it is quite difficult to find open and lengthy discussions of incidents of cruelty. Divorce records, in part, offer a solution to this problem in that they provide intricate accounts of disappointments in marriage. Divorce in antebellum America was not a private process but a public one that reflected the needs and desires of the community, state, and nation. We, as historians, get an intimate glimpse of household dynamics as antebellum men and women came before the courts and placed the contents of their private lives on public display. It is necessary to approach these documents with the reasonable caution afforded to most historical records, but the advantages of working with case files far outweigh the possible drawbacks. All of the cases included in this study come from the courts of original jurisdiction, making it possible to keep the focus on local processes and concerns. And I only included those petitions in which litigants or witnesses brought up allegations of cruelty. No attempt was made to quantify the exact numbers of cruelty cases filed in each county or state. Due to damage, theft, and other concerns, the remaining local court records would not sustain an accurate quantitative analysis. When these issues are paired with the degree of unreported incidents of marital cruelty, even in divorce cases, it becomes clear that the best way to avoid the numerical inaccuracies is to explore violence and abuse on the qualitative levels of description and perception.[19]

Based upon divorce records, newspaper accounts, moralist tracts, and personal papers, this work presents a multipart argument. It finds that many antebellum marriages were characterized by open enmity. Violence and cruelty between spouses often arose as part of ongoing struggles for power in the household and in the relationship. With the rise of companionate marriage during this period, one would expect to find an emphasis on positive emotion within the records. However, this was not the case. Husbands and wives instead described a baseline requirement for marriage in which both partners performed their respective duties adequately. Even in the face of liberalizing divorce grounds, it was violations of duty, not love, that were the focus of discussion. New marital forms, including companionate relationships, influenced spouses by emphasizing the importance of equal contributions in those traditional roles. For the cases studied, cruelty then did not mean—on the one hand—the absence of love but, rather, a failure to fulfill marital labor expectations. On the other hand, husbands and wives also used cruelty as a tool when they tried to brutally force their own, often traditional, understandings of marital duties onto their partners.[20]

This work explores the degree to which region shaped reactions and responses to cruelty. It finds that, contrary to what is generally understood about the American South, marriages in Texas and Virginia were not exceptionally violent, at least not when compared with those in Wisconsin. The presence of marital cruelty was most pronounced in environments suffering from gender role instabilities. In the southern states studied, the primary concern was refining the practice of domestic mastery and its relationship to violence. Honor, in situations of marital chastisement, limited rather than encouraged brutality. Cruelty for southern husbands and wives meant the pursuit, or employment, of inappropriate mastery over one's spouse. In the two frontier states studied, multiple traditions defining the roles of husband and wife combined with unique environmental challenges to create widely varying perceptions of what proper household mastery entailed. The absence of a dominant gender role tradition often bred confusion, fostered marital anxieties, and prompted much, rather intense, violence. Frontier husbands and wives turned to cruelty as a tool to reaffirm the importance and positioning of mastery and dependency in their relationships. The definition and perception of cruelty varied according to the gender of the victim and perpetrator. Antebellum wives were indeed capable of committing a wide variety of cruelties within marriages, and were often willing to do so.

The work is organized thematically according to particular categories of marital cruelty. Chapter One explores verbal cruelty, including the particular meanings behind ethnic epithets and sexual rumors. Chapter Two focuses on physical cruelty. Chapter Three discusses sexual excess, notions of sexual propriety, and the transference of venereal diseases as cruelty. Chapter Four examines intemperance and marital cruelty, especially as related to interpretations of cruel neglect. Chapter Five looks at third-party interventions in situations of marital discord, paying particular attention to local networks of rumor and report within the three states. The conclusion provides an overview of the comparative findings while suggesting additional ways to approach the study of American domestic discord.

Historians possess a significant amount of information regarding those couples who were trying to achieve the perfect companionate marriage, but we know substantially less about those spouses who were simply trying not to kill one another. I do not attempt to create a comprehensive picture of antebellum marital attitudes, but I do "sketch the outlines" of what it meant to be married in nineteenth-century America. Studying marriage from the "way, way below" allows us to move beyond ideals to examine the messiness and unhappiness that often characterized conjugal unions.[21]

CHAPTER 1

"As Much Pain as Blows and Kicks"

The Verbal Cruelties of Husbands and Wives

Rebecca's marriage started off on an unpromising note. Shortly after saying "I do" to Robert Harper, she learned that on the very night of their wedding another woman, from the same county, stood waiting "all dressed with her family and guests" to marry him as well. This attempt at a dual wedding shocked the couple's small Texas community and, living up to his reputation, Robert only played the part of a doting husband for a short time before revealing a cruel and violent disposition. Wandering around the house murmuring vulgarities and obscenities, he would burst into anger when even asked the most civil question, telling his wife, "not to speak to his head but to his——." If Rebecca combed her hair, Robert would come by and rumple it. If Rebecca was sick and in bed, Robert would order her to get up, pushing her if she did not move. Despite these incidents and others, Rebecca continued to pray for her husband's reform and the preservation of her marriage.[1]

Robert dashed all hopes of improvement, however, when he began to publicly defame his wife. While she still resided in the household, he placed notices in local newspapers stating that she had left his bed and board and now lived as a known adulteress. In addition, joining together with his father, Robert verbally abused Rebecca in private on a regular basis. On one occasion the two men called her a "whore" and "bitch" and then proceeded to accuse her of committing adultery with her brother-in-law. They also declared that her mother "was a whore and that she had raised a large family of daughters to be whores." Ignoring Rebecca's sick condition at the time, the two men forced her out of the house, making her walk three miles on foot to her father for protection. Upon completing the long trek to her parental home,

Rebecca initiated divorce proceedings with the goal of severing her three-month marriage. In her bill, she asked the court to recognize Robert's words as not only slanderous, but cruel. After a short trial, the judge acknowledged the existence of verbal cruelty, found in Rebecca's favor, and granted the separation.[2]

Drawing upon the spousal struggles of Rebecca and others, this chapter explores how antebellum men and women defined verbal cruelty in marriage. It asks: How were husbands and wives verbally cruel? Why were husbands and wives verbally cruel? It finds that the verbal attacks employed by spouses generally fell into three categories: epithets, character assaults, and threats. Antebellum husbands and wives used verbal barbs to draw attention to perceived deficiencies in their partner's performance of marital duties. As a result, the vast majority of verbal attacks centered upon questions of labor or issues of sexual morality. Antebellum men and women believed that verbal cruelty occurred if a person could demonstrate a "reasonable apprehension" of physical injury based upon the comments of their partner. Cruelty also took place if the words of one spouse caused the other to sustain emotional distress that in turn crippled his or her ability to function in society.[3]

Across the three states studied, local communities pressured lawmakers and the higher courts to expand the definition of cruelty beyond black letter law. In Virginia, the legislature clung to an ideal of verbal cruelty that relied upon the potential for bodily injury. This interpretation, again, adhered closely to English legal precedent. In Texas, the Supreme Court and lawmakers appeared increasingly willing to investigate the idea that cruel words could fit within an excesses, outrages, or general cruel treatment category. This transition to a more liberal interpretation can be seen over the course of just a few years. In the 1852 case of *Nogees v. Nogees,* the Court cautioned against "vagueness and uncertainty" when presenting verbal cruelty claims. Yet by the 1855 case of *Pinkard v. Pinkard* the court opined, "The charge of adulterous intercourse against the wife, if groundless, is undoubtedly an act of gross cruelty." At the same time, the Wisconsin Supreme Court's ruling in *Johnson v. Johnson* sought to limit their permissive divorce grounds by stating, "Abusive and opprobrious language, which wounds the feelings merely, unaccompanied with any bodily injuries, actual or menaced, is not considered a ground for a divorce." This chapter will show how communities departed from these formal limitations to create cruelty definitions, and divorce decrees, based on local needs and understandings. The chapter begins with a discussion of epithets before moving on to examine harmful accusations and threats directed at spouses.[4]

Husbands and wives often used epithets to enact not-so-subtle commentaries on the work habits of their partners. For disgruntled husbands, this generally meant emphasizing a woman's failure to behave properly as a productive wife. It was not uncommon for men to refer to their wives as "lazy trifling worthless & of no account." And within that series, the term *lazy* made the most frequent appearance. Husbands employed this particular epithet out of an attempt to force their wives to conform to their ideas of what industrious, hard-working housewives should act like. However, in an interesting twist, the critiques made by these men implicitly recognized a woman's critical role in a household's success while simultaneously denigrating the extent of her efforts.[5] The records demonstrate that frontier husbands, especially those residing in rural Texas, particularly relied upon epithets. *Lazy* and other derogatory terms served as tools that frontier men used to stress the ways in which their wives detracted from, instead of adding to, the family's worth. Reeling from the clashing of transplanted southern gender ideals with the harsh realities of settlement, some Texas husbands gave vent to their frustrations via name-calling. The continuous presence of terms such as *lazy* in the court documents hints at the possibility that Texas husbands expected their spouses to take on even heavier labor loads while simultaneously not challenging their husband's position as master of the house. It was critical for Texas men to maintain marital mastery because, as historian Randolph Campbell has shown, the frontier lifestyle created circumstances in which women could "direct their lives in ways that were anything but docile and submissive." While the courts were sympathetic towards women who suffered from the ill effects of name-calling, the isolated usage of epithets still did not make a husband guilty of marital cruelty.[6]

If a husband paraded his name-calling in a public way, a woman could pursue a cruelty ruling by emphasizing the physical consequences of mental anguish and embarrassment. Within their bills, injured wives recounted how insults especially stung when made publicly where other members of the community were placed in a position to evaluate a woman's essential "value." Take, for example, the case of Victoria Frederic, who suffered from continual ridicule by her husband, Samuel. She recounted to the court how, after their marriage in March 1856, she expected them to live a peaceful and happy life together. Unfortunately, her dreams turned into nightmares shortly after the marriage as Samuel "disclosed an angry, turbulent & brutal disposition." On one occasion, he even pointed a loaded gun at her and threatened to shoot. In addition to threats and physical violence, Samuel also emotionally crushed Victoria by proclaiming publicly and privately that "she was worthless & no value." As she related to the Gonzales County court, Samuel's public comments caused her much "mental suffering" and damaged her quality of life. Fearing for her general welfare, Victoria fled their house after less than six months of cohabitation.[7]

Name-calling focusing on the nature of a woman's economic contribution could cause tension in a marriage, but the majority of epithets and accusations made by husbands towards wives centered upon issues of sexual morality. Out of all the epithets directed at wives across the three states, the terms *whore, bitch,* and *strumpet* appeared the most frequently. All of these negative labels carried explicit, and nationally understood, connotations of sexual licentiousness. In a fashion similar to the use of labor epithets, a husband could lob sexual insults at his wife with impunity within the confines of the private sphere. If he chose to regularly employ such comments in public arenas, he ran the risk of being accused of marital cruelty. The nature of these public "performances" of verbal cruelty by husbands varied a great deal depending on the individual couple. In many cases, for emphasis and elevated drama, husbands combined the above epithets with a "damned," such as when Henry Carlisle drew a knife on his wife, threatened to kill her, and called her a "damned whore and strumpet." On other occasions, the base insult remained the same with the addition of a colorful cultural curse phrase. One husband, a former English citizen residing in Wisconsin, referred in public to his wife as a "bloody bitch." Vile terms of this ilk quite often served as the opening salvos of extended verbal attacks that would progress into detailed attempts at character defamation.[8]

An accusation of illicit intercourse was the most serious allegation that a husband could level against a wife. As legal understandings of marital discord expanded in the late antebellum period, adultery accusations were increasingly recognized as satisfying the minimum threshold for a divorce on the basis of cruelty. For example, as early as 1827, Louisiana law recognized defamation of character as a category of cruelty and reasonable justification for divorce. In that same vein, in 1855, Texas Supreme Court chief justice John Hemphill authored an opinion in which he argued that false allegations of adultery made against a wife "undoubtedly" constituted "an act of gross cruelty." Hemphill's ruling existed as a forward-thinking acknowledgment of the extreme "mental pain and anguish" resulting from cruel words and of the need to penalize accusatory husbands, when possible.[9]

The story of Anne Souther, a Virginia wife, is illustrative of the damage wrought by sexual allegations. After tolerating almost two years of abuse by her husband, Simeon, she filed for a divorce on the grounds of cruelty and adultery. In the usual form, Anne claimed that she married her husband out of sincere attachment, but soon realized that he possessed a jealous demeanor. Shortly after the match, he began "to make the most insulting and unmerited charges against" her. For example, on one occasion a nearby neighbor ran into the Southers' house looking for a missing dog. Simeon was not home at the time and the neighbor left without finding the dog. Anne thought little of this incident until her husband returned and accused her of "being together" with the said neighbor. Needless to say, Anne was shocked and outraged. But even worse, Simeon was consistent in his allegations. He constantly accused her of committing illicit intercourse with anywhere from six to eight men. Simeon's jealousy reached its height when he "prevented her from joining the church as she desired saying, 'she designed it as a cloak for her wicked purposes[.]' He said, 'her reading the holy scriptures was only for the obscenity they contain.'" In his answer, Simeon admitted that he disliked the church but never forbade Anne from attending. He refused to comment on any of the other cruelty claims presented by his wife.[10]

Although many of the couple's clashes took place in private, Anne still feared for the general damage inflicted upon her reputation. She wondered how her suburb of Richmond community would react. As aptly described by Laura Edwards and Ariela Gross, while white southern men possessed the right to perform and practice honor, white southern women claimed their own versions of honor through the concepts of "character" or "credit." According to these interpretations, women gained credit by performing their familial roles in a proper fashion and avoiding any hints of societal deviance. A woman's credit then determined how she was treated by the entire community. So it made sense that Anne evinced concern regarding how her husband's verbal attacks might alter her social standing. The couple's neighbors recounted how Simeon rarely missed an opportunity to denigrate his wife in public. Without remorse, he would call her sexual epithets, such as "Damned Old whore and old strumpet." It eventually reached a point where Simeon's public allegations required an equally public response. In the southern states studied, it was an unspoken societal rule that unchallenged accusations were true; therefore it was imperative that Anne defend herself or forfeit her character wholesale. As opposed to engaging in a war of words on the street, Anne took the civilized approach and filed a divorce petition. She would suffer some stigma contingent with pursuing a separation, but the court documents gave her an opportunity to present herself as a victim of cruelty as well. Anne recognized that she had to defend herself from her traditional defender, her husband.[11]

Damaged wives also claimed that knowingly making false allegations of adultery constituted cruelty. Angry at being accused of being unfaithful with "several men," Harriett Smith made sure to stress to the court that her husband "well knew" that his statements were "utterly false." His charges "affected her character as a chaste & virtuous woman," thereby impairing her ability to fully function in society. According to Harriett, her husband behaved in a calculated manner and intended to destroy her life. Mentioning such calculations proved important because an antebellum judge and jury might have felt inclined to excuse the cruelties if they believed that the statements fell under the same premise as crimes of passion and stemmed from intense emotional anguish.[12] In contrast, intentionally making false statements demonstrated a desire to inflict crippling mental suffering on one's spouse, an outcome recognized as cruelty across the three states studied. Acknowledging the importance of intent, men accused of verbal cruelty initiated damage control by gesturing towards their uncontrollable emotions. Garland Mallory avowed that "out of fullness of the heart, the mouth spake." Admitting partial guilt, Mallory understood the true social injury caused by "cast[ing] an imputation upon" one's wife but, nevertheless, he resisted being labeled a cruel husband by the court.[13]

The records show that some men embraced verbal cruelty as a creative outlet for their marital frustrations. These men knew that their words would continue to haunt their spouses even if they made far-fetched allegations that were generally dismissed and immediately refuted by others. Robert Harper, of Texas, charged his wife with committing adultery with her sister's husband, because she was a whore raised in a "large family" of whores. The jury found him guilty of cruelty via false adultery charges and granted his wife a divorce. Wisconsin citizen Caleb Creswell divided the entire community when he accused his wife of having an illicit connection with his own brother. In another case, Torrence Hughes, fueled by liquor, made a similar charge. He "publikcly & privately" accused his wife, the self-proclaimed daughter of a respectable Virginia family, of committing "incestuous intercourse with her own son, a boy then about 14 years of age." Regardless of the truthfulness of the actual charge, residents documented that Hughes's pronouncements continued to linger in the rural Campbell County air long after they were issued. As one witness to a divorce case stated, "such charges against a virtuous woman was like sending a dagger to her hart." In honor-driven southern communities, a woman might flee to avoid future social stigma on the basis of false allegations. In Wisconsin communities, a woman's reputation was also important, as strangers settled near one another and used gossip as a means to create and enforce social order. As such, a label of "troublemaker" was almost impossible to shake off.[14]

Staying within the territory of sexual slander, cruel husbands also expanded on the epithets of "whore" or "strumpet" and gave detailed accounts of their wives being prostitutes or contracting venereal diseases. Following accusations of this nature, the marriage of Fredericka and Charles Nordhausen fell apart rather quickly. Married in June 1854, Fredericka filed for divorce, citing cruelty, less than a year later. She described how Charles, his mother, and his brother would verbally abuse her, calling her whore and other false names. Hoping in vain for Charles to defend her honor, Fredericka was alarmed when he instead publicly identified her as a prostitute and alleged that she was diseased with the clap. Charles, for his part, admitted the above incident to the court, but asserted that he spoke the truth. He claimed that it was only after marriage that he discovered his wife's disease. And to make matters worse, her infection resulted in a "noxious and sickening" smell so foul that he could not "come near or stay about her." In an acknowledgment that Fredericka's social life was ruined by the case and the accusations contained therein, Charles offered to pay to send her to Europe. We do not know if she accepted his proposal, but his actions indicate that he wanted to obliterate their marriage from memory. In this case, the truth of whether or not Fredericka did indeed have the clap is not as important as the community reaction to the allegations. Antebellum American gender ideals stressed female sexual innocence and passionlessness, and therefore even allegations of prostitution and disease could ruin a woman's future possibilities. The Fayette County jury believed Fredericka's claims and severed the union.[15]

The evidence shows that communities possessed little tolerance for public displays of epithets and accusations by cruel husbands. To encourage the peaceful resolution of marital troubles and to guard against public disruptions, antebellum citizens mobilized certain defensive measures. Morality sections in local newspapers would instruct spouses to maintain emotional control at all costs. As the *Clarksville Standard* (Texas) in an article entitled "Guard Against Vulgar Language," admonished, "There is as much connexion between the words and the thoughts as there is between the thought and the words; the latter are not only the expression of the former, but they have a power to re-act upon the soul and leave the stains of their corruption there." This newspaper expressed the forward thinking opinion that verbal cruelty, even in private, was a public problem and, quite often, a precursor to serious physical violence. When assessing whether or not verbal cruelty had actually occurred, the community would often take into account the intended audience. As part of the chivalric code of honor embedded in southern ideology and the general understanding of decency in the North, husbands were supposed to watch their language towards their wives, children, and other women. Serving in the role of protector, husbands were called upon to temper their passionate natures as a sign of respect for womanhood.[16]

Under these terms, John Pratt was no respecter of southern women or his wife. In her bill for divorce, Elizabeth Pratt enumerated her husband's physical and verbal cruelties, including hitting her in the mouth with a turkey leg, striking her in the forehead with a fire shovel, and calling her a "damn worthless bitch" in front of the neighbors. Elizabeth's sister, Jane, resided with the couple and wanted the court to note for the record that John was "harsh and very cruel in both words and actions." To drive her point home, Jane concluded by stating, "He treated her more like a slave than a wife." And she would know, as they lived in the slaveholding county of Gonzales, Texas. With the assistance of her sister, Elizabeth was granted a divorce.

In another cruelty case, describing the harsh verbiage of a neighbor, Jacob Mason observed, "I should not suppose that all men or young men should use such language when ladies are present." In a fashion similar to that of many deponents, he declined for reasons of decency, respect, or simply lack of information to provide examples of the specific terms. But he was able to convey the general message that vulgar husbands were not socially acceptable anymore. It still fell to the wifely litigant to prove that the foul language in question not only caused emotional distress but actually resulted in tangible injury to her standing in society, thereby constituting cruelty.[17]

Drawing attention to the ways in which cruel words were just as harmful as physical abuse was one tactic employed by wives and deponents. Sally Baggs of Walworth County, Wisconsin, was just fourteen years old when she married Horace in 1847. In the seven years following he frequently refused to provide any household support, forcing her to take in sewing to pay for groceries. Known in the neighborhood for forcing his wife out of the house on a regular basis, Horace's physical abuse in the form of choking, kicking, and hitting Sally reached the point where neighbors intervened and filed an assault charge against him. But this did not stop Horace who, along with the physical attacks, made sure to swear at his wife whenever possible. Regarding his profanity, Sally commented that it had caused her "as much pain in her feelings as have his blows and kicks." A boarder in the household, Elvira Fairchild, agreed and added, "I think the language he used was worse than the blows he gave I should rather a man strike me than to call me such names as he called his wife." Sally's case rested upon the assertion that her husband's physical and verbal cruelties were one and the same. They both caused mental suffering and physical debility. Through her petition, Sally warned her peers that they ran the risk of losing a productive member of the community if they failed to recognize Horace's cruelties and grant her a divorce.[18]

Sally and other wives called upon the courts to shield them from cruelty that surfaced as part of a man's nature and natural temperament. Antebellum society believed that men suffered biologically from tendencies towards passionate behaviors. Mastery of one's emotions therefore made one a capable master of others. However, not all men could harness their emotions into productive channels. Take, for instance, the case of a man whose continual reliance upon epithets led to his neighbors' referring to him as the "swearing fellow." This "fellow" simply could not restrain himself and "his course was to speak well of nobody." And in support of a divorce proceeding, community members related to the court how this man's wife was exposed to his swearing ways on a regular basis.[19] When faced with allegations such as those found above, the husbands in question often turned the tables and accused their wives of wearing down their masculine restraint with constant nagging or harassment. They would claim that they only broke down and used terms regarded "by ears polite" as "low and vulgar" after "incessant and severe cross fire" from their wives. Regardless of the excuses presented, antebellum judges and juries appeared to have felt little sympathy for those husbands suffering from uncontrollable cruel passions. They especially expressed concern regarding those cases that suggested the possibility of escalating violence.[20]

While some women sought out ways to escape from their husband's verbal attacks, in other situations wives were the ones accused of committing verbal cruelties. The verbally cruel wife in antebellum America joined a long historical tradition of women using their tongues to challenge, as Terri Snyder has argued, "traditional political and domestic authority." Through the very act of speaking up in a negative way, a wife contested her husband's ability to govern dependents and "gave lie" to his pretensions of absolute mastery. Southern husbands, in particular, could ill afford to have their authority questioned so openly. It was perhaps for this very reason that the records show almost no Virginia wives accused of committing verbal cruelties in marriage. As honor depended on the display of mastery, the cost of pursuing such cases was too great for the husbands in question. Protecting one's manhood in Virginia meant privately dealing with a wife's unruly tongue or providing more egregious evidence for a divorce. Verbally aggressive wives undoubtedly existed in Virginia marriages, but their stories usually do not make it into the available records.[21] If we turn our attention to the frontier communities of Wisconsin and Texas, we find divorce cases focusing on the actions of verbally cruel wives. In particular, husbands presented complaints alleging that their wives would refer to them in animalistic ways. Edward Luxton, a Milwaukee man, found no solace with his wife as she, aside from neglecting her household duties, bit and pinched his arm, all the while calling him a "beast and brute." His bill went on to lament that she has "frequently told him to shut up his head."[22] When a wife called attention to a man's beastly nature, this charge could be perceived as cruelty, since it mocked what many men considered to be a real internal struggle.

Frontier husbands also described how their wives relied upon another manner of attack, namely applying cruel labels intended to ruin or destroy a man's moral and financial standing in society. Liar, scoundrel, swindler, rogue, blackguard, villain, rascal, and thief appeared the most often in the petitions, answers, and depositions. Each of these terms implied that a man possessed a faulty moral compass. They also suggested that the wife in question had had her trust violated in some way. For John Miller it appeared as if his wife Eliza believed that his constant trips between their new homestead in east Texas and their original home in Alabama led him to disregard his duties in their household. Henry McNealy, who lived with the couple as an overseer, overheard a conversation in which Eliza suggested that her husband "did not govern his family." Eliza's public verbal cruelties, including calling John a liar and a fool, did not begin until he first suggested moving to Texas. Of course, Eliza's implications proved particularly harmful because John was trying to establish himself in a new community, and his honor was critical to that goal. He needed people to know that his word was his bond, and for his wife to call him a liar in public did not aid in that cause. Even the appearance of lying could damage a man's honor irrevocably. Being "given the lie" was a tragedy indeed for any man.[23]

In addition, wives committed cruelty if they publicly or falsely accused their husbands of sexual deviancies. Interestingly enough, in a scenario opposite to that discussed above, society did not generally consider it cruel for a woman to accuse her husband of extramarital dalliances. A man's reputation, whether in Wisconsin or Texas, could withstand, or even embrace, a straightforward adultery accusation. On the contrary, false or public allegations that suggested extreme sexual indulgence or sexual deviance were problematic and cruel. This category of verbal cruelty proved particularly problematic in urban areas, where men struggled to establish their reputations amidst a sea of strangers. Husbands may have believed that city-based courts would interpret the grounds of cruelty in a more flexible way, prompting additional claims. Therefore, Houston resident Erva Barzak was cruel when she called her husband a "whoremonger." And Milwaukee wife Almira Brown behaved cruelly when she included "whoremaster" in a stream of insults to her husband. Almira may, or may not, have been responding to her husband's calling her a "dirty whore." For added emphasis, wives paired these epithets with "old" as in "old whoremaster" or "you old devil," the implication being that a husband was no longer fit and able to maintain his duties in the relationship, especially providing for the family, as compared to a younger man.[24]

Some women continued with their insults and accusations until the point of suggesting outright physical impotence. While living in Nacogdoches, Texas, Harriet Brewer not only called her husband impotent and other "foulest names and epithets," but she also deserted him to cohabit with one William Taylor, who lived only three hundred yards from her marital home. Seeking to reclaim his manhood, Harriet's husband filed for divorce on the grounds of cruelty, adultery, and desertion.[25] In late 1850s Dallas County, Elisha Lovell came to court precisely to defend his mastery and to cut off an unruly dependent, his wife Mary Ellen. He made the trip to court after learning that she had circulated scandalous reports about him in their community. In particular, she told their friends and neighbors that her husband "had tried on several occasions to make her cohabit with one M.A. Durrell a neighbor for the purpose of raising an heir" as he "was physically unable to beget one." Elisha assured the court that he had several children by a former wife, and therefore Mary Ellen was clearly acting out of an "utter want of love or even respect for him." James Brewer and Elisha Lovell came before Texas courts out of an effort to reassert their compromised manhood. Their honor demanded that they respond promptly to the allegations made by their partners because "a mere statement" whether "true or untrue" was "among strangers" enough to injure a man's reputation and bring scandal upon him.[26] Husbands and community members alleged a wide variety of motives that inspired vitriol-tongued wives. They pointed to nature and the fact that some wives, in a fashion similar to that of their husbands described previously, simply possessed "quarrelsome & abusive tongue[s]." In fact, when one Fayette County, Texas, judge delivered his orders to the jury in a divorce proceeding, he cautioned, "It would not only be farsical and ridiculous but extremely dangerous to the morals and well being of society to allow a divorce for every little manifestation of temper and indulgence in ill natured harsh or abusive language, particularly by a woman." According to this judge, a woman's words, while admittedly cruel, did not always meet the legal qualifications for cruelty because such language was almost expected as part of the marital package. Even though they faced difficulties in securing divorces based upon a woman's harsh words, husbands from Wisconsin and Texas still presented cases centering upon verbal attacks. They stood a better chance at success if they could demonstrate a pattern of verbal abuse or if they could hint at the possibility of future physical violence. Thomas Dickinson of Dallas County, Texas, believed that his wife's abuse and mistreatment emerged out of her general "malignity of feeling" towards him. He offered no additional explanation. Another Dallas husband described how his wife called him a villain and blackguard and confessed that "she did not love him, she wished she had not married him and she would not live with him much longer." For the antebellum period, historian Norma Basch has observed that "Men, no less than women, gave evidence of suffering unrelenting psychological cruelty." However, emotional injury alone was not sufficient to warrant a divorce on the grounds of cruelty.[27]

Therefore, husbands emphasized the ways in which a woman's verbal cruelties could compromise a man's ability to rule his household. Verbal attacks that took place in front of other dependents were considered to be particularly problematic. Although the stresses associated with mastery in a slave society did not weigh upon them, two complaints by Wisconsin husbands hint that they too, like their southern counterparts, felt the need to exert unblemished authority over their household and business dealings. They understood, as

Stephanie McCurry states, that "Dependence was the stuff of which independence and manhood were made." Albert Bowker came to the court alleging that his wife "commenced a course of cruel conduct" within the previous two years (after almost two decades of marriage) and refused to let him manage his household affairs. Aside from neglecting the washing and mending, she "has been in the constant habit of interfering with & preventing plaintiff from governing & correcting their children and addressing to him in their presence the most abusive vulgar and insulting language." Neighborhood witnesses came forward to corroborate Bowker's account, stating, "I never saw a woman treat her husband so unkindly & cruelly." Just when the case seemed quite clear, Mereda Bowker delivered her answer and admitted that she did interfere with his management of the children, but only when it was necessary due to his "brutal & inhuman" treatment. As such, she defended herself by asserting that her actions were not cruel at all because of her primary motive of protection of the helpless and the prevention of Albert's cruelties. In the end, the court determined that the couple could no longer live together peacefully and dissolved the union.[28]

Julius Strauss, a blacksmith from Milwaukee, in his answer to his wife's petition for divorce, provided evidence as to his own understanding of cruelty. Quickly passing over the fact that he had been fined $25 for a physical assault against his wife, Julius moved on to describe how Anna would come into his shop, which was attached to the house, and abuse him in front of his laborers. She called him names and "also abused & asailed said workmen in like manner" so much so that he "had great difficulty keeping them in his employ." In a state of growing frustration, he determined to lock the door against her because he had reached his limit of tolerance as a "man of passions as other men, and sensitive to and impatient of abuse, though from the hands or lips of his wife." Aside from annoyance, he claimed that his wife's actions prevented him from earning a proper living, as the city's residents began to avoid him and his shop. Julius and Albert presented stories of mastery under attack, and looked to other men in their communities for sympathy and assistance. After all, they argued, the problem of unruly dependents was an issue that affected all men, regardless of position.[29]

So far this chapter has discussed verbal attacks ranging from sexual and labor epithets to accusations of adultery. Within all of the cases, injured husbands and wives had to not only show emotional distress but an impaired quality of life if they hoped to win a divorce on the grounds of verbal cruelties. Judges and juries hoped to protect the productive potential of individuals by recognizing the connections between emotional, social, and physical damages. The third category of verbal cruelty found within the records, threats, lent itself quite easily to cruelty rulings on the basis of "reasonable apprehension" of physical injury. According to the premise of the law, threats of imminent danger severely reduced quality of life. The recognition of this category of cruelty reflected a desire on the part of judges and juries to respond to deadly threats before the action alluded to was actually carried out. As such, threats were viewed as the type of verbal cruelty that was as close as possible to physical violence. Not surprisingly, threats appeared in a majority of the court cases examined for this study.[30]

The regulation of threats against wives assumed particular importance as the nineteenth century progressed due to a growing discussion focusing on the physical consequences of anxiety. Popular and medical literature from the antebellum period described how a woman's body was exceedingly frail in composition. Following this logic, even the smallest hint of discord could wreck havoc on a woman's overall health. In accordance with this interpretation, wives within the court records attempted to clearly demonstrate how the foreboding words of their spouses not only ruined their daily quality of life but also left them unfit to perform the simplest of tasks. One example of anxiety-induced debility comes from the case files of Charlotte Cowen. Charlotte appeared before the court and recalled how her husband would, when intoxicated, take up an axe, hold it above her, and proclaim his intention to split her head open. His actions led to Charlotte's existence being "one of continual uneasiness anxiety & misery." Years later and across the country, Isabella Clark complained that her husband's verbal cruelties and personal violence left her "prey to constant anxiety." For wives such as Isabella, the historical evidence demonstrates that the settlement conditions found within frontier Texas and Wisconsin were stressful enough without the addition of abuse. Chronic anxiety was also a concern for general society because it was widely believed that women such as Charlotte and

Isabella might have trouble bearing children as a result. Historians of sexuality and the body reference how "The uterus, it was assumed, was connected to the central nervous system." The cruel words of a husband could potentially endanger the life not only of a wife but of her future unborn children.[31]

The general threat to take a spouse's life, made by both husbands and wives, was frequently found within the court records. A threat against a person's life was, at its core, a simple way to instill fear. Petitioners also relied upon testifying to life-threatening statements because they satisfied the legal definition of cruelty, at the most fundamental level, while requiring only minimal detail. This was a type of cruelty recognized quite broadly in the antebellum period. A Kentucky appeals court judge in 1829, for instance, allowed that reasonable apprehension of bodily injury, as seen via violent threats, satisfied the threshold for divorce. Texas, Wisconsin, and Virginia all followed in this tradition. Based upon court documents, it appears as if this particular type of threat was tossed around fairly freely within unhappy marriages. The daughter of one Texas couple related to the court how her father threatened "so frequently" to kill her mother "that I cannot remember all the times and places it was a common threat used almost daily." Not content with simply declaring their general intentions, cruel husbands and wives would often try to emphasize their murderous intentions. Peter Madden, for no reason his wife could later understand or relate, drew his knife and declared that he would "have her [his wife's] life if he had to die the next minute, and that no person could stop him." Other husbands went into even more specific detail, providing an exact time for their planned assault. Nancy Hilburn of Texas and Catharine Crandall of Wisconsin both lived with husbands who declared at various points that "murder would be done before night" and murder would happen "at the dead hour of night." For Nancy and Catharine, cruelty no doubt brought many sleepless nights.[32]

Although we commonly associate threats with firearms or knives, the records indicate that many cruel spouses leveled threats in which their bodies would serve as the weapon of choice. A husband could hint at his lethality, for example, by saying that he would "stamp the life out" of his wife. Or, he could indicate a desire to mar her face. Married in the fall of 1854, Christy and Evan Mattison of Wisconsin never lived peacefully together. Evan became a habitual drunkard, coming home from binges and striking, kicking, and calling his wife names. During one brutal encounter, Evan attacked Christy, all the while promising "that he would smash her face so she could not talk any more." The graphic image of brain injury also appeared with regularity within the records. One man threatened to "smash" his wife's "head almost every night." However, it would be a mistake to assert that only men proved capable of threatening severe violence. Women also swore that they would "beat out the brains" of their husbands.[33]

Aside from creatively worded warnings, cruel spouses particularly favored threatening their partners with imminent bodily harm while using "traditional" weapons as props. Traditional, in this case, can refer to the use of a knife or gun, as opposed to a weapon of opportunity, such as a heavy spoon or water pitcher. Antebellum judges and juries viewed these types of interactions as particularly worrisome because only a thin line separated a deadly threat from murder itself. Consider the case of Ann Chick, a Virginia wife tortured by her threatening and often outright violent husband, Littleton. Aside from inflicting blows on Ann and their children, Littleton developed a pattern in which he regularly threatened to cut Ann's throat. In these moments of terror, he would "hold a knife in one hand" and a lump of her hair in another and "threatened and indeed seemed earnestly endeavoring to cut her throat." She generally escaped his potentially deadly embrace aided only by her "state of terror and alarm." Her husband also tended to get extremely upset over seemingly trivial occurrences. In one situation, he was sick and requested a pillow, which she handed him. Then, he yelled that he did not want a pillow, so she asked what he did want. He jumped up, "took a knife out and swore he would cut her throat." She ran to another room in the house where she happened to meet arriving visitors who "saved her."[34] An interesting aspect of Ann's bill is that the image of cutting a throat was a dramatic one. The spouses, more often than not husbands, who relied upon this threat intended it to have an exaggerated effect, as compared to a threat to stab, which may or may not be immediately life-threatening. In her study of domestic violence in mid-nineteenth-century New York, Pamela Haag describes how verbally assaultive husbands tended to "underscore an unnegotiable right over wives and control of the private sphere by reveling in their capacity to determine the very life and death of their families." Men such as Littleton wanted to make clear their level of control: they could take a life at will.[35]

A knife threat undoubtedly escalated the level of tension within marriages. Three cases, out of many, from Wisconsin are illustrative. One woman, married to a confirmed drunkard, described how she had been turned out of doors on numerous occasions. Even her home was not a haven as her husband "had a knife hid with a standing threat that he would kill [her] with that knife." Almost a decade later, another Wisconsin wife lamented to the local circuit judge how her husband, also a drunk, tormented her when "he took out his pocket knife and began to sharpen it and threatened to kill" her. For Lucinda Benson's husband the use of a knife was intended to cause anxiety of a different type. Charles Benson wanted his wife to know that if she ever revealed his general cruelties to anyone, he would kill her. The couple only managed to live together for a few months, and he "disregarded the feelings and happiness" of Lucinda the entire time. She finally was forced to flee to a relative in February 1850 when he drew a knife on her and threatened that if she ever told anyone about his treatment of her, "she would tell it but once before he would stop her." In these situations, husbands employed very traditional weapons to elicit a very expected emotion, terror. This description of threats involving weapons would be remiss if it did not include a mention of the importance of guns and angry words. The divorce papers show that across all three states, cruel husbands quite often leveled threats with firearms in hand. The standard story included a man loading a pistol or shotgun and aiming it at his wife, often accompanied by cruel statements, many described in this chapter.[36]

Although wives were far less likely than husbands to resort to threats with traditional weapons, it was still possible. Those wives who grabbed a knife or gun to threaten their husbands were, unknowingly, broadening the understanding of cruelty during the period. The cruel woman with a weapon was not able to be identified on sight. She could be anybody. For example, the *Daily Milwaukee News* described how "a rather good looking woman, with a fur cape, black velvet cloak, clear teeth, brown hair, and a nervous looking eye, went into a gun shop down town, and purchased a neat little revolver, and was particular to learn how to load and fire off the institution." Evidently, considering the "wrath in her countenance," the newspaper editor was certain that she was off to shoot and kill somebody. Lacking the physical force to carry out their threats, other women took up knives to emphasize their dangerous intentions. After four years of marriage, John Fowler of Texas decided to divorce his wife Eliza. Aside from using "vexing" language and proclaiming that she could no longer love him, Eliza decided that she wanted him to leave his own house. Grabbing a knife in her hand in a threatening manner, she told him that "she was one of the sort that would stick the knife into him." Clearly, John claimed, he could not live with that "sort" of woman and required a divorce.[37]

While certain women handled weapons to their advantage, the records show that wives included excessive weapons-carrying as fitting within the boundaries of marital cruelty. The very presence of weapons was enough to cause anxiety and terror within the hearts of women, as in the case of Dorcas Nelson, a resident of rural Virginia. She married Moses Nelson in 1851. They immediately set off to visit his relatives in Tennessee, and it was on this trip that Dorcas "first discovered in part the true character of her husband." Upon arriving at the family home, her husband's brother took her aside and avowed "that her husband was a dangerous man and advised" her "to endeavor to induce" him "to lay aside his deadly weapons, with which he was constantly armed." Following the brother's advice, she requested a disarming, which her husband absolutely refused. Upon the couple's return to Virginia, Dorcas was in such a state of fear that she convinced her husband to agree for them to move in with her father so that she would be afforded some protection. The situation only worsened, and Moses abandoned her in 1854; but up until that point "her life was one of continual fear and trouble" due, in part, to her husband's habit of constantly carrying deadly weapons on his person. Although she never alleged that her husband actually made a statement about using the weapons against her, which weakened her legal case, Dorcas believed her husband was cruel because of the constancy with which he armed himself. He was never without a firearm. As a result, Dorcas was unable to relax and enjoy a normal home environment. Because "he thought every body was his enemy," she was forced to bear his anxieties as well as her own. The court agreed and granted the divorce.[38]

While husbands in all three states declared their right to possess arms of various sorts on their persons, their wives cited cruelty to make claims to the contrary. Descriptions abound in which men are described carrying around "a gun, ax, cutting knife, & other weapons." On occasion the information would include exactly the type of knife, clasp-bladed, etc., or style of gun, "five or six shooter."[39] In response to these allegations, husbands replied that they carried weapons for specific, useful purposes. Garland Mallory, a Virginia resident, in response to his wife's cruelty petition, stated that he owned a revolver "not to take his wife's life, but to protect her virtue." He even went so far as to surrender his bowie knife to his wife with "lamb-like meekness" upon her request, thus clearly indicating that she never stood "in great peril" from him. For Garland, his revolver and knife were symbols of his manhood, and therefore he could only submit partially to his wife's demands of disarmament.[40]

In court, wives presented arguments that the presence of deadly weapons violated the sanctity of the domestic sphere. Susan Menefee, of Virginia, complained that her husband, Banks, was in the habit of shooting off firearms within the house. He answered that he did shoot a gun out of the bedroom window but only to "scare off a pack of wild dogs." In this situation, it is clear that Susan would have preferred Banks to pursue this impulse out of doors. One Wisconsin boarder recalled how the couple who owned the house he boarded in would quarrel on a regular basis. He went on to assert that cruelty clearly occurred when the husband "when in his cups" would "load his rifle, and pistols, and stride up and down his room, and conduct himself like a madman." Needless to say, this boarder was happy to leave after two-and-a-half months. In particular, wives complained that their husbands brought weapons to bed on a regular basis. One Botetourt County, Virginia, husband habitually carried "weapons about his person" that he then took "with him to bed at night, with a view, either to alarm or terrify" his wife. Ira Hall, a Wisconsin resident, would take his gun to bed and "has slept with the same in his arms thus loaded with powder and ball all night." John Cooper "placed a razor under the pillow of their bed" for the purpose of intending to take his wife's life. In stereotypical Texas fashion, Anton Leitenberg took a "large bowie knife" into bed in order to "frighten and intimidate" his partner. These "weapons violations" bred anxious wives because they could imagine no other purpose for firearm use in the house, much less keeping a gun in the intimate space of the bed, except to harm them. As the moral guardians of the domestic sphere, women felt uniquely positioned to ask for an end to these behaviors. They argued that the presence of weapons made it difficult for them to create a peaceful and calm household, one of the principal tasks allotted to their sex. Husbands usually refused to compromise on this ultimate sign of manhood.[41]

Just as the presence of weapons could alarm wives, the threat of poisoning seemed to strike fear into husbands. By the antebellum period, the possibility of poisoning hovered in the southern air and coincided with a growing fear of slave defiance. According to rumors, slaves, often in charge of preparing food, could dispatch plantation owners with relative ease. Historians will never know the exact number of individuals who lost their lives in this way; but it was this context that, in part, made threats of poisoning a particularly effica-cious form of wifely cruelty. After a wife made a poisoning threat, her husband, in order to avoid a painful death, would refuse to drink or eat food prepared by her. As such, one man left the coffee brewed by his wife untouched. Another wife let it be known that "she would in a certain contingency (in case she should again become pregnant)" poison her husband and their two children. She also poured "vitrial" in her husband's eyes while he was sleeping. Impressed by the graphic nature of these claims, the court divorced the couple in question. The anxiety and stress caused by these toxic threats led one man to de-clare that "if the cruelty had not been extreme I should not know what extreme cruelty would be." When wives made poisoning threats, they pointed out their husband's vulnerability stemming from a woman's domestic role. As a result, they gained extra maneuvering room in the marriage. Few men would order a wife to cook dinner if they feared she would poison the food.[42]

Petitioners also came before the courts citing a spouse's threats to burn down the home as a form of cruelty. The twenty-three-year-old son of Betsey and Archibald Carter described how his father was "very quarrelsome" and said that "he would burn the house and run away by its light." This was after his father piled all of the family's bedding and curtains on the floor and attempted to burn them. Burn-ing the house would not only possibly kill the entire family but gen-erated the specter of total property loss and poverty. Men understood that a woman without any real or personal property faced a difficult road ahead, especially if she was without familial resources. This threat was taken very seriously by Virginia's courts, and records from the Eastern State Hospital show female patients admitted due to insanity caused by the progression from threats of burning the house to physical violence. Marital duty required that a husband provide basic goods for his family, so cruel men could turn the threat of abandoning these responsibilities into a way to leverage for more power in the relationship. After bearing sixteen children over more than two decades of marriage, Mary Crowell described in her bill how her husband, Joseph, used just such a threat. He "expressed an intention to sell his property and abandon her, leaving her penniless." It was an idle threat in this case; he never left. Nevertheless, Joseph's statement served to remind his wife of her subordinate place in the relationship. He could cause her physical pain, which he did. But he could also injure her by wrecking her chances of survival.[43]

In addition, husbands could frame threats around child injury or removal. William Crawford was a local drunk who failed to support his family and would leave for intervals of time with no notice. When he was home, Martha, his wife, continually avoided any close physical contact with him due to a fear of harm to her or her child. Upon returning home from one of his drunken sprees, William even "threaten[ed] to tear the child from her arms and dash its brains out against a tree." As a result of these threats, Martha filed for, and received, an absolute divorce. She was seriously concerned that in a fit of drunken rage he might carry out his threats and kill her and her child. Although the wife might be the primary caretaker of a child, a husband could quickly demonstrate that he was still the most important authority figure in a child's life. Threats to remove a child from a mother's custody were viewed as cruel during the antebellum period. Recognizing that a woman's mobility was somewhat limited, her husband could also threaten to take the children to a far-off locale, such as Georgia. These threats represented attempts to make it clear to women that motherhood was a privilege granted to them by their husbands. Threats of this nature were deemed cruel because they flew in the face of an increasing recognition of the significance of the mother's role, as is evident from the rise of custody decisions favoring mothers.[44]

While threats could arise out of seemingly random situations, spouses often used them to encourage their marital partners to perform certain tasks. For example, a husband could tell a wife to leave the home and never return, or else. The "or else" aspect of the threat quite often involved a death by shooting or some other means. Isaac Farrell of Frederick County, Virginia, kept a gun ready in case his wife returned to the house, refused to leave, and "needed" to be shot. According to witness accounts, a Wisconsin man, Samuel Galbreath, carried a gun on his person and "said that he had long intended to kill her [his wife] and that he would do so unless she should quit the house and leave him within a specified time which he named." Galbreath and others were also accused of failing to provide necessary goods for their families, so perhaps forcing their wives to leave was a way for them to drop all appearances of marital obligation. The fact that they threatened violence to achieve these aims, however, made their behaviors cruel.[45]

Across all three states, husbands and wives cited a spouse's temper as one of the principal contributing factors behind marital verbal cruelties. This emphasis on tempers deserves a quick treatment at this point but will also be a theme carried throughout later chapters. In particular, husbands called wives to task for possessing frightful and cruel tempers. Within court papers, a reference to a wife's temper did not always require additional explanation in order for it to be taken seriously. It was understood that temperamental women, otherwise known as shrews or scolds, could hound their husbands until the men, in a fashion similar to that of the threatened wives, lived in a constant state of anxiety. However, men's reactions usually combined anxiety with annoyance. Their wives' temper held more of a danger to their mental state than to their well-being in a physical sense. References to a woman's temper could describe it as "high" or "bad" or "violent" or "ungovernable." Women with high tempers were not calm and soothing in accordance with womanly ideals. Women with bad or violent tempers could be prone to making physical assaults. Women with ungovernable tempers were a danger to society's hierarchical structure, wherein a wife should always be obedient. By describing a temper as ungovernable, husbands admitted their own failure to govern their households and invited the entry of other men into their domestic sphere.[46]

It was believed that a wife's cruel temper could lead a man to de-

struction. In a treatise on family government, one author described
how a man who was "industrious, sober, temperate, and entirely
amiable" was driven to drink by his wife. The man proved "mistaken"
in his choice of wife and "wedded a lovely form, but it enshrined
the temper of a demon." Men also claimed that part of the damage
wreaked by a woman's temper was that it brought out the cruel side of
men as well. L.D. Spragins recalled how, after "being provoked by an
incessant and severe cross fire" from his high-tempered wife, he then
"may have used expressions that were not very witty or fashionable
and that might have been regarded by 'by ears polite' as 'low and vulgar.'" Hence, his wife's cruelty drove him to vulgarity. Charles Yearout
admitted that his wife's "exceedingly peevish and fretful" demeanor
led to his using "abusive language" towards her. Other men would
respond with physical violence.[47]

Interestingly enough, the problem of a woman's temper was not
unsolvable. Treatise and newspaper writers expounded that cruelty,
in this case, was avoidable. To prevent the development of an unruly
temper, a wife should exercise constant diligence with respect to her
own emotions. She should focus on her wifely duties as opposed to
romantic longings. *The Young Wife's Book* cautioned that "continued
differences and bickering will undermine the strongest affection,"
and therefore, "a wife cannot be too careful to avoid disputes upon
the most trivial of subjects." Of course, *trivial* is a subjective term and
the husband defined it in these cases. To achieve a peaceful marriage,
"Every wish, every prejudice must meet with attention, and the first
thought of a woman should be the pleasing and providing for her
husband." Under these instructions, a wife pursing any other focus
than her husband's needs ran the risk of developing, and displaying,
an unwomanly temper.[48]

It should be stated that concerns about men's tempers also appeared with regularity within cruelty cases. While women were
cautioned to cultivate pleasant dispositions, men were told to control their passionate natures. Essentially, in all three states, those
husbands who could not regulate their own tempers were unfit to
lead separate households full of dependents. As one treatise author
argued, "He is an unworthy head of household who cannot control
his own temper, who is constantly breaking out with angry remarks."
Cruelty, as elaborated in divorce cases, was the natural outcome of an

uncontrolled masculine temper. A Wisconsin wife recalled how her husband "was a man of violent ugly temper, got mad quick, when he had no reason for it, got mad very often. . . . He would get so mad he couldn't help himself." In the process of court proceedings, male deponents would act as expert witnesses in the use of mastery over self, pointing to the moments when husbands "did not appear to exercise any control" over their brutal passions.[49]

This chapter opened by asking how and why antebellum husbands and wives were verbally cruel. It has shown that verbal marital cruelties could take a variety of forms. Epithets, character attacks, and threats used by spouses demonstrated the degree to which marriage was often an ongoing power struggle. Cruelty was a tool that antebellum spouses employed to control the behavior of a partner. However, society on the whole did not sanction verbal cruelties. In particular, judges and juries were sympathetic to claims by injured spouses alleging crippling emotional distress or a "reasonable apprehension" of physical injury. They believed that words could, and did, hurt.

CHAPTER 2

"A Kind of Hell upon Earth"

The Physical Cruelties of Husbands and Wives

After five children and over a decade of marriage, Albert Bowker finally reached his breaking point. In a detailed bill, he described to the Dane County, Wisconsin, circuit judge why he no longer wished to stay married to his wife, Mereda. He explained that shortly into their union he discovered that she possessed a demon temper, a fault he was willing to tolerate. However, over the past two years, Mereda conducted an all-out war on his domestic authority. During regular "fits of anger and rage," she fell into the "constant habit of kicking, striking, scratching, & pushing" him. She even took her aggression so far as to hit him on the head with an "iron stove hook." In addition to feeling cowed by her physical prowess, Albert related to the court that his wife sought to undermine his parental rule by "interfering with & preventing" his governance of the children. A witness confirmed Albert's account, adding that the Bowker household was a "kind of hell upon Earth." Julia Barnes, a former boarder, provided additional insight regarding the day-to-day operations of the Bowker family. Barnes claimed that Mereda not only refused to do the cooking, washing, or mending, but she acted in an outright confrontational manner towards Albert. During one incident, Mereda shook her fist in her husband's face and "dare[d] him to put his hand on her, and said if he did she would knock him over with the first thing she could get hold of." Albert declined the invitation and walked away. In the end, Mereda behaved cruelly by not allowing Albert to be the master of his household and by positioning herself in his rightful place. As a result, Albert received his divorce.[1]

This chapter examines how antebellum men and women in Virginia, Texas, and Wisconsin defined and perceived physical cruelty in marriage. It asks: How were husbands and wives physically cruel? Why were husbands and wives physically cruel? Isolated outbursts of violence, whether in the form of a slap or a blow, were understood by many to be unpleasant but tolerable parts of marriage. The records show that nineteenth-century Americans drew the line between impulsive violence and cruelty, at willful and systematic physical attacks, evidenced by blood, repeated blows, etc. Moreover, reasonable chastisement shaded into cruelty if a spouse perpetrated a punishment in an overly emotional way or if the action resulted in permanent physical injury. A fine line existed between chastisement and cruelty, proper mastery and improper mastery, honorable and dishonorable manhood. Unsurprisingly, violence between spouses often arose from a struggle for power in the household and in the relationship.

In the southern states studied, husbands attacked wives in an attempt to assert mastery (and were divorced for it), and they also claimed to have been victimized by abusive wives who sought inappropriate mastery over their husbands (and were granted divorces on those grounds). Southern cultures of honor and mastery buttressed traditional gender roles, and men's violence within households helped them to violently affirm those roles. In Wisconsin, on the other hand, fewer traditions defined the roles of husband and wife; indeed, many new conditions of daily life demanded improvisation. How much of traditional gender roles remained relevant in the pioneer context? Such a question, and the confusion it reflected, apparently grated on couples and prompted much rather intense physical violence. All in all, the actions of cruel husbands and wives in Wisconsin led to more permanent injuries and generalized brutality within marriages than can be seen in either Virginia or Texas for the period.

It is important to note that, at the appellate level, the three states studied all understood extreme bodily injury as constituting cruelty. However, despite being the oldest recognized brand of cruelty, physical violence still presented a bit of a definitional quandary. The rulings of higher courts provided only minimal guidance for the local communities encountering such actions on a regular basis. Much emphasis was placed on the local knowledge held by juries who could, in the words of the Supreme Court of Texas, "appreciate and place the proper estimate on [their] conduct" better than a distant court. Jurors were to use their "discretion" to separate the wheat from the chaff. After all, "Among persons of coarse habits, blows might pass for very little more than rudeness of language or manner." To interrogate how communities across the three states interpreted instances of physical cruelty at the ground level, we begin by examining the physical cruelties of married men before turning our attention to the actions of cruel wives.[2]

Cruel husbands manifested their ill feelings towards their spouses in a wide variety of ways, often relying upon sheer physical superiority to carry the day. By far the most prevalent form of physical abuse was the "slap" or "blow." A slap was an open-handed hit, frequently directed at the facial area. In contrast, a blow occurred when a person struck the other with a closed fist. Most people considered a closed handed attack the more dangerous of the two, although a slap could hold perils of its own. For this reason, judges and juries gave full consideration to spouses who came before the courts claiming injury due to cruel hand-based assaults. Wives, for their part, relied upon language that recognized the potential utility of the slap or blow, while pointing out their husband's individual failings in usage. As Laura Edwards argues, "The issue was not *whether* they should be subordinate, but *what* their subordination should entail." Wifely litigants conceded that chastisement required physical force but took issue with what they perceived as the overzealous application of domestic punishment. They wanted to refine the practice of marital mastery, not destroy it. After all, the vast majority of women who received divorces due to cruelties would go on to marry again.[3]

In particular, wives and witnesses called attention to those moments in which out-of-control negative emotions, as opposed to sound logical principles, guided a husband's violent hands. Assaults of this nature could come out of nowhere, as Lucy Burwell described to a Virginia court. Once when her husband was "angry with her for some cause," he snuck up behind her, pushed her so that she fell down, and then "twice slapped her in the most humiliating manner." She lived with the markings from this attack on her face for more than a week. Lucy and other wives successfully argued that the causal agent of "anger" moved a slap or blow out of the category of benign "discipline" and into cruelty. Proper domestic mastery required control, consistency, and a careful application of violence on the part of the master. A husband who ruled unpredictably could foster potentially contagious feelings of dependent discontent and rebellion. Therefore, any and all instances of inept mastery represented a community problem, especially in southern areas. By the late antebellum period, the South was trying to project the image of a benevolent society in which dependents, especially white women, received fair treatment.[4]

Struggling to erect boundaries between acceptable and unacceptable behaviors, antebellum citizens repeatedly emphasized the importance of assessing the exact number of slaps or blows. This, perhaps, reflected a desire to impose a sense of order on otherwise chaotic scenes of marital conflict. While the victim and perpetrator of the supposed assault might provide a numerical summary of the incident, the most valuable information usually came from witnesses. Out of the direct fray, these individuals carefully listened and observed as scenes of discord unfolded. One household servant recounted, "he hit his wife with seven blows two with open hand, one with closed fist." She did not specify further, but we can safely assume the other four blows involved shoving or perhaps the use of a weapon. Children provided some of the most detailed estimates. Sixteen-year-old Emeline Giese told the court about a family quarrel that ended when "father struck mother with his fist in her face, and on her head, on her arms, and breast, all over. He struck her five or six times." Witnesses argued that a single blow might be forgiven as an emotional outburst, but a series constituted a larger threat. Cruel husbands escalated their attacks while simply inept ones lashed out infrequently, only causing minimal injuries.[5]

Could a single blow satisfy the legal threshold for marital cruelty? The simplest answer was that yes, it could, but most of the time it did not. Husbands accused of committing cruelty understood this and often mounted a defense by saying that they required only a single slap to set their entire household back to order. They tried to limit the damage by admitting to a lone act of violence, a singular moment of weakness in an otherwise solid record of mastery. They reached out to other men with a question: if faced with a wife like mine, wouldn't you do the same? However, on occasion, the ferocity of a solo blow captured the court's attention. Sarah Budd's statement began ominously with a description of her husband's unpredictable fits of temper. In a particularly violent assault that left their marital bed drenched in fresh blood, John Budd relied on his fists to do his cruel work. Upon his wife's return from helping a neighbor, John pounced on her and threw her on to the bed. While she was on her back in an obviously vulnerable position he then "struck her a violent blow in the face which caused the blood to run from her nose & mouth in a frightful manner," ruining the bedsheets. Managing to slip free, despite the blood, Sarah then ran into the street screaming for help. To secure a divorce she needed the judge and jury to recognize her husband's fist as a potentially deadly weapon.[6]

To gauge the ferocity of a marital confrontation, judges and juries encouraged witnesses and litigants to provide detailed descriptions of where exactly a husband's hits landed upon his wife. The location of the blows might offer an indication as to intent, the assumption being that those husbands who planned to seriously injure their partners generally concentrated their energies on the critical areas of the head and neck. In Virginia, Elizabeth Binn's husband slapped her on the jaw. The Amelia County, Virginia, jury found him "guilty of using inhuman violence against her" and dissolved the union. Meanwhile, one Texas husband struck his wife in the face so hard as to knock a pipe from her mouth. The said pipe then fell onto the child the woman was holding, "badly burning" the infant as a result. The man continued by pulling the woman out of the chair by her hair while at the same time proclaiming that "she had better go back to Indiana." By the end of the attack, this Texas woman was left out of doors to nurse her own injuries and those of her child. She believed that her husband initiated the confrontation out of a desire to drive her from the home and enact an informal separation. Historian Norma Basch has documented how frontier husbands, in particular, "created de facto divorces" while "women sought out legal ones." If divorce was not something that a man wished to pursue, or if a wife refused to leave, then violence could be used to push a wife out of the domestic space. In the end, cruelty offered husbands an avenue, albeit a cowardly one, to effectively end cohabitation.[7] Although gendered ideals of modesty traditionally dictated that a woman's body was not a suitable topic of public conversation, court participants expected and anticipated graphic testimony. This represented another indication of the extent to which marital disputes blurred the boundaries of public and private. In the antebellum period, when a woman such as

Delia Tubbs walked around with her face "blue" from a recent attack, her body made her private sufferings public. Her visible injuries invited members of the community to comment on and explore not only her particular circumstances, but the degree to which their society tolerated cruelty.[8]

The courts and community members across the three states studied reserved their harshest critiques for cruel husbands who chose to pursue attacks while their intended victims attempted to flee or fell to the ground. The sheer physical force employed by violent men virtually guaranteed that many women would end up on the floor at some point during an assault. Quite often the most dangerous injuries resulted from the fall itself and not the prior blows. Witnesses described how Lynchburg City resident John Mullens, during his four-year marriage with Mary Ann Mullens, would strike his wife with such "great violence" as to make her "stagger" and nearly collapse. As an indicator of the force that John used, in one instance when a blow intended for his wife missed its mark, it "fell on the stove pipe—in which it made a deep indention." Fearing for Mary's future safety, the court granted the divorce. Once a woman was down on the ground, the attack could develop in a variety of ways. In the best of circumstances, the husband would choose to end the assault. Then, the determination of cruelty would be based upon his actions up until that point. Unfortunately, this was usually not the case. Part of the progression could involve a wife being dragged around the floor by her husband, generally by the hair, continuing the assault. He "did then and there, in a violent and brutal manner drag her over the yard," read one Texas woman's account of cruelty. Another wife recalled how she escaped from her irate husband only to be found again by him, at which point he "draged her about by the hair for the half a mile back home." Grabbing a handful of hair from above generally prevented a woman from attempting to make a successful escape, or possible counterattack. In this very primitive manifestation of physical dominance, husbands forced their wives into submission. Dragging resulted in few visible injuries, thus making it possible for a man to plausibly deny a woman's allegations of cruelty in court. This defense, of course, only worked if no other witnesses came forward to describe the assault.[9]

As a wife lay upon the ground, her husband could escalate the degree of bodily injury by kicking. Wisconsin wives, in particular, requested relief from kick-prone cruel husbands. The specific nature of their complaints can be partially attributed to the attire of the region. Many Wisconsin men worked as loggers, lumberjacks, and outdoor laborers and regularly wore heavy boots. Their choice of footwear made any ensuing kicking assaults all the more brutal. The *Baraboo Republic* newspaper reported that a "miserable brute of a husband" appeared before the Police Court on charges of "kicking his wife with great heavy boots, so that she was nearly killed." He was freed after she refused to testify against him. Although legal officials recognized her husband's behavior as worthy of censure, she may or may not have agreed. Even if she believed that he had behaved cruelly, the necessities of survival might have required that she rescue her abuser and attempt to salvage the relationship. After all, life for a single woman in rural Wisconsin possessed many kinds of hardships.[10]

Other wives related how husbands employed kicking as a form of general harassment. Take, for example, the Hersey marriage, which lasted less than one year. On their wedding trip, George Hersey demonstrated that aside from being borderline suicidal, he also possessed a maniacal temper. When traveling in rail cars he would push his wife, Caroline, up against the side of the car, injuring her "very much." Then, upon their arrival at one of the hotels, he "insisted in sleeping with his feet" in Caroline's face, which could have been harmless except for the fact that he then proceeded to kick her in the face "with all his might." He also held her against the bed wall "with his feet for some time" until she begged for release. On the same trip, he grabbed a pair of "heavy soled cow-hide boots" and swore that he would knock her brains out. George used his feet and footwear as weapons until he finally deserted his wife in April 1857. She then successfully pursued the dissolution of their union. Under normal circumstances, the wedding tour represented an opportunity to enjoy one's spouse and revel in the marital state. In contrast, George embarked upon this journey with a goal of showing his new wife exactly what it meant to live under his rule. His actions suggest a desire to literally trample his wife's health and happiness underfoot.[11]

Unlike George, the vast majority of husbands preferred to use the power of their hands to perpetrate cruelties against their wives. Choking, or placing both hands around another person's neck and applying pressure, appeared frequently within the records. Wives and witnesses who sought cruelty rulings on the basis of choking incidents argued that this particular form of intimate violence was almost always detrimental to life and served no purpose related to domestic mastery. Because it did not fall under the rubric of chastisement, choking was an illegitimate use of violence requiring regulation by the courts and community. To bolster their arguments, wifely litigants described being choked "nearly to death," all the while listening to their husband's snarled death threats. When husbands expressed their lethal intentions during choking attacks, their comments would then be repeated in a courtroom setting. For example, a Milwaukee court heard how John Curliss seized his wife by the throat and declared, "I believe by God I'll shut off your breath and the sooner it's done the better." John's comments turned an already violent attack into a clear situation of cruelty by uniting deadly intent with harmful action, thereby justifying a divorce. Moreover, wives and witnesses framed choking as a particularly intimate and opportunistic form of cruelty. The records indicate that husbands generally initiated choking attacks in the bedroom, the most sacred of domestic spaces. A pattern emerged in which a man would sneak up on his wife while she lay asleep in bed. Then, when he was close enough he would wrap his hands around her neck, perhaps smothering her with a pillow as well. This manner of approach provided maximum surprise as well as leverage. After properly positioning his hands a man could squeeze and, in the process, cut off all oxygen available to the victim. In a manner similar to hair-pulling, choking could be used to place the victim's body under the attacker's control.[12]

Armed with limited medical knowledge, antebellum men and women struggled to identify and understand the biological hazards associated with choking. Modern-day society, fed by a variety of academic and popular studies, recognizes choking as one of the clearest indicators of malicious, even fatal, intent on the part of husbands towards wives. However, antebellum observers and courtroom participants acted without the benefit of wide-ranging scholarly studies. To determine the extent of choking injury, they focused on body markings and the degree of oxygen deprivation. To fulfill this evidentiary requirement, a rural Texas wife, Sarah Burdett, asserted that the bruises on her throat from her husband's attack lingered for a "long time." The jury found her account to be compelling enough to justify a divorce. It was not uncommon to find wives within the records who lived with fingerprints on their necks for weeks or months. Although an asset in a divorce proceeding, the presence of bruises prompted much public gossip and questioning. As such, some women devised ways to conceal the physical evidence of abuse. The eleven-year-old son of Rachel and Augustus Gardner recalled in his deposition how his mother "wore a handkerchief on her neck for several days" following a physical domestic dispute in order to "hide the marks." Interestingly enough, the records suggest that bruises alone were generally not enough to sustain a cruelty ruling. Indeed, as the argument went, some women bruised easily and wounds of this sort, typically, did not impair overall functionality.[13] To get a divorce, a woman needed to prove that choking was a form of wife torture. Elizabeth Waid's case is illustrative in this context. In her bill to the Franklin County, Virginia, chancery court, Elizabeth claimed that her husband "several years ago in a fit of drunkenness and rage, while in bed . . . caught her rudely by the neck and violently choked her, leaving the prints of his fingers upon her flesh for many days." A few weeks later he choked her again, but this time he also hit her about the head and "kicked her in the abdomen & groins with great violence, knocking her speechless and senseless, and biting out of her hand a large piece of flesh." Determined to pursue a divorce after these two attacks, Elizabeth approached the court only to delay filing after her husband promised to reform. He later continued his cruel actions, albeit in new forms, and she reinstigated her divorce action. Within her statement to the court, Elizabeth emphasized how her husband acted out of "rage" and without reason. His animalistic attacks, including hand-biting, were intended only to humiliate and injure her. Moreover, Elizabeth drew attention to the brutal elements of their confrontations by using terms such as "violently" and "rudely" to describe her husband's behaviors.[14]

The most legally compelling choking cases centered upon those moments in which a woman's breath left her body and the attack became imminently fatal. Depriving one's spouse of vital oxygen clearly qualified as cruelty, if not attempted murder. The challenge for litigants was to convince a judge and jury that the physical conflict in question had gotten to that point. As such, injured spouses called upon those witnesses who could provide minute-by-minute commentaries of the day's events. A person requested to appear in court in this capacity might give an estimate as to the number of minutes that the victim went without breath or the ability to speak. Common sense dictated that the severity of the overall injury coincided with the length of any impairments.[15]

George Compton, a child witness, appeared before the court and described how he was awakened from sleep one night by his mother running to his bed claiming that his father was going to kill her. Almost immediately his father then arrived and caught her and "pulled her loose" from George's hands. Then, as George recollected, "my father put his hand over her throat for her breath seemed to stop." The recognition of the lethal possibility of the attack prompted George to action and he "caught hold" of his father, allowing his mother to escape to a neighbor's house. While the son knew that his father was behaving cruelly, he waited for a certain level of danger before acting in defense of his mother. If he interfered prematurely, he ran the risk of being subjected to abuse as well. George's testimony demonstrated with clarity that his mother suffered under cruelty via the application and apprehension of severe bodily injury at the hands of her husband, George's father. George's statement provided sufficient evidence for a rural Virginia court to dissolve his parents' marriage contract.[16]

As we move away from direct, body-to-body, physical assaults by men, we turn our attention to those husbands who perpetrated cruelties against their wives with the aid of outside weapons. Unlike slapping, pinching, kicking, or choking, whipping appeared to constitute, if anything, a traditional form of chastisement. The practice of whipping appeared within American households well prior to the antebellum period. In colonial families, husbands served as the hierarchical heads of households and, as such, they sought to keep their dependents in line, even if this required corporal punishment. In order to ensure that all men chastised their dependents with restraint, an informal "rule of thumb" developed and eventually made its way into courtrooms as a general assessment of proper correction. According to a recent scholar, the "rule of thumb" in England and the United States stated that if a husband beat his wife with a stick or switch "about the size of one of his fingers (but not as large as a man's thumb)," he should be left "immune from prosecution." In theory, this restriction limited the possibility for an emotional outburst while lessening the severity of damage inflicted on a wife's body. The "rule of thumb" also contained a significant class element in application. Simply put, a person of the lower classes might be deemed more suited to this chastisement style than an individual of middling or well-to-do means. Thus, even in its early forms, a sliding scale of cruelty was informally acknowledged by the legal system. Although colonial courts regularly applied this threshold in domestic management cases, historians have generally argued that the "rule of thumb" was all but gone by the antebellum period. In fact, the court records suggest that this was only partially true. Virginians rarely referenced the rule of thumb because they were already in the midst of tightening the restrictions connected with marital chastisement. In this context, they believed that the rule allowed for too much tolerance for the practices of domestic tyrants. On the other hand, Texans looked to the rule as a general guideline. They hoped to use it as a tool to regulate mastery with an eye towards the needs of frontier families. Wisconsin residents mentioned the rule the most frequently, with husbands claiming the concept was too restricting and wives lamenting that it allowed brutal husbands too much behavioral freedom.[17]

As their differing applications of the rule indicate, citizens of the three states took varying approaches to cases involving whippings perpetrated by husbands towards wives. Many men in Virginia and Texas utilized whipping as a tool in the management of household dependents. According to the logic of southern mastery, a whipping kept dependents in line while lessening the possibility of a power struggle. In their divorce documents, husbands repeatedly referenced a dialogue of familial control that all members of society understood, even if some of them disagreed. The general belief was that a chink in the husband's armor of authority caused, for example, by a disruptive wife, could result in other dependents questioning or challenging their positions within the household. Masculine authority in the South proved particularly important as it was critical to maintaining a slave society. Whipping was a common form of punishment used upon the enslaved, and this practice extended to other household members as well. Southern husbands, therefore, employed whipping as a way to remind their wives of their position in the family order. One husband was overheard stating that, "he had as much right to whip her [his wife] as he had to whip one of his horses." However, as the antebellum period progressed, even southern husbands found their rights of chastisement coming increasingly under attack. This placed whipping at the center of a growing discussion regarding the line between the proper practice of authority and domestic cruelty.[18]

With reference to matters of authority, James Flinn's answer to his wife's divorce petition is instructional. Following the standard format, he admitted that they had married many years prior to his wife's bill. He also mentioned that, yes, he was indeed hurt by his wife accusing him of insanity. Accusations such as these, according to James, "were well calculated to make a bastards heart bleed." But he was prepared to live with her oddities until the point at which she attempted to subvert his direct authority in his own home. Namely, she placed herself in the doorway of the house with a knife and refused to allow him entrance. Claiming to be at the limit of his benevolent tolerance, James "thereupon broke from the bough of a peach tree, a switch with which he restored peace to his house and family." His wife, "alarmed at this exercise of authority . . . ceased with her menaces & became quiet." According to this logic, the most effective way of bringing about peace in a southern home was to use violence. James recognized that he should not resort to such violence immediately and, in his closing remarks, reiterated that "he has not exercised over her [his wife] any authority, much less practiced cruelty, over her, which was not in his judgment essential to the due regulation and peace of his family." James's statement reinforced the idea of a controlled, and limited, chastisement as an unpleasant but essential part of society. In James's opinion, cruelty only occurred when a husband moved closer to enacting the rule of thumb. It is interesting to note, however, that James also dehumanized his wife by never mentioning any of the physical consequences of the whipping itself. She "became quiet" but he offered no other information on her bodily condition post-incident.[19]

When looking at the experiences of James Flinn and other Virginia husbands, a historian discovers significant evidence to support a theory of embattled southern domestic authority. These husbands operated in an environment in which the relationship of honor and mastery was increasingly fraught. To be perceived as honorable and to maintain the stability of southern society, a man must not only govern his dependents but do so in a proper manner. The definition of "proper" served as the battlefield for debates over domestic authority. In the face of criticisms focusing on the violence and inhumanity of the southern slave system as well as general campaigns against corporal punishment, Virginia husbands continued to argue for their right to chastise dependents. But this was an increasingly limited right, at least with regards to marital rule. The whipping of slaves, according to historian Ariela Gross, "did not amount to cruelty because it was the usual punishment."[20] In contrast, the whipping of wives potentially constituted a cruel violation of southern conjugal norms.

Household heads could face challenges from the unlikeliest of sources. Consider, for example, the case of Margaret Compton of Rappahannock County, Virginia. She filed a divorce petition claiming that her husband had choked her, whipped her, and kicked her out of their house. A nearby neighbor, Elizabeth Dowden, recalled one of the conversations that she had with John Compton regarding the treatment of his wife. When Elizabeth asked him to "quit abusing" his wife, John replied by saying that "he would do as he pleased . . . if she [his wife] did not do better he would get switches and whip her or confine her in some place, until she was better." In his response, John not only asserted his right to chastise Margaret, but also made it clear that he was the person who determined if she acted "better" or not. This case file demonstrates how community members, such as the neighbor Elizabeth, could call into question a man's right to rule. Although James and John might have felt justified in their actions, they lived in a society increasingly skeptical of the traditional practices associated with chastisement, especially when those "punishments" were visited upon southern white women.[21]

Texas men also struggled to delineate the boundaries of proper mastery, yet they differed from Virginians by more freely turning to cruelty as a tool for marital management. The environment of frontier Texas presented many challenges for settlers, and traditional gender norms began to erode under the pressures of such conditions. Husbands would often respond to these changes by using cruelty to push their wives back into a state of "proper" subordination and dependency. When questioned about his actions, one Texas husband defended his cruelties by stating that his wife insisted on "interfering with his business and wished him implicitly to follow her rule, indeed desired to be master of all and was not content to be mistress of his house." Therefore, he would whip her or hit her in an attempt to "maintain the dignity of his position as husband." The home sphere was one area in which men demanded to maintain control, a haven of authority in an unsettled environment.[22]

Unsatisfied with merely accepting a husband's word that his wife deserved corporal punishment, southerners created an active dialogue focusing upon the varying degrees of cruelty encapsulated within wife whippings. When assessing the severity of a whipping and, therefore, the possibility of cruelty, they considered a variety of factors. To begin with, what weapon was used? The weapons can generally be divided into sticks and proper "traditional" whips. Sticks were often small branches grabbed from nearby trees. A "good" whipping stick or branch was pliable enough to support a quick striking motion while also not breaking under the pressure of the blows. A traditional whip was usually an item used around the house, often to control animals, which became a weapon upon its usage against a human being, usually a dependent of some sort. Cowhide, wagon, and horse whips were all mentioned frequently in the records. A whip was an easily accessible weapon of choice. If an area had trees or animals, a husband had a ready-made whip.[23]

Some husbands cruelly prepared in advance to administer whippings. This type of premeditation demonstrated that their actions were not in response to a domestic breach, but rather the outgrowth of a twisted habit. This is only somewhat surprising considering that, as other studies of violence have shown, instruments of violence can occasionally be the focus of fetishization. Essentially, an individual or group can develop an almost obsessive focus on a certain weapon; such was the experience of John Clopton. He was a husband, a father, and a violent abuser. He preferred to injure his wife with whipping assaults in which he would "attack with horse whips, cowhides, sticks, anything he could get ahold of." Not to be limited in his behaviors, Clopton perpetrated these cruelties in front of neighbors and even while his wife was pregnant. At one point a female friend of his wife observed "splinters" in Mary Clopton's head after an assault. But, as a Clopton daughter later claimed, her father truly preferred to mete out abuse with his special "cowhide which he said he had made for that express purpose." The daughter described how her father tested out this device by hitting her mother on the body and head until "her eyes were so swolled that she could not see." Apparently satisfied with his work, her father then proclaimed that he intended to use the cowhide whip to kill her mother "by piecemeals" so that he would have no fear of "being hanged" as a wife murderer. Clopton's preparation and planning transformed what could have been a "typical" cruel whipping into premeditated wife torture. Mary Clopton lived in a state of constant apprehension of physical violence, which John fed by his bizarre behaviors. He was found guilty of cruelty by the court, and Mary received custody of the children and a divorce from bed and board.[24]

Southerners took particular note of the number and nature of the "stripes" inflicted on a woman's body. As the emotions of the situation often did not allow an exact count, witnesses often provided an estimate as to the number of blows. It was generally believed that a "few" stripes, though cruel, were excusable, whereas "many" were, literally, harsh beyond measure. Again, when in doubt, individuals focused on the body itself for answers. During one episode in which James Fulford "inflicted punishment" on Rosina, his wife, he left long bloody lines on her back and "contusions of the flesh which remained for one week." A beating such as this could result in Rosina's being permanently disfigured, a gross violation of the protection owed to wives by husbands in Virginia and Texas. The location of the blows was also important, with the majority usually falling on the body but occasionally on the face. Stripes on the face were deemed very serious because they could lead to scarring or even blindness. A resultant facial deformity could then diminish a woman's public standing, thus satisfying the cruelty threshold of permanent damage.[25]

The violation of a wife's body by her husband reached another level of unacceptability if, by chance, a whipping exposed her nakedness. This then damaged a woman's chastity by presenting her body to other dependents and to the general public. As historians of slavery have shown, the abolitionist movement was particularly effective at using these types of images of slave women to elicit empathy among white women and men. Even in Virginia, the whipping of a white woman to the point at which she "lost" her chastity, meaning her naked body was on display, represented a major misuse of mastery and a case of marital cruelty. In a moment of deep intoxication, William Waid committed such a cruelty on his wife Elizabeth when he "jerked her off of the bed, stripped her clothing above her waist, and inflicted upon her naked limbs and the lower part of her person a most severe and cruel whipping with switches, cutting her skin in a number of places." As a result, she was unable to sit for numerous days. To heighten the humiliation, her fifteen-year-old son witnessed the entire incident. The son, Wingfield, later recalled how his mother begged his father to desist even as he continued to "wear out" a "handful of switches" on her. Southern honor dictated that a husband protect his wife's chastity and virtue, by lethal force if necessary, so whippings of this sort violated marital norms on multiple levels. And "as white women were not expected to defend insults on their own behalf," victimized southern wives looked to the courts for assistance.[26]

However, it would be a mistake to stereotype these women as shrinking violets in constant need of male rescue. In fact, their court statements indicate that injured women not only desired, but expected, justice. Lawyers in an 1843 case would sarcastically claim, "It is for the Court to say whether striping an aged and respectable Female of her clothing and inflicting stripes upon her back with a cowhide" constitutes "legal cruelty." Their sixty-year-old client, Anne Souther, had been whipped in this manner on at least one occasion by her forty-five-year-old husband. As Anne related to a friend of hers, she had decided that she could put up with a variety of cruel acts on the part of her husband, but she would not submit to whippings, and she filed for divorce. Anne's lawyers believed hers to be an open-and-shut case of marital cruelty. By proceeding in an overly deferential manner to the court, they implied that the public consensus was already formed in their client's favor.[27]

Aside from using their hands, whips, and sticks as weapons, spouses would also transform regular household items into dangerous objects. As a continuation of the pattern discussed up until this point, it appears as if husbands in Virginia used the most "innocuous" weapons set, followed by Texans, with Wisconsin husbands opting for more deadly tools of cruelty. While husbands might have reached for weapons in a spontaneous fashion, they chose the items that best suited their overall intent. Men also had the option to use objects that women were less able to wield as effectively, such as chairs. In Texas, we find a wide variety of weapons used. Chairs, boards, glass bottles, and tailor's shears were only a handful of the weapons mentioned.

For example, John Pratt struck his wife "in the mouth with a wing of Turkey which bruised her face." And Peter Betz threw an umbrella at his wife, while James Barrett preferred to lob socks and glass bottles in his wife's general direction.[28]

If we turn our gaze to Wisconsin, we find the same weapons listed above with the addition of more purposefully deadly items, handled with a desire to commit serious injury. Many Wisconsin husbands looking for a domestic weapon would perhaps throw a washbasin at their wives or strike them with a fire shovel, pitcher, pail, iron spoon, teacup, table fork, candlestick, teapot, or hammer. If those items did not result in the degree of physical damage desired, a husband might reach for a more dangerous item. Husbands could even throw pitchforks at their wives. Given the general agricultural nature of Wisconsin society, this tool was readily available and could be injurious from quite a distance. William Bryerton, after a fierce drinking fit at his family farm, grabbed a pitchfork and threw it at his wife through a window, in the process breaking out "three or four lights of glass." Luckily, his wife managed to dodge the fork and escape mostly unharmed. Wives recognized that a pitchfork was a "deadly weapon" and, in the case of Margaret Lewis, they would state this fact to the court.[29]

The axe was one of the most frequently mentioned, and one of the most harmful, weapons wielded by Wisconsin husbands. Regular articles in local newspapers described what could happen when husbands took their cruelties too far and actually murdered their wives with axes. The particularly violent story of Adam Rettig provides a singular example of marital discord. As reported by the *Daily Milwaukee News,* Rettig was a farmer near Milwaukee who, while his wife was kneeling down performing housework, grabbed an axe and "dealt her a dreadful blow on the head, breaking in her skull, and knocking her senseless to the floor. Not satisfied with this, the wretched man then took a kettle of boiling water and poured it over her from head to foot, while she still lived and shrieked in tortures worse than death." He then fatally shot himself in the head with a rifle.[30]

Although this was an admittedly extreme situation, Wisconsin wives in divorce papers described scarily similar scenarios within their own households. Harriet Ann Davey lost the use of her left arm after one such attack. Harriet and her husband Thomas, both English emigrants to Wisconsin, never lived peacefully together. He always found fault with her and could quickly turn violent. In one incident, Thomas knocked her to the floor and then swung an axe at her "which she partially avoided," the blow landing on her neck and shoulder. As she lay "senseless" on the floor, he then took a razor, dipped it in her blood, and spread the report that she had cut her own throat. His plan did not work, however, because she lived to tell the tale and it became "understood in the neighborhood that he had struck her with an axe." Thomas Davey's action led not only to a divorce suit, but also a criminal assault case. Although this work does not focus on criminal cases, the evidence suggests that domestic disputes in Wisconsin were walking a very fine line between life and death.[31]

The elevated and ferocious nature of marital violence in Wisconsin owed a great deal to husbands' reactions to the pressures of maintaining domestic control in a topsy-turvy society. Wisconsin society in the 1840s and 1850s was still a frontier, characterized by clashing cultures and harsh environmental conditions. As such, husbands and wives looked to a wide variety of gender models when creating their own households. Unlike in the South, Wisconsin men did not have a system of honor or the subordination of an enslaved people to bolster their domestic rule. Therefore, it appears as if Wisconsin men took their cues from the violence that they witnessed in their communities and perpetrated physical marital cruelties as part of a quest to reinforce their authority as the head of the household. In a manner similar to what Christine Stansell observed for antebellum New York, this study finds that Wisconsin's violent men often acted out of "an attempt to recapture and enforce older kinds of masculine authority." In this context, every domestic argument could be seen through the lens of embattled masculine rule. These anxieties partially explain why violence could erupt out of seemingly trivial disagreements. For example, Horatio Castle threw a butcher knife at his wife because he "wanted a different piece of meat on his plate." In general, Wisconsin husbands reacted in cruel ways because they felt as if constant displays of domestic control might somehow shore up their fragile frontier mastery.[32]

Thus far, this chapter has discussed the behavior of, and societal perceptions surrounding, the physically cruel husband in antebellum America. It has argued that physical cruelty occurred if a man "punished" his spouse in an overly emotional way or if his actions resulted in permanent bodily injury. Across the three states studied, communities expected male household heads to behave in a controlled manner and to protect, not hinder, the productivity of their dependents. While it is clear that husbands were the most frequent perpetrators of physical marital cruelty, the cruel actions of wives should not be overlooked by scholars. The current historiography of marital discord focuses primarily on the actions of men, at the same time painting any evidence of violence by women as trivial, rare, or defensive. In the works that do mention women as violent actors and men as victims, only a few pages are devoted to the topic. In his multiple studies on antebellum domestic violence, David Peterson del Mar refrains from discussing violent women and defends his choice by asserting that "husband abuse" was "rare." While Peterson del Mar is factually correct, the minority presence of violent women is not a valid reason to exclude them from study. As Linda Gordon and Victoria Bynum have astutely argued, "placing subordinate people center stage need not trivialize the effects of institutionalized oppression. Nor should viewing women as active agents of their own lives suggest that they were to blame for their own oppression." Studying the lives of violent women does not minimize or trivialize the challenges posed by patriarchal rule in antebellum America.[33]

Utilizing a gendered approach to the study of cruelty, the remainder of this chapter explores what happens when we take women's marital physical violence seriously. It considers what it means for antebellum men to be victims of physical abuse. This analysis is significant in part because we, as historians, know a great deal about the ideals of womanhood, yet we still need information regarding the actions of those women who lived at the opposite spectrum of the norm. As individuals struggled to understand the actions and motivations of cruel wives, they outlined how wives and husbands should behave and how marriages should proceed. An antebellum wife committed cruelty if she permanently injured her spouse or if her actions severely impaired his labor productivity. The records indicate that southern wives generally refrained from committing the most lethal forms of cruelty against their husbands. When they contested a husband's domestic authority, they did so in ways calculated to achieve maximum impact with minimum danger. In contrast, Wisconsin wives were more likely to use dangerous weapons, include threats against life, and conduct attacks focusing on a husband's domestic and business contributions. The presence of frontier conditions fostered gender role instabilities whose result in Wisconsin was that wives felt uncertain as to their exact place within the home. This, in turn, led to women pushing for more autonomy in their marital relationships.[34]

Finding extended descriptions of physically cruel wives within the court records poses a research challenge. As mentioned earlier, fewer cases exist because women were less likely than their male counterparts to perpetrate physical assaults upon their spouses. In addition, husbands were generally hesitant to pursue a divorce on the grounds of physical cruelty. A claim of this nature required a man to come before a group of his peers and relate a story of how his wife had managed to physically dominate him. This admission would speak directly to a man's inability to control dependents on the most basic of levels. For southern men, these statements could also signify the loss of a man's honor, leaving him in a position of weakness and womanhood. Essentially, the assault itself was the initial trauma, but coming before a court to relive the incident was damaging as well. With an awareness of the limitations presented by the source materials, it then becomes necessary to look very closely at the existing petitions that describe women's physical cruelties.[35]

In general, wives were less likely to perpetrate direct physical attacks on their husbands sans weapons. Engaging in hand-to-hand combat required a measure of physical superiority that many women clearly did not possess. If a woman attacked in this way, she could very quickly find the tables turned on her and end up the recipient of abuse at the hands of her intended victim, her husband. Women generally understood the dangers of close physical proximity when conducting their assaults and therefore attempted to proceed from a distance. However, some women ignored all dangers to their own well-being and proceeded to boldly attack their husbands with blows and slaps. One husband described how his wife used abusive language and "beat [him] with her hands" which "greatly annoyed and injured his feelings." In stark contrast to the complaints presented by injured wives, when husbands were the victims they rarely counted the number of blows or slaps or even recorded the location of their injuries. Instead, they typically described a frenzy of hits. Riley Pratt, a Texas man, alleged that soon after marriage his wife "commenced such a system of persecution, upbraidings and criminations as to make his house a place of torment." Aside from expressing a general "aversion" to him, Elizabeth Pratt also "struck him and fought him a number of times." His recollection of events was intended to draw attention to Elizabeth's prolonged attack on his authority; therefore the stories he related only needed to sketch the outlines of her cruelties.[36]

Husbands also argued that a particularly violent solo blow by a wife could constitute cruelty, depending on the physical aftereffects. Hits on the face garnered particular attention. After nine years of marriage, the union of Mary and Oliver Richmond was in a state of disarray. Mary came before the Portage County, Wisconsin, court claiming that Oliver was an exceedingly cruel man, often in the habit of whipping and choking her. In response to Mary's petition, Oliver denied everything and countered that his wife was actually the cruel partner. As such, he provided a detailed account of a September 1858 incident in which Mary struck him with her fist on the cord of his neck, "which raised a lump thereon as large as a hen's egg and rendered it exceedingly painful." To Oliver, this assault constituted cruelty since it resulted in the unnecessary infliction of pain. Moreover, he wanted the court to recognize the public humiliation associated with carrying around the physical evidence of this confrontation for all to see. The records indicate that wives also disfigured their husbands by scratching the men's faces, arms, or other body parts. These attacks were generally described as animalistic in nature, characterized by the spontaneous release of angry emotions. A Virginia husband, for example, complained that his wife "repeatedly attempted to chastise him" with a broomstick. When he then pulled the broomstick out of her hands she flew at his face, serrating it "severely" and leaving "three imprints of her nails." He immediately went to the local justice of the peace and exhibited the marks upon his face as evidence of her assault. In similar complaints, other husbands attested to the fact that scratching attacks could result in deep facial lacerations and even scarring.[37]

Wives also relied upon nonbodily weapons during instances of domestic discord. Eschewing traditional weapons, such as guns or knives, women most frequently transformed household items into assaultive tools. They used what they knew. A domestic cleaning implement might turn into a club while in the hands of a cruel wife. Men, including Wisconsin's Robert Vill, complained to the courts that their spouses had assaulted and beaten them with "broomsticks" on the head or on other parts of the body. Vill's wife also "tried to strike him on the head with an iron pot." Archibald Hinton, of Texas, was beaten severely until he managed to remove the broom from his wife's hand. Some wives grew creative in their efforts and actually tried to utilize all parts of the broom. In Harrison County, Texas, Alfred and Susan Council were married in December 1855. Only a few years later, Susan attempted to poison Alfred by mixing toxins in with his daily medicine pills. While he lay in bed near death, Susan taunted him by saying that "the pills were curing him and that he looked better than he ever did." After making a partial recovery, Alfred had more obstacles awaiting him. One day when he returned home from the field with sores on his legs from the bugs, his wife proceeded to stick the "jagged and rough ends" of a broom into the open wounds. Susan turned a regular household item into a weapon, catching Alfred off-guard, although he clearly considered her actions to be cruelty and felt confident that others would agree.[38]

When wives reached for items that they felt comfortable handling with force, their hands might grab shovels, candlesticks, fire tongs, or even churn dashes (the pole used in a butter churn). In his daily diary, Virginia resident William Matthews Blackford recalled how one "domestic feud" between a neighbor couple "came to a head" due to a battle over candlesticks. A Mr. Dabney was attempting to take a pair of candlesticks to be restored when Mrs. Dabney decided that she disagreed with his plan. She suddenly pounced on her husband and "hit him on the head with one of the candlesticks . . . then put the fragment into the fire." As Blackford recalled, this scene quickly became the "town talk" due to the gossip of slaves who had witnessed the entire episode. It was hinted that Mrs. Dabney, in part, committed this action out of desire to protest her husband's perceived infringement on her domestic authority. As such, she ensured that her husband would think twice before even attempting the slightest alteration to "her" possessions.[39]

In particular, the kitchen served as a prime location for wives to express themselves in cruel ways. To begin with, as Jeffrey Adler has observed, this was a spot literally busting at the seams with possible domestic weapons that women handled with great dexterity and expertise. After all, a wife was generally either the primary cook or she oversaw the cooking process, thus making it possible for her to throw hot coffee or tea on her husband without the man suspecting anything prior to the attack. Unlike the presence of traditional weapons, kitchen items aroused no alarm, thus allowing wives to get closer to their targets. The court records relate how angry wives would look around the kitchen and take up all sorts of items that could inflict injury. A witness to one such attack, Hannibal Cox, recalled how the wife would strike her husband "with any instrument that she could get ahold of." While eating in the kitchen, she would "take up cups, plates, knives, forks etc" and throw them at her husband, accompanied by words of hatred. Interestingly enough, even a seemingly innocuous table fork could turn into a dangerous weapon in the hands of a cruel wife. By resorting to personal violence and abusive language, Sarah Lee made her household a place of discord instead of harmony. After her husband had successfully gathered a crop of wheat from the field, she proceeded to scatter the wheat on the ground and on the floor of the house, thereby ruining it. When her husband tried to interfere, she "gethered a table fork and attempted to stab" him in the chest. Failing at this initial attack, she then "gathered a skillet or baking oven of some six or seven pounds weight which [she] then threw" at him with apparent success. Almost a year after the above incident, Sarah again attempted to take the life of her husband by mixing poison in with the family's milk supply. By the time Sarah's husband filed for divorce, the couple could no longer even eat in the same room together without breaking out in conflict.[40]

Why was the kitchen such a prevalent site of cruelty by women? At its core, the kitchen represented ongoing marital conflicts focusing on gender roles and labor expectations. Across all three states, husbands expected their wives to be involved in the food preparation process. The final meal appearing on the table, even if not made by her own hands, was the wife's responsibility. Wives, in contrast, could view the kitchen as a location of oppression. Daily food preparation, especially on the frontier, could descend from an art form into a stream of endless drudgery, which many wives resented. They also, of course, took issue when their husbands decided to criticize the meals, down to the smallest details. Therefore, the kitchen environment was primed for domestic conflict at its core. While living in Texas,

Eveline Wade continually tried to demonstrate to her husband that she was the dominant actor in the kitchen space. Upon his arrival at meals, she would call him a wide variety of epithets before she would serve the food. On one particular morning, David Wade came into the kitchen area to find Eveline setting up two breakfast plates, as usual. However, she held back the plates and waited for a gentleman boarder to arrive. She then sat at the table with the boarder and ate breakfast. David stood by in a state of clear shock. Not only did she leave him without breakfast, she gave his food to a paying stranger. Aside from this statement of control and choice, Eveline intermixed physical cruelty into the relationship as well by sometimes grabbing a hammer and hitting her husband on the temple. As a result of this combination of cruelties, David received a divorce.[41]

The records suggest that, while some wives might attack perfectly healthy husbands, many others proceeded in an opportunistic fashion. Mounting assaults when their husbands were sleeping, weak, or injured, these women attempted to eliminate the male advantage of strength. The situation of John and Charlotta Allridge, a Virginia couple, is illustrative. After nearly thirty years of marriage, John claimed he could no longer tolerate living as a "perfect martyr to the shrewish tempers of his wife." He claimed that for many nights past he had been forced to leave to sleep in other locations due to her continual night attacks. Charlotta "often awoke him at night by the application of hot irons to his body and . . . would often seize him when asleep & scratch & abuse him with the ferocity of a tigress." John admitted that he was particularly vulnerable while lying down. Other husbands complained that their wives behaved cruelly while they were sick and in bed. Texas wife Elizabeth Veasy hit her husband with a shoe three times while he was confined in bed and barely able to rise up. It is important to note, however, that the above accounts were based upon the words of husbands, so it is possible that a man emphasized his own incapacity in order to minimize the damage to his manhood involved in admitting to being beaten by his wife.[42]

It also appears as if men tried to excuse their own ineffectiveness in dealing with cruel wives by claiming that particular women might possess exceptional levels of strength. Again, a man could more readily explain why he succumbed to a beating by his wife if she was an Amazon and simply too strong to restrain. Appearing before the

Wisconsin legislature, one husband asserted that he had to build a separate dwelling for himself in order to escape the evil machinations of his wife. According to his account, she was "a woman of remarkable physical prowess, stronger in muscle than most men." He elaborated with examples of how she would stride around the house ripping off doors from hinges and breaking out windows with her bare hands. He concluded with a plea, "I fear that she will take my life, will beat and bruise me whenever she can get a chance."[43]

Conflicts over the nature of household productivity often served as precursors to cruel actions perpetrated by wives. While the possibly lazy husband could earn the ire of a wife, women might also assault husbands for not performing domestic tasks in the "correct" way. In frontier areas, a thin line often separated the marital contributions of men and women, thus creating the possibility for battles of authority focused on specific tasks. Lucinda Smith, of Wisconsin, regularly interfered with her husband's farm work. She would refuse to cook meals for the hired help or would threaten suicide to distract him from his labors. While working with many other men to fence the perimeter of their property, Samuel Smith noticed that Lucinda came out to inspect their progress. Thinking nothing of her presence, the men continued to work until Lucinda commanded them to halt and ordered that they use a different sort of rails. When the men brushed her aside, she then ran over to the wagon and pushed the rails off. As Samuel shoved her away, she "raised her fist and struck" him on the nose, making it bleed as a result. In an unusual turn of events, the couple sat down later that evening and discussed what had happened. They "had a conversation in relation to their respective duties towards each other." However, no real progress was made. While Samuel argued that he was the "head of the family and as such to be regarded by her," Lucinda replied that she did not respect him in that role, whereupon she left the house. During her extended absence, Samuel requested and received a divorce decree. Through their critical actions and words, Lucinda and other wives attempted to impact the productive processes of their own households.[44]

Wives also perpetrated cruelties in order to enforce their right to perform their household tasks as they saw fit, without being subject to oversight by their husbands. Cruelty, in this sense, could provide a pathway to some measure of labor independence. Husbands often complained jointly of cruel neglect, described in a following chapter, and physical cruelty. For example, one man related to the court how his wife refused to cook or do any other domestic work. As a side note, he added that she regularly inflicted blows and scratches on his face. Wisconsin women, in particular, pushed for more autonomy in matters related to household productivity. Daily life on the frontier was difficult and couples required the labors of both partners to succeed. In this tense atmosphere, confusion over the basic distribution of domestic tasks prompted wives to commit rather severe acts of violence against their partners. One woman, Jane Patrick, grew tired of the stifling behaviors of her husband and his refusal to allow her to travel to nearby Madison to procure household goods without his "immediate inspection & surveillance." Perhaps pushed too far by these constraints, Jane lashed out with sudden acts of violence, even seizing him by the throat during one altercation. In effect, Jane responded to her husband's efforts at control with her own tactics intended to bolster her authority in the marriage.[45]

In addition, if a husband behaved cruelly in a marriage, his wife might respond in kind. Essentially, a peaceful woman could grow violent in response to constant abuses at the hands of her husband. This phenomenon appeared within the divorce records and was part of criminal cases from the period. Fourteen-year-old Caroline Brenig recalled how her mother and father had a difficulty one day that led to murder. Her father arrived home and demanded supper, at which point her mother placed some butter and cheese on the table. He then ordered her to make some coffee, which she put on the stove. As Caroline remembered, her father then "said it took to long and then he hit her [Caroline's mother]." When Caroline asked why he struck her mother, he then slapped the girl "more than once" so that her "nose bled." The mother and daughter both left the house at that point to complete a few chores. A little while later Caroline's mother ran out of the house screaming for her children to flee. It soon became clear that the mother had struck her husband in the head with an axe several times, resulting in death. She was later found guilty of murder and sentenced to four years' imprisonment. Clearly, not all abused wives went so far as to commit murder, but retaliatory cruelty or violence existed as a definite possibility.[46]

Physical cruelty was often a by-product of marital power struggles.

Recognizing the stresses associated with marriage, society generally tolerated a limited amount of physical violence between spouses. A line was crossed, however, if a partner behaved in an overly emotional manner, resorted to violence with regularity, or permanently injured their counterpart. In Virginia and Texas, cruelty was understood in the context of chastisement and mastery. However, in Wisconsin spouses used cruelty as a tool as they jockeyed for position and power in the household and in the relationship. From the experiences of men and women across the three states studied, we learn that many couples were heavily invested in refining their marriages towards the ideals of the period, while other couples were simply trying to limit the bloodshed.

CHAPTER 3

"Every Twenty-Four Hours and Almost Every Day"

Sexual Mistreatment

Five years after her 1847 marriage, Christiana Wadkins appeared before a Texas district court requesting a divorce on the grounds of sexual cruelties, excesses, and outrages. She related a tale of deep discord, describing how her husband, Samuel, spent most nights lost in drink, only occasionally getting up from his chair to chase her around the house. If and when Samuel managed to catch her he would either drive her from the home or wrap his hands around her neck, applying pressure until she would pass out. Christiana told the court that she tolerated her husband's violent behaviors, but drew the line when Samuel began to make sexual demands that she deemed dangerous, including forcing her to engage in intercourse even when she was "far gone with child." In these moments of intimate terror, Samuel would proclaim that "if he could not kill her any other way he would in that."[1]

When Christiana approached the court she did so out of a desire for protection, but in the process of presenting her claims she fostered a judicial conversation that pushed at the boundaries of Victorian moral conventions. Her success depended upon the growing belief that society could, and often needed to, regulate the sexual practices of others. Even in the face of these developing concerns, passing judgment on the intimate actions of private citizens proved no easy task for judges and juries who struggled with how to differentiate between expected marital obligations and dangerous demands. Using personal documents and divorce records, this chapter explores how men and women in communities and households across Virginia, Texas, and Wisconsin understood and defined possible situations of sexual cruelty, as found within antebellum marriages. Not only did local citizens make supposedly private sexual practices the fodder for public discussion, they also struggled to align larger legal interpretations with community behavioral norms. In light of expanding conceptions of cruelty and a growing awareness of bodily pain, residents actively explored what constituted proper sexual practices in Victorian America. The discussions surrounding sexual cruelties often reflected ongoing struggles to control the productive processes of women's bodies. Concerns over how certain sexual practices affected a woman's bodily integrity varied according to region, with frontier cultures stressing the importance of sustaining a woman's labor potential.[2]

Looking to the higher courts in Virginia and Wisconsin for guidance generally proved unfruitful, as they had yet to delve into the intricacies of sexual cruelty claims. The Supreme Court of Wisconsin, for example, considered intimate cruelty charges under the statute of that which "renders the living and cohabitating together unsafe," essentially offering a vague and unsatisfactory definition for an increasingly complex, and visible, problem. The Texas Supreme Court agreed with Wisconsin's assertion and used the addition of excesses and outrages to expand the definition of cruelty into typically private concerns. As Chief Justice Hemphill mused, "These are cruelties of the most base and aggravated character; and they are such, not because any of them are violative of the laws of the country, but because they are outrages to the feelings . . ."[3]

This chapter opens with an analysis of divorce proceedings in which the absence of sexual relations was the primary complaint. It then transitions to look at cases centering upon excessive or bizarre sexual practices. A vast array of behavioral oddities prompted wives, in particular, to come before the courts and describe nascent scenes of marital rape. The discussion concludes with an examination of whether or not the transmission of a venereal disease to one's spouse constituted marital cruelty in antebellum America. In addition to the topics listed above, those moments in which pregnancy violence intersected with sexual cruelty are also examined. Not only the product of sexual relations and a key moment in a woman's productivity, pregnancy was significant in that communities consistently set the bar for sexual cruelty lower in cases involving pregnant women. Therefore, moments of pregnancy abuse give historians glimpses of varied trajectories of cruelty interpretations in nineteenth-century communities.

Although they generally perceived marriage as something beyond a physical relationship, antebellum spouses anticipated some degree of sexual interaction within their unions. When selecting marital partners, men and women took care to choose individuals who appeared physically sound and prepared to participate in the creation of offspring. If a husband or wife refused, or was unable, to engage in intercourse, this suggested an unnatural element within the relationship, which in turn opened up the possibility for community regulation. Biological impotence was an accusation leveled at both husbands and wives within the records. The vast majority of spouses who requested divorces on these grounds claimed that, beyond the condition itself, the premarital concealment of vital biological information constituted cruelty. Mary Dennis, for example, argued that her husband, John, hid his impotence by "artfully and mischievously plotting." Following three years of childless marriage, Mary discovered the truth in the midst of a heated confrontation when her husband confessed that he had knowingly misled her. She then filed for a divorce citing cruelty, not fraud, as the principal cause. The records show that the courts were generally inclined to grant separation requests in which one spouse, such as Mary, presented uncontested allegations of impotence. Appearing before a judge and jury of one's peers to level charges of biological dysfunction was an embarrassing proposition, to say the least, and it appears as if the majority of spouses did everything they could to avoid a public trial. Recognizing the concomitant shame of separation on sexual grounds, many couples even chose to relocate prior to pursing their cases.[4]

Seemingly simplistic impotence proceedings held the potential to spin out of control if a spousal defendant felt obligated to tender a statement in opposition and, in the process, attempt to rehabilitate his or her tarnished reputation. Peter and Susan Moore "contracted a matrimonial alliance" in 1843, and they resided together for two years before Peter discovered "to his utter surprise and astonishment" that his wife was "not a natural woman." Armed with this knowledge, Peter felt compelled to leave her and to file for a divorce. To cement his case, Peter's petition to the Virginia legislature included the request that a court-appointed surgeon examine Susan in order to verify his claims that she suffered from an "unnatural malformation." Peter refrained from offering any further explanation as to what Susan's supposed "malformation" entailed. However, he underestimated the resourcefulness of his conjugal mate. Susan refused to give in to his request and countered by presenting a statement from her personal physician. Her doctor not only refuted the accusation of malformation, but stated that Susan clearly engaged in regular intercourse, as evidenced by her "missing hymen." Humiliated yet vindicated by this testimony, Susan told the legislators that she presented her physician as a witness so that Peter would understand that she would not stand by and be publicly shamed for a fault that was not her own.[5] In the end, the Moores' case aptly illustrates the extent to which sexual cruelty proceedings, even more than other types of cruelty conversations, relied upon the opinions of supposed medical professionals. Medical jurisprudence flourished in the nineteenth century, fed by the idea of trained insight into intimate matters of the body. Even with a medical advantage in one's corner, court conversations centering upon impotency and cruelty often strayed into embarrassing territory and involved great sacrifices of personal privacy.[6]

Regardless of whether the case centered upon biological dysfunction or an outright refusal of intercourse, winning a divorce on the basis of sexual dissatisfaction required not only evidence as to the problematic practice, or lack thereof, but a statement as to why the behaviors in question proved injurious. A relationship sans intercourse might satisfy some, so it fell to the dissatisfied to present a compelling case to the contrary. Husbands were far more likely to appear before the courts lamenting the absence of conjugal interactions, and it proves useful to consider how they approached these delicate matters. Historians have traditionally placed male criticisms of female sexuality within a duty-based paradigm. According to this interpretation, wives owed husbands sex in exchange for protection, shelter, etc. So, we would expect to find husbands arriving at court stressing their wives' duty to provide them with sole sexual access.

The records present a picture that is a bit more complex. Husbands within Wisconsin and Texas frequently based their cases upon the existence of marital rights, duties, and obligations. Jacob Chancellor's wife "deprived him of all conncubinal rights." John Edgrine's partner "entirely refused and neglected to comply with her legal obligations as his wife, and the obligations of the marital contract." And Shepherd Adams simply wanted to "exercise his right as a husband." In contrast, Virginia husbands appeared more reticent to argue for the right to sexual intercourse, and when they did file under this heading, they utilized language that emphasized the emotional aspects of sexual marital relations. Take, for instance, Leonard Bailey, who pleaded to the Virginia legislature that his wife "seems to have become to a considerable extent abandoned in her feelings [and] has wholly abandoned her sexual intercourse with your petitioner." Jacob, John, Shepherd, and Leonard all suffered from the same problem, so what explains the differences in framing, language, and approach?[7]

By the mid-nineteenth century husbands across America felt increasingly under attack as various conjugal rights came under growing scrutiny. According to prominent marital historian Hendrik Hartog, an antebellum husband "knew—or might suddenly discover—that he was no longer sure of his legal rights over his wife. . . ." The gender role instabilities present in frontier Wisconsin and Texas only magnified these anxieties, leaving male heads of household feeling overwhelmed and under attack. To shore up their flailing mastery, frontier husbands emphasized the contractual elements of matrimonial unions. This explains why male partners in frontier locales often presented the courts with extensive lists of rights complaints in which sexual interactions appeared alongside cooking or washing duties. Clinging to traditional contractual understandings provided the illusion that the duty-based paradigm of marriage still held true in a time of perceived social chaos. It also allowed for an interpretational mechanism by which men could continue to harness and control all categories of women's productive potential, including childbearing.[8]

In contrast, husbands in Virginia hesitated to place marital sexuality within a rights discourse. Perhaps they believed, due to long-standing patriarchal traditions, that they could reap the benefits of the rights of duty without making overt references in that direction. Or maybe they acted under the influence of the growing ideals of romantic love. Either way, the records show that Virginia's men proved far more likely to create an association between a woman's sexual failings and her general immorality. In some cases this meant bookending cruelty complaints with hints of adulterous behavior. In his petition for divorce, Jacob Cool alleged that his wife cruelly refused to sleep with him any longer. As a possible explanation for her behavior, he offered up the possibility of adultery. Stopping short of accusing his wife of outright infidelity, he instead intimated that the couple's neighbors and friends doubted her faithfulness. Sexual innocence and virtue existed at the core of a southern white woman's identity, so Jacob's comments held the potential to severely damage his wife's social credit or character in the local community. By drawing attention to his wife's potential moral weaknesses and by directly refraining from mentioning what he felt he was owed, Jacob successfully painted himself as a masculine victim saddled with a wifely villain. He received a divorce.[9]

Aside from unnatural malformations or extramarital entanglements, and despite their husband's claims to the contrary, antebellum women had good reasons to avoid intercourse. First and foremost, sex led to pregnancy and childbirth, two experiences characterized by physical danger. Antebellum women greatly feared motherhood for the trials contained therein. Despite harboring anxieties, the majority of wives continued to fulfill their marital sexual obligations, even if begrudgingly. However, women could also push their marriages to the brink by enacting elaborate plans to avoid sexual intercourse.[10]

Although various abortificants were available to antebellum wives, the preferred way to steer clear of pregnancy involved occupying a separate bedchamber from one's spouse. It is important to note that husbands generally considered this act of physical separation and sexual denial cruel in and of itself. A man living with a woman under these conditions not only relinquished his right to her body, he lost management over a portion of his own home. The records show sexually spurned husbands frequently complaining to the courts that they cohabitated as strangers alongside their spouses. Mary Hawley, a Texas wife, allegedly told her husband that she would live with him "as a boarder but never as a wife" and refused to share a bedchamber with him. In another case, Harriet and Cornelius Dow lived in a Wisconsin household together, yet they refrained from speaking to or sleeping with one another. When questioned about her distant demeanor, Harriet admitted to the court that she "did object to raising more children" and behaved in a manner designed to avoid the possibility of impregnation. After bringing up twelve children with only minimal assistance from Cornelius, she had had enough and was determined to enact a de facto sexual separation. She remained unapologetic as she described their rare interactions to the court. As the Dow case amply illustrates, separatist actions centering upon the bedchamber quite often spread to include living spaces and eating areas as well, as spouses avoided even the most basic of contact.[11]

Not content with simply staking claim to a separate sleeping area, some women chose to employ threats and physical violence to defend new domestic arrangements, much to the consternation and chagrin of their mates. Striking at the base of the issue, they used threatening language in an attempt to create a negative association in their husband's minds between sexual intercourse and pregnancy. Simply put, they wanted men to fear the possibility of pregnancy as much as women did. So, defensive wives would warn their husbands that various catastrophic events would occur upon the discovery of a pregnancy. Poisoning was one of the most effective threats that a woman in this position could make, as it exposed the degree to which men relied upon the food preparation skills of their wives. Stephen Miles, a Texas husband, told the court that he was afraid to ask his wife for intercourse after she, quite shockingly, proclaimed to relatives and neighbors that she would poison her husband and their two children if she was to become pregnant once again. Suffering from shame at his own inept mastery, Stephen waited years before coming to the court and asking for a divorce on the grounds of cruelty. Within his bill he grudgingly admitted that his wife's actions had the intended effect as he avoided approaching her bedchamber due to her virulent verbal barbs. The court sympathized with him and dissolved the marriage.[12]

If threats failed to prove effective, wives occasionally relied upon a combination of advance planning and physical action to maintain distance from their spouses. The possibility of engaging in hand-to-hand combat was an undesirable outcome, as wives recognized that they would, generally, be outmatched in term of physical force. One approach was to bar the door of the bedroom to prevent entry. Another tactic wives employed involved ordering a husband from the bedchamber for the entirety of evening and night hours. If a husband ignored his wife's admonishments and proceeded to the bed he might receive serious injury. After only a few months of marriage, Elcana Blair learned that his wife no longer welcomed him in bed. She requested that he stay away and when he tried to get closer, she "procured a knife and took it to bed with her," telling him that if he approached the bed she would kill him. Not always making idle threats, some wives enforced their orders with potentially deadly force. Consider the case of Joanne Lamkin, a Texas wife, who stabbed her husband with an iron poker when he entered her bedchamber, after ignoring admonishments to the contrary. Silas Lamkin received a divorce because the jury, while not wholly sympathetic to his complaint about the absence of sex, was convinced that cruelty occurred when Joanne proceeded to physically injure her spouse. They found that Joanne was "guilty of excesses extending to personal violence and abuse insufferable."[13]

The evidence indicates that frontier wives, in particular, evinced a willingness to defend their personal space with physical aggressiveness. Caged in by isolation and with limited opportunities to call on others for assistance, defense-minded wives in frontier spaces drew upon extra levels of force to counter the challenges directed at them by their husbands. Through their acts of sexual resistance, Lamkin and other women expressly denied the idea that husbands should enjoy unlimited access to marital conjugal interactions and instead demanded the right to maintain control of their own reproductive processes within marriages. Those husbands who sustained injuries in intimate spatial contests hoped to show the courts that the physically aggressive actions of their wives demonstrated that their marriages were damaged beyond repair. Refusing sex may not have been a divorceable wrong, but permanently injuring one's spouse in the process of avoiding intercourse constituted cruelty.

Whereas men were the vast majority of spouses who appeared before the courts complaining about the lack of intercourse, it was women who generally mounted protests on the basis of excessive or bizarre sexual practices in marriage. Through their divorce bills, women forced the courts to engage in uncomfortable conversations regarding exactly what constituted "normal" sexual relations. They asked: at what point did intimate requests or demands become excessive and satisfy the legal requirements of cruelty? In general, wives who pursued divorces on the basis of sexual deviance faced an uphill battle in proving their cases. To begin with, they held the unenviable position of pressuring their peers to discuss matters that generally remained hidden behind closed doors. They also asked a group of men to recognize the need to regulate sex which, in turn, could place these same men in a position of being vulnerable to judicial sexual policing. And in order to satisfy the "clean hands" doctrine of adversarial divorce, a wife needed to maintain an aura of innocence and virtue while presenting information to the court that was anything but innocent or virtuous. This posed quite a challenge. Victorian society felt a marked reticence about broaching sexual matters in public, and the litigants who did so ran the risk of being labeled vulgar or rude just for their initial efforts. On the other hand, injured spouses could use increasingly common indignities clauses to their benefit when discussing sexual matters. As mentioned earlier, Texans in the 1840s followed this precept, and other states, such as Arkansas from 1839 onwards, did so as well. Under these laws, various types of sexual cruelties would be included alongside ridicule, disdain, etc.[14]

Although justices across the country increasingly recognized mental anguish as a viable cause for separation, winning a divorce on the basis of sexual excesses required clear evidence of physical injury or the reasonable apprehension of it. Eliza Wyman's case is illustrative of the antebellum evidentiary requirements. Married only a short time, Eliza filed for divorce, claiming that her husband's ongoing physical violence compromised her already delicate health. In particular, William Wyman "was excessive in his demands for sexual intercourse." To support her allegations, Eliza's physician Alman Lull appeared and described how he diagnosed her with a "local inflammation of the womb." He recalled how she had been "unable to turn herself or sit up in bed" due to being "completely goded out with sexual intercourse." Based upon his observations of her body, he felt as if he could conclusively tell the court that her condition directly stemmed from "too much intercourse." Satisfied with Lull's testimony, the court dissolved the Wymans' marriage. By issuing this ruling, the court found that William needed to more fully embody the growing Victorian ideal of masculine self-restraint and emotional control. While society admonished women to follow the precepts of passionlessness, it increasingly called upon men to control their baser animal instincts, especially in marriage.[15]

While many men heeded this warning, others went to the opposite extreme and forced their wives to engage in intercourse. Marital rape as a legal concept was just beginning to gain traction in the years leading up to the Civil War. Under the earlier legal model of coverture, courts could not convict husbands of marital rape because they could not hold a man accountable for damaging what was considered his own property, his wife's body. In the words of seventeenth-century legal theorist Matthew Hale, "The husband cannot be guilty of rape committed by himself upon his lawful wife, for by their mutual matrimonial consent and contract, the wife hath given up herself in this kind unto her husband, which she cannot retract." This perspective began to change when women's rights advocates operating in the 1850s compared marriage to slavery and pushed for expanded bodily rights for wives. Other social reformers took up the call as well, and by the late antebellum period a significant number of tracts circulated advocating for the legal recognition of marital rape. One such work, *The Fugitive Wife* (1866), proclaimed, "If we will save the institution of marriage, we must protect the wife, as we do the unmarried woman, against the passions of man, and give the husband no more control over the person, *body or soul,* of the woman, after marriage than before." As the language of the quote makes clear, the very survival of marriage in society was at stake.[16]

Despite the developing public conversation regarding marital bodily ownership, it would be a mistake to assert that accusations of spousal rape appeared with great frequency within the divorce records. Undoubtedly, spouses continued to question whether or not coerced sex could sustain a cruelty ruling in and of itself. When this is considered alongside the fact that female sexual submission, at least in the South, was still touted as a hallmark of femininity, it is not surprising that the southern court records, in particular, yield few results. Turning to Wisconsin, we find far more women willing to come to the court on these grounds. Sparing very few details in their pursuit of justice, Wisconsin wives laid out their private lives before the courts. One woman, Harriet Hubbard, decided that simply gesturing towards excessive behaviors would not prove sufficient for a ruling in her favor, so she quantified what she meant by excess. According to her account, Harriet's husband Mortimer forced her to have sex "twice to three times in every twenty four hours & almost every day." His actions entirely destroyed her health and constitution. To compel a woman to submit, the records describe how a husband could use a wide variety of forcible techniques, including pushing her against the bed or holding a weapon against her neck.[17]

For mid-nineteenth-century society the existence of marital

rape proved problematic in numerous ways. Forced sex constituted an excessive behavior, and it was generally believed that any action beyond moderation could yield severe physical consequences. The female nervous system, in particular, was perceived as "prone to over-stimulation and resulting exhaustion." A husband's ongoing sexual assaults could create catastrophic consequences, including the inability to bear children. Society could not tolerate such direct attacks on a woman's future productivity. That is one reason why husbands who forced their wives to engage in sex at an advanced state of pregnancy met with particular scrutiny. Men such as Samuel Wadkins, whose story opens this chapter, mortgaged their wife's productive future for the sake of present pleasures. If a woman could document specific instances of coerced sex and provide evidence of a resulting miscarriage, it was difficult for juries and judges to rule against her.[18]

Injured wives could also find a sympathetic audience if they engaged with a growing discourse focusing on the nature of pain. In her history of pain and humanitarianism, Margaret Abruzzo describes how antebellum men and women came to understand cruelty as the infliction of unnecessary pain. In this context, "Cruelty at once undermined refined civilization and human nature." Therefore, a woman's case was immeasurably strengthened if she could chronicle in detail the physical sensations accompanying scenes of coerced sex.[19]

Pain played a central role in the divorce bill presented by Elizabeth Bruss. After only a month of cohabitation with her spouse, Elizabeth came to the Milwaukee court seeking a separation. According to her account, Frederick, her husband, regularly "compeled and forced her to have sexual intercourse with him." His actions "gave her extreme pain" as the "unnaturally large" size of his genitals led to widespread damage to her "private parts." In an interesting twist, Frederick provided an answer to his wife's complaint in which he denied forcing her to do anything sexual. He also questioned, and evinced surprise at, the fact that "she could pronounce his penis and know it to be unnaturally large as compared with others" when, in actuality, "his penis is rather smaller than the usual size." Through his statements, Frederick intimated that his wife was not nearly as sexually innocent as she attempted to appear. A "thick set, square built, stout and healthy woman," she could withstand her marital obligations without experiencing pain. Frederick made a point to emphasize that their relations were pain-free. Through the graphic descriptions provided therein, the Brusses' case turned the judge and jury into voyeurs who gained glimpses into a bundle of potentially disturbing marital dynamics. Armed with this knowledge, they needed to determine if the suffering and pain inherent in her marriage to Frederick violated Elizabeth's right to bodily integrity. The stakes were particularly high for Elizabeth who, much like other frontier wives, needed to maintain her productive capabilities in order to survive. Unfortunately for historians, the final verdict in the case was not recorded.[20]

Whereas marital rape was a relatively new legal concept, the willful transmission of disease existed as one of the oldest generally recognized categories of cruelty. Even with its long pedigree it was not an easy violation to pinpoint. The term "willful," in particular, posed all sorts of interpretive difficulties. In theory, to be found guilty of cruelty, a spouse not only had to infect their partner but they had to do so with "willful" intent. In the face of an onslaught of medical studies postulating a relationship between sexual disease and catastrophic bodily dysfunction, antebellum citizens began to place less of an emphasis on intent and more of a focus on the ways in which an illness altered a person's productive potential in society. As a result, spouses who infected their partners were subject to growing condemnation within the records. Although this study does not examine those cases filed as adultery proceedings, venereal disease claims usually existed at the intersections between adultery and cruelty. The disease itself served as convincing evidence of adultery, while the transmission of the illness to one's spouse potentially constituted cruelty.[21]

The patterns present in venereal disease cruelty cases varied little according to region, although the manner of infection differed somewhat. In the southern states studied, continuous sexual assaults upon enslaved women by white men fostered a virulent disease environment. In accordance with the southern sexual double standard, husbands in these areas engaged in extramarital liaisons with little thought as to consequences. That is, of course, unless they managed to infect their wives in the process. If we turn our attention to Wisconsin, many of the disease cruelty claims there still possessed clear links to adulterous practices, but the coercive nature of racial sexual exploitation did not hold as prominent a place in the records.

In all of the locations, the records consistently show infected spouses torn between the desire to conceal their condition and the need to find solace by telling others of their troubles. Hiding the disease from one's marital partner might involve avoiding intimate contact during flare-ups or even leaving town for brief periods of time. Regarding this exact dilemma, one diarist noted, "Clapp—much itching in my flopper—must keep away from wife." However, on occasion, men and women failed to behave covertly in their extramarital dalliances, and this same lack of caution characterized their disease responses. Mansfield Seymour, a Mecklenburg County, Virginia, resident was known for his trysts in the forest with lewd women. A local man even witnessed him buttoning up his pants after one such encounter. Another neighbor, George King, became Mansfield's unwilling confidant. According to King, Mansfield told him that he had been involved with a local mulatto woman and had caught a disease from her. Asking for advice, Mansfield then pulled down his pants and showed King his "much diseased" private parts. Not stopping there, he also removed a secreted chest and showed King "the instrument for injecting his penis" and "the boxes of capsules, which he said he was using for a cure." Even in a culture tolerant of male sexual infidelities, Mansfield went too far. His irresponsible actions rendered his penis, the very symbol of his manhood, useless and deformed. As such, his male neighbors, including King, participated in the case in order to ensure that Mansfield's display of inept mastery did not go unpunished. After all, his lack of caution threatened to draw attention to extramarital relationships on the whole.[22]

As Mansfield's actions demonstrated, many carriers of venereal diseases sought curative options and then placed the blame on medicinal failures if they happened to infect their partners. Although the biological details of infectious disease were a growing topic of conversation in the antebellum period, reliable information regarding these illnesses was still quite limited. This meant that many spouses could not identify the exact ailment or combination of ailments they suffered from, thus making effective treatment much more difficult. When and if an infected individual obtained a diagnosis, their problems were by no means over. Studies of venereal disease wards during this period have shown how the supposed cure could actually be more harmful to the person than the disease itself. This was certainly the case if the patient happened to be pregnant. Mercury treatments, for example, often led to the birth of stillborns. Even with the potential for a negative outcome, antebellum citizens continued to trade supposed remedies, magnifying the potential for curative damage. In addition to medical excuses, spouses under scrutiny for spreading diseases also mounted defenses by accusing their partners of other categories of excess, including drinking. Washington Chiles, for example, countered his wife's allegations that he had a "dangerous and loathsome bodily disease" by alleging that she was "in the constant habit of indulging in the use of ardent spirits." Another far less persuasive defense involved a husband lamenting that his wife refused intercourse, thereby driving him to commit adultery and become diseased. According to this argument, if a sexually frigid woman was infected it was as a direct consequence of her own conjugal failings.[23]

All defenses generally came to naught if a victimized partner could provide physical evidence as to bodily damage caused by a venereal disease. Unfortunately for injured spouses, making a case based upon impaired physicality proved difficult, because even medical professionals remained divided as to the effects of illness on the body. While doctors frequently provided statements to the courts diagnosing particular types of diseases, they refrained from elaborating on the long-term consequences of infection. In a case of medical hesitance, the physician Frederick Vail diagnosed a defendant wife, Lansany Batten, with gonorrhea but refused to elaborate on the consequences of her transmitting the disease to her husband. This hesitancy broke down if the victim in question happened to be filing for divorce on the basis of a disease-induced pregnancy disaster. Women in these situations often stood to benefit from the diminishing importance of intent and the escalated probability of success if they could provide clear indications of outright damage to the child in question. As such, they made it a point to call upon physicians to prove to the courts that infants born to an infected mother faced unique health challenges. In a fitting example of medical jurisprudence, one doctor operating out of Texas even presented his theory to the court that the "filthy and loathsome" disease of gonorrhea produced a "shock upon the brain," killing children shortly after birth.[24]

In addition to eliciting supporting medical testimony, wives with problematic pregnancies presented some of the most detailed bills found within the records. Consider, for example, the disastrous marriage of Peter and Eliza Julien. Amid the bustling seaport of Norfolk, Virginia, the Juliens' relationship foundered as a result of Peter's conforming to the naval pattern of disease transmission. According to the standard narrative, husbands employed in various naval professions would spend long periods separated from their marital partners, engage in sexual liaisons, return home, and infect their long-waiting wives. Then, they would head off again, leaving the wives to suffer in solitude. This pattern took hold in the Juliens' relationship almost immediately, with the couple marrying young and Peter beginning work as a sailor soon thereafter. It quickly became evident, however, that his return visits home were not a cause for celebration. Following one short leave he gave his wife a venereal disease identified by a physician as the "China Pox." After a period of intense questioning at the hands of his mother-in-law, Peter admitted his error and promised to do better in the future. He then promptly returned to his life at sea, leaving his pregnant and infected wife with no means of support. When he saw his wife the next time, five weeks later, he got her sick again, this time with the clap. Again, he admitted his actions and apologized. Only a few weeks after the receipt of this latest apology, Eliza Ann gave birth to a sickly child who died shortly thereafter. Blaming her husband for the infant's death and frustrated by her own continuing bouts with illness, she filed for divorce, claiming cruelty, not adultery, as the cause. Proving that the transmission of a venereal disease constituted cruelty was not always an easy task, but Eliza's physical trials held the power to sway an otherwise hesitant jury.[25]

Sexual marital cruelty in antebellum America took a variety of forms, including refusals of intercourse, excessive behaviors, coerced sex, or the passage of disease to one's partner. When an injured spouse approached the court claiming one of these violations, they initiated a conversation that blurred the boundaries of public and private in Victorian society. Winning a case necessitated providing abundant explicit detail, thus turning average men and women into voyeuristic observers wrestling with graphic judicial quandaries. In accordance with the growing professionalization of medicine, physicians shaped understandings of sexual cruelty to an extent beyond that of other categories of abuse. It was difficult for everyday men and women to determine the outlines of sexual misbehavior when the very nature of sex remained shrouded in biological mystery. Despite these interpretive challenges, the records clearly show that the court conversations regarding sexual cruelty revolved around how to effectively control, manage, and protect the productive potential of women's bodies.

CHAPTER 4

"The Poison That Maddened His Brain"

Drunkenness and Neglect

As the daughter of a middling Virginia family, Harriett expected nothing less than a loving, stable marriage. To cement her ideal spousal partnership she brought significant property, both real and personal, to the marital altar when she wed William Smith. The couple enjoyed a comfortable married life until William's affinity for ardent spirits began to disrupt the household. Determined to fulfill her wifely and motherly duties, Harriett waited thirteen years before filing for a divorce in the Botetourt County court of chancery in 1847. Unfortunately for her, according to legal precedent, Virginia did not recognize intemperance alone as a viable cause for divorce. To receive the result she desired, she needed to prove that William's habits constituted, and contributed to, cruelty in their marriage. With that legal need in mind, Harriett regaled the court with the real life account of how a man could transform from a proud husband into a dangerous wastrel.[1]

The most damaging evidence pointed to the fact that William repeatedly made financial decisions that threatened the stability of his household. Instead of carefully managing his wife's inherited property, he wasted it and spent his time "wandering about" without occupation. To fund his local meanderings he would spontaneously seize and sell his family's possessions, frequently leaving Harriett and the children penniless and without support. During one intoxicated rage William even threw out all of their furniture, ruining the great majority of it. Perturbed by the constant upheavals within the Smith family, locals gave colorful testimony in support of Harriett's claims. After fifteen years as a neighbor to the Smiths, Merryman Sanford felt qualified in asserting that, "It is generally known that he

[William] has been in the habit of using ardent spirits whenever he thinks proper, and that he is apt to take more than does him good." Other deponents contrasted Harriett's "smart industrious" work ethic with her husband's inability to hold gainful employment due to "sprees." The general consensus was that, while William's intoxicated singing, dancing, and praying provided community-wide amusement, his general manner proved "very disagreeable." In response to these allegations, William appeared before the court and admitted to drinking to excess on occasion. However, he fervently denied that this habit impaired his ability to conduct himself as a proper Virginia patriarch. Not convinced by William's answers, the court found that his behaviors violated Harriett's "natural rights" and granted the divorce.[2]

In a period marked by the rise of the ideal of the companionate marriage based on love and affection, the Smith case is notable for the degree to which the participants emphasized duty over romantic emotion as the key ingredient of a successful partnership. Like the Smith proceedings, this chapter lies at the intersection of two prominent subjects of antebellum conversation: intemperance and marital cruelty. Even with the development of a reformist rhetoric focusing on the hyperbolic drunkard's broken home, in the first half of the nineteenth century the meaning of cruelty was contested and the definition of intemperance was uncertain. The divorce laws adopted by the states reflected and embodied this atmosphere of confusion. By the 1840s, various northern locales, such as Connecticut in 1843, added drunkenness as a possible cause of divorce. The South followed suit, and in the antebellum period six states (Arkansas, Florida, Georgia, Louisiana, Mississippi, and Missouri) explicitly included intemperance as well. This was all part of a larger plan to combat society's evils, as Mississippi, Arkansas, and other states passed acts designed to suppress "the Vice of Drunkenness."

Of the three localities examined, Wisconsin proved the most liberal in allowing divorce as a result of male and female intemperance. This progressive decision was prompted, in part, by an ever-growing temperance movement in the state. Many urban residents of Milwaukee and Madison began to resent the lingering lawless traces of frontier culture and sought to eradicate all categories of vice. However, the Wisconsin Supreme Court was careful to assert that plaintiffs must petition for a divorce with "clean hands" in order to achieve success. Essentially, a spouse who was known to have his or her own "lewd and lascivious behavior" would find no shelter in intemperance or cruelty as grounds for divorce. Texas, in contrast, followed an "excesses" clause that permitted divorce under a variety of behaviors practiced beyond normal measure, the concern being that a state of drunkenness beyond "a few months" could only aggravate any other cruelties present in a marriage. Like Texas, Virginia did not recognize intemperance as a sole cause for divorce. As a result, across the three states, adept husbands and wives pursued separations based on multiple grounds to increase their likelihood of success. This chapter explores those cases in which men and women claimed that their spouses were intemperate to a cruel degree. Not all instances of intoxication constituted cruelty, and divorce proceedings give us an indication of the dividing line between acceptable and unacceptable imbibing.[3]

Antebellum society believed that intemperance constituted marital cruelty if and when it contributed to a further breakdown of traditional gender roles and diminished household productivity. Labor expectations varied according to myriad factors, but at the most basic level a husband was supposed to generate income to support his family and a wife was generally admonished to maintain an orderly and efficient household. The following pages trace how intemperance played a key part in triggering catastrophic role reversals. The alcoholic habits of husbands could result in the loss of their ability to contribute financially to the household, which in turn often forced their wives into the marketplace as wage earners. The equally destructive female inebriate might engage in excessive spending and, as a result, expose her husband to community ridicule as a feminized man who could not regulate household consumption and production practices. Moreover, a comparative approach reveals that intemperate marital cruelty pushed an already taxed frontier labor system to the breaking point. Texas and Wisconsin residents stressed to the courts that intoxicated spouses represented too much of a family liability in environments, in which even the most minute financial missteps made the difference between survival and death.

The majority of divorce petitions from this period alleging cruelty and intemperance opened with an overt statement regarding the importance of mate selection. Not simply the product of nostalgia, this introspective exercise spoke to the legal requirements of conjugal separations in nineteenth-century America. As an adversarial procedure, divorce required a plaintiff to shoulder the burden of displaying their own innocence as well as their spouse's guilt. An injured spouse needed to convince the court that, at the time of marriage, they remained unaware of their future partner's weakness for ardent spirits. Paying homage to the ample literature on the subject of courtship, husbands and wives described how their personal situations existed in spaces where guidebooks could have rendered little to no assistance. They might blame their transgressions on immaturity in age, as Elizabeth White did when relating how she was "induced" to marry at the tender age of seventeen. She implied that society could not expect an innocent youth to identify the potential for inebriate behavior in a partner. Another frequent refrain connected one poor moral decision with a sequence of others. Norfolk resident Eliza Miller related how she eloped and evaded the law only to marry a future drunk. By recognizing that a marriage that began with uncontrolled emotions could only end badly, she hoped to secure a modicum of sympathy from the court.[4]

To fully prove their own innocence, a plaintiff often found it necessary to provide a detailed narrative explaining how their spouse transformed from sober to intemperate. Counting out from their marriage date, they would attempt to recall the exact moment when their partner's behavior underwent a change. As described within the record, the period of initial marital tranquility could last anywhere from days to years. Texas residents Augusta and Christian Rhodius made it a single year before he "became dissipated and a confirmed inebriate." In contrast, Catharine Chadwick's partner "contracted intemperance" after two decades of marriage. While the word "became" hints at a mysterious transition, the word "contracted" suggests a view of intoxication as a disease or illness. Both explanations were viable because no clear definition of what constituted inebriation existed during the antebellum period. The argument that a potential drunk was difficult to identify was amply supported in local newspapers. An 1853 article from the *San Antonio Ledger* stated, "The danger of this vice lies in its almost imperceptible approach." Another significant moment of transformation occurred if a person transitioned to drinking ardent spirits. Keeping opening statements fairly brief, spousal litigants moved quickly to the body of the complaint, where they enumerated specific examples of cruel intemperance.[5]

Emphasizing the reciprocal rights of marriage, wives appeared in court claiming that cruelty occurred if a husband's drinking habits led to his inability to labor adequately for his family's support. Of course, this obligation of support varied according to a person's class position. Society did not require that husbands keep their wives in luxury beyond the norm. Moreover, antebellum men and women did not always equate alcohol consumption with impaired work performance. In fact, laborers from the colonial period onward partook of intoxicants as a stimulus for increased productivity. The benefits of this practice, however, were illusory. A temporary rush of warmth hid a suppressed immune system. A surge of caloric energy masked a liquid lacking any valuable mineral content.

Society generally downplayed the negative side effects of alcohol consumption until the early 1820s, when the appearance of an alcohol-fueled ailment, delirium tremens, focused new attention on the destructive potential of intoxicants. Individuals suffering from the tremens manifested a variety of symptoms, including shakes, spasms, paranoia, and anxiety. Adding to the fear factor, a drunken spree could come on suddenly and last for an extended period of time. Because of its unpredictability, determining the exact cause of delirium tremens presented a challenge for nineteenth-century physicians. Even so, by the 1850s, they could safely say that "heavy drinker[s]" were the most likely to suffer from the tremens, with the majority of bouts occurring after "a binge, an illness, or a withdrawal from accustomed portions of alcohol." Historians have even considered the possibility that a rise in the consumption of distilled liquors heading into the nineteenth century helped to create a generation of drinkers particularly susceptible to the tremens. Regardless, by the mid-nineteenth century reformers and members of the medical community spread the image and story of the ill-drunk across all categories of media. The resulting popular castigation of tremens sufferers led to elevated court censure for those men and women accused of this ailment.[6]

One of the most detailed descriptions of delirium tremens in the case files comes from a Wisconsin divorce in the winter of 1853. The husband in question, Fletcher Brooks, met his wife Elizabeth six years earlier in Pennsylvania. Shortly after marriage, the couple migrated to the Midwest as part of Fletcher's larger goal to make a living by touring and lecturing in the Washingtonian tradition as a reformed inebriate. Unfortunately, everything did not go smoothly upon their arrival in Wisconsin. In her petition for divorce, Elizabeth recalled how her husband's career plans failed due to his continued drinking. Entire neighborhoods would turn out for his temperance lectures only to find him intoxicated and unable to speak. One such patron, a local Waukesha physician, attended various events that billed Fletcher as the main attraction. He later testified that he treated Fletcher over ten times for the tremens. According to this doctor's notes, the intoxicated lecturer was never an easy patient. A bloated Fletcher would request "stimulants in large doses," with the doctor refusing to administer them because, as he told the court, "there was no use in doing any thing" for a drunkard this far gone. Interestingly, his assessment represented a conservative approach for the time; in contrast, many medical practitioners aggressively treated the tremens with opium and its derivatives, thus possibly causing a fatal drop in blood pressure. Fletcher suffered no such fate, and Elizabeth's chief complaint was that her husband's illness caused him to miss business appointments and speaking engagements, which, in turn, left him unable to pay the bills. His irresponsible ways forced her to rely on her father, living in Ohio at that time, for assistance and housing. As such, she felt confident that the court would look favorably upon her desire for a divorce on the basis of marital cruelties and intemperance.[7]

Additional wives mirrored Elizabeth's concern for the ways in which drinking impaired a husband's mental functions and could render him unfit for business and work. It was popularly believed, and women argued, that alcohol suppressed a man's natural abilities in areas of control and logic. Illness in body and mind led to a withdrawal from roles typically associated with manhood, including household and labor leadership. In Virginia, if a husband abdicated his conjugal duties in this manner, his actions threatened social stability as a whole. As the argument went, morally and physically ill masters drew attention to the perversions of southern society. Patriarchs of all classes at the very least needed to give the impression of healthy vitality and productivity. Additionally, in the frontier areas of Texas and Wisconsin, any weaknesses in manpower and leadership were felt in an even more critical sense. Families in rural communities required the contributions of every member simply in order to survive. Developing frontier economies historically placed great labor pressures on all settlers.

The challenges only multiplied in times of economic downturn. For instance, by the middle of the century the rural county of Kenosha, Wisconsin, was suffering economically. It was during this period that a leader in the community, Michael Frank, recorded in his diary how the area's farmers had fallen "deeply in debt." Desperate circumstances forced locals to make difficult decisions in defense of their personal financial well-being. As such, Frank recalled how a Kenosha woman pursued a claim for damages against the community's liquor sellers. The justice court awarded her one hundred dollars, the maximum sum possible, finding that the businesses in question sold her husband liquor "by reason of which sale her husband became sick and incapable of rendering her any support." This "great" trial captured the entire region's interest as it held up the possibility of placing a monetary value on the suffering endured by drunkards' wives. The ruling supported the belief that wives possessed a right to receive the benefits of their husband's labors and to sue for damages if that right was violated.[8]

Even aside from moments of delirium tremens, drunkard husbands developed additional habits directly at odds with regular, gainful employment outside of the home. Few employers willingly tolerated the emotional and angry mood swings exhibited by inebriates. In addition, punctuality fell by the wayside as sleeping patterns altered in conformation with drinking binges. Wives who discussed this type of intimate information in court often appeared openly distressed. Such was the case when a very dismayed sixteen-year-old Sarah Briley complained to the court that her sixty-year-old husband took to drinking every day and usually slept until noon. He failed to find gainful employment, even in the bustling city of Milwaukee. Recognizing her dilemma, the court dissolved the marriage. Like Sarah, many women overcame their initial trepidation and appeared anyway because these habits impacted a marriage beyond simple annoyance and actually indicated a man's inability to maintain consistent employment. In the very mobile areas of Wisconsin and Texas, job losses connected with drinking combined with other factors to create a mass of unemployed, roaming men with families to support. Responding to the fact that one category of mistreatment spawned others, wives complained that cruelty occurred when a husband purposefully disregarded his spouse's desire for a permanent home and instead uprooted the family on a regular basis. Citing economic and emotional needs, "homeless" women blamed alcohol for exacerbating already difficult settlement scenarios. The frustration felt by Texas wife Martha Smyth was evident when she told the justices that she was tired of her husband dragging her "from one part of the country to another without any fixed residence for any considerable time in one place." Martha understood that the law bound her to follow her husband, but she believed that forcing her to acquiesce to his alcohol-fueled ramblings constituted cruelty. With her expectation of marital stability not met, she questioned whether she still owed her spouse allegiance in all his movements.[9]

While many wives dealt with husbands who were unfit for employment due to alcohol-induced illness or habits, other women faced intemperate spouses who openly refused to engage in any domestic labors. Gesturing towards the violation of an implicit labor contract within marriage, injured wives claimed their husbands acted cruelly by denying responsibility for maintaining the public areas of a family's domicile. Simply put, if a woman took care of the interior of a home, the private space, the man should exert an equal degree of effort on the exterior, the public space. Not to be undervalued, a man's home labors could either earn him the respect or ire of the entire community. If a husband chose not to "pursue any occupation" on the home front, then marital discord surely followed.

To fully recognize the implications of having a house or farm fall into disrepair, one must understand the widespread antebellum belief that connections existed between physical and moral imperfections. According to this logic, unsatisfactory outward appearances served as indications and a warning to others that interior circumstances were in a similar condition. Antebellum reformist tracts asserted that the outside estate of a drunkard always displayed the moral failings of its owner. Benjamin Rush, an avid temperance activist, described a drunkard's home as follows: "Behold! . . . their houses with shattered windows—their barns with leaky roofs,—their gardens overrun with weeds,—their fields with broken fences. . . ." For the wives of drunkards, occupying such a home presented numerous challenges. Aside from a loss of basic domestic functionality, the attendant shame could almost cause a woman to withdraw from society. For example, the embarrassment was palpable in a letter composed by a young Virginia woman to a distant friend. In the note she expressed her desire that the other woman come for a visit; however, she warned her potential visitor that the household and the company may disappoint. As a result of her father being a "lover of strong drink," the family house had fallen into a state of general disrepair and was not even properly furnished. The author explained that she wanted her friend to "not be surprised" at the lodgings or her father, but rather to understand everything in its appropriate context as a case of parental neglect. Much like the letter writer, the wives of drunkards suffered the shame of having their struggles with inebriated partners cruelly displayed for all to see via households in varying states of disrepair. Fortunately, community members quite often recognized the source of the chaos.[10]

When a husband pulled out of the labor market, the bulk of the household tasks naturally fell upon the other marital partner, the wife. Although some women could and did flee to relatives for sanctuary, as will be discussed in the following chapter, this option was not always available. As such, many wives argued that marital cruelties occurred when a husband's intemperate habits forced his wife to labor to support the household. They expected, at minimum, a degree of labor partnership in marriage. Elizabeth Doyle and other women arrived in court prepared to explain why they refused to live with men who insisted on "prostituting" them for support. These women often hailed from urban locales, such as Milwaukee in Doyle's case.[11]

Regional differences emerged, however, in the execution of these demands. Wives in Virginia were more likely to present their claims on the basis of physical differences between the sexes. Citing the fragile nature of a woman's constitution, they stated that the forcing of women into men's work could bring disastrous consequences. Sarah Robinson entered into marriage anticipating that through the "united exertions" of her and her husband they might be able to "sustain themselves in comfort, happiness, and independence." Unfortunately, her plans failed to materialize due to her husband's taste for intoxication and other vices. Forced by circumstance to labor night and day, Sarah experienced "excessive fatigue and exposure" that wore down her naturally "delicate constitution." She appeared before the court asking to be spared an early grave. The court granted her a divorce on the basis of her husband's "habits of intoxication," his being "indolent and neglectful of family," and "turbulent and tyrannical in conduct." Historians have described how Virginia women such as Sarah could present portraits of frailty because southern slave society was heavily invested in the appearance of white women's gentility. Of course, the ideal of the pedestal rarely matched the reality, especially for the lower classes. But injured wives could draw upon ample common knowledge to support a sexual division of labor in marriage. A woman's fragile uterus, for example, could be strained to the point of destruction by heavy lifting. Then, as the argument went, the inappropriate labor would have effectively made a woman unfit to perform the most important work of all, motherhood. Antebellum society considered it marital cruelty if a woman ruined her health by performing tasks to support her family that normally should have been completed by her intemperate and lazy husband.[12]

The line separating gendered categories of labor was blurred even further in frontier areas, which led to the development of a work choice argument by suffering wives. New arrivals to both Wisconsin and Texas brought with them a wide variety of understandings regarding the ideal economic responsibilities of married couples. They then adapted these ideas to the challenging living conditions found in both states. This process has been well documented by historians, such as Mark Carroll, who have asserted that new gender roles emerged out of these processes of adaptation. Women completed tasks typically reserved for men, and occasionally the reverse happened as well. With these conditions in mind, when did a husband's intoxicated refusal to perform work put enough of a labor burden on a wife to constitute cruelty? The responses of frontier wives show that they rarely attempted to argue for protection based upon the notion of female fragility. Instead, they reserved the right to choose which labors they would complete, and cruelty took place when a husband burdened his wife with a task not of her own choosing.[13]

Consider, for example, the marriage of Wisconsin residents Catharine and John Crandall. The couple only lived together for two years before receiving a divorce from the Dane County district court. In Catharine's bill she alleged that John would get intoxicated and violent, even throwing a tin dipper at her head. Frances Wilson, a fifteen-year-old staying with the Crandalls, described how John broke Catharine's collarbone during a drunken rage. However, Frances's most damning statement was, "I have heard him [John] say that if she [Catharine] done her duty she would support him." This desire, in Frances's assessment, made John not "much of a man." Within two months of the conclusion of the Crandall case an article appeared in the *Daily Milwaukee News* arguing that "It is the paradise of marriage that man shall work for the woman; that he alone shall support her. . . ." It can be argued that this article and others reflected a backlash against Wisconsin husbands who took flexible gender norms too far and expected an entire role reversal into dependency.[14]

This disregard for duty by husbands forced wives into difficult and often unpleasant labor situations. In many cases the only outside employment available for women involved performing "wifely" tasks such as cooking or washing for single men in the area. These opportunities were particularly available in Wisconsin, where mining and logging enterprises created concentrations of single working men. Wisconsin wives who earned money by taking in washing or cooking for others did not object to the labor itself, but rather to the fact that it took their attention away from the needs of their own homes. Susan Hull received a divorce based on intemperance and cruelty after she described her routine of "working out by the week in the kitchens of private families," only for her husband to seize her earnings and spend them "in idleness and in liquor." Similarly, Ida Schmidmeyer traveled from house to house in her Eau Claire community, taking in washing to support her household. Mary Moore completed piecework for local stores in order to feed her children and send them to school. Moore's ten-year-old daughter confirmed her mother's hard work when she declared, "She takes care of us the best." Each of these women survived despite having intoxicated albatrosses for husbands. They all came to court seeking relief from cruel spouses and citing their own accomplishments in the face of patriarchal abuses.[15]

The use of alcohol by husbands could cripple a man's ability to properly manage household resources. Antebellum society expected husbands to serve as the principal stewards of the real and personal property of families. To adequately fulfill this responsibility, a man needed to carefully guard against financial waste by delineating between fruitful and wasteful expenditures. Of course, not all heads of household succeeded in creating stability or even prosperity for their family groups. However, failure alone did not make these men cruel husbands. The wives who appeared in court argued that husbands behaved cruelly when they wasted resources by placing personal needs before family duty. By spending money on various vices, including alcohol, cruel men diminished the protection a steady income provided and exposed their wives and children more fully to the whims of the market system. As a result, the spouses of intoxicated husbands often watched helplessly as their family's financial stability evaporated.

To highlight the difference between a proper patriarch and an inebriated wastrel, wives recalled situations in which their husbands chose to purchase intoxicants instead of provisions for the family. In the majority of households in antebellum America, each partner procured items for the home, usually sticking to their particular areas of expertise. Women might purchase fabric while men might buy farm implements. It is clear that this balance began to shift when one person developed a thirst for alcohol. The individual with the habit would demand an increased portion of the purchasing power, and in the case of men, this often meant taking control over all money in the home. Instead of funneling this cache of cash, however meager, into purchases necessary for survival, a drunk spent "every penney" on liquor. In Texas and Wisconsin the catastrophic effects of this practice deepened, as men would leave their residences on provision trips only to return home with nothing of use. Wives spared few words when describing how their husbands abandoned them to starvation for the sake of a good time. A Texas woman, married to a blacksmith, told the court that her husband could support the family if he so chose, but instead "money that should have been expended in procuring food . . . was dissipated in procuring the poison that maddened his brain and transformed him into a demon." To demonstrate this point even more fully, some bills contained estimates as to how much money husbands wasted over time. Maintaining a state of perpetual drunkenness or being a "soaker," a person "constantly soaked with liquor," clearly required a great deal of monetary investment. Margaret Zimmerschitte estimated that her soaker husband spent "about $3000" over the course of three to four years. As a result of his extravagant expenditures and lifestyle, he could not afford to take care of her when she fell ill. Margaret's bill made it clear how much suffering ensued when a husband jettisoned his family's only defense against a heartless market—his control and care—in the reckless pursuit of booze.[16]

It would be a mistake to assert that all inebriated husbands in antebellum America behaved in the exact same way. In fact, drinking habits developed differently across the three states. In Virginia it was far more common for wives to complain if their husbands drank within the home environment. They described how the men purchased alcohol at a local tavern or store only to return home to indulge. This does not necessarily mean that all Virginians drank at home exclusively, but it does gesture towards the importance of domestic drinking practices. In contrast, the wives of Wisconsin and Texas consistently cited the development of a public drinking culture in which saloons held center stage. This is not that surprising when we consider how public drinking houses grew in importance in frontier areas during the 1850s.

Although the tavern initially served as a drinking site for travelers, many establishments found that they needed to attract local customers in order to survive. By acting as the social centers of frontier communities, these businesses secured themselves a place of importance in developing societies. Of course, not everyone welcomed these establishments. New arrivals to both states noted with disgust the settler's propensity for alcoholic indulgence. In describing her neighbors, one woman wrote, "one would suppose that old Mother Earth had got drunk and emptied her huge stomach into this goodly land of Wisconsin." Despite this type of protestation, the numbers of saloons in operation in both states continued to rise throughout the antebellum period. As an indicator, the first Madison village census in 1853 revealed forty-three saloons in operation, or one for every ninety residents.[17]

Caught up in this public drinking culture, Wisconsin and Texas husbands often chose to spend time in saloons instead of at home. As a result, descriptions by wives of men "coming home intoxicated" regularly appeared in the records. In fact, it was not uncommon for inebriates, such as William Burch, to establish a pattern of never leaving home without returning intoxicated. It appears as if Burch would not resist the lures of Milwaukee's local taverns. The actions of Burch and others existed as perversions of a market ideal in which household heads were supposed to leave the house and return enriched financially as a result of work. Alcohol-related absences led many women to argue that they were bereft of the protection supposedly provided by marriage. They made the case that leaving a pregnant wife alone until midnight in the wilds of Wisconsin, without a legitimate excuse, was not acceptable behavior but an act of cruelty. Women also, rightly, feared that short absences from home might lengthen into permanent ones. A growing temperance movement in Wisconsin, in particular, served to remind wives that abandonment was an ever-present possibility; and saloons posed a serious threat to family stability by contributing to societal pressures injuring a man's connection to his home. This antialcohol sentiment fed upon stories of husbands who stepped out for a drink and eventually ended up in California gold rush towns.[18]

According to contemporaries, it was no easy feat to resist temptation in antebellum Wisconsin or Texas. While some communities managed peaceful existences, others experienced regular disturbances and lawlessness. As a result, it was not altogether uncommon to witness men and women, in the words of Texan Helen Chapman, "violating all laws, human and divine." The apex of immorality often existed in saloons, where adherence to morality proved optional. Excess ruled the day with advertisements for cigars and images of female nudes papering saloon walls. Concerned wives warned the courts that drinking served as a gateway into other dangerous and costly vices. Gambling, usually card or dice playing, and carousing with lewd women existed as objects of particular concern in the records. To prove cruelty a wife needed to demonstrate that her husband's participation in these activities damaged a family's financial stability. Women did this by linking the vices together to show a pattern of poor choices on the part of the husband. The mother-in-law of Charles Rossiter recalled how he was a regular in Milwaukee-area gambling houses. Even when his wife was home pregnant, Charles was out on the town. On a January evening in 1847 he returned home drunk and "very cross" after a losing night. As it turned out, he had gambled away the couple's rent money. When questioned by his wife he proclaimed that "he would do as he dam'd please." The court decided that he could do so alone and dissolved the union. In contrast to the lengthy Rossiter petition, short lists of their husband's vices were compiled by other women to prove the point of cruel financial mismanagement.[19]

In addition to protesting wasteful spending on immoral vices, antebellum wives contended that drunkard husbands regularly destroyed and damaged items in the household. Their claims fell on sympathetic ears because it was common knowledge that individuals under the influence of alcohol could prove extremely dangerous to people and possessions. However, sympathy alone would not result in verdicts finding marital cruelty. So, women attempted to show how they suffered inordinately following ruinous drunken sprees. To begin with, inebriated men tended to concentrate their destructive potential on items within the home. Clothing, bedding, and personal trinkets were all fair game. A man "cutting up" or in a state of intoxication might even break "windows, tables, crockery." He could target the stove and kick it over, scattering ashes everywhere. Thomas Dowling of Wisconsin would regularly arrive home intoxicated, strip the table bare, and throw everything in his reach into the fireplace. Despite the fact that Harriett Dowling was well aware of this ruinous pattern she, along with other wives, proved helpless to prevent its recurrence. To avoid a fiery death, Harriett eventually fled the home.[20]

While Thomas's destructive behaviors bordered on homicidal, other husbands let loose of all inhibitions by vomiting or urinating on items in the home. These men were not simply occasionally ill due to indulgence in spirits, but actually used their bodily fluids as weapons to inflict pain on their wives. Virginian William Waid, for example, took particular pleasure in "making water" on his sleeping wife. As a witness to multiple incidents, Waid's son testified that his father, although intoxicated, acted deliberately by pulling the sheets off of the sleeping woman and standing over her during the process. If disgusting actions of this nature took place with regularity, a case could be built upon them alone. This was the approach taken by Milwaukee County resident Sarah Roper in her 1847 divorce petition to the Wisconsin Territorial Legislature. Sarah requested a separation on the basis of her husband's inability to conduct the most basic business due to his constant state of inebriation. Although the majority of the incidents described in the petition took place in New York, the couple's original residence, the details are still relevant to this work as an example of the damage that bodily fluids could cause. William Roper fell into an alcohol-induced illness so frequently that numerous members of the household commented on it. Servants of both genders recalled him staggering about the house and vomiting on any and every thing. As a result of this perpetual regurgitation, his breath grew so "offensive" that the servants would actually get "sick at the stomach" upon speaking with him. His stepfather, John Newell, castigated William's actions in court. Newell stated that William would "vomit about the house on the carpet & in the bed & some times attend to the calls of nature, in the house, in so much as to render it almost insupportable to remain in the house, on account of his filthiness." And finally, Sarah herself recalled how she was forced to sleep on the floor in the parlor or on the couch in order to avoid her husband's "loathsomeness" in the bedroom. However, she wanted the court to note that she did not escape entirely, or abdicate her domestic duties, as she would rise in the early morning and attempt to clean the items her husband had "fouled" the night before.

In courts across the three states, Sarah and other wives presented the claim that society should not tolerate alcohol-fueled destructive behaviors. The women had numerous reasons for focusing their bills primarily on the damage done to items in the home. To begin with, domestic possessions were considered part of a woman's domain and, therefore, wives were the most qualified to assess the extent of the injuries. In addition, when men damaged common household items, they also crippled a woman's ability to perform basic household tasks, laying the groundwork for additional economic problems. Finally, historians have noted how antebellum women were particularly inclined to assert possessive rights over personal items in the home. In situations of cruelty and intemperance, the affected wives felt an even stronger desire to protect their financial well-being by approaching the court and placing domestic property beyond the reach of irresponsible spouses.[21]

The "reckless management" of family finances perpetrated by the husbands in question opened the door for women to request increased property and earnings protections in the face of demonstrated patriarchal abuses. As discussed throughout this chapter, intoxication often hindered a husband's ability to participate fully and properly in the market. A man's potential incompetence placed a remarried widow, in particular, in a difficult position. Yielding to the norms of traditional marriage and despite possible indications of incompetence on the part of their intended partners, widows generally permitted their current husbands to control their property accumulated from prior marriages. In other cases, male heads of household simply assumed responsibility over all possessions of both partners without any consideration of the opinion of their spouse. Regardless, the divorce records provide evidence of those women who later regretted these arrangements. Widows might appear in court to request a divorce along with a payment for properties squandered. Or they might want legal assistance to prevent their spouses from seizing and selling additional holdings acquired before the marriage. Simply put, the waste of properties due to "imprudence intemperance and mismanagement" was unacceptable.

Widows who married intemperate men often benefited from changing laws regarding the control of married women's property. The 1848 Married Women's Property Act passed by New York is probably the most noted of these types of acts. However, almost a decade prior, in 1839, Mississippi adopted a similar act. And in the 1840s, Texas passed provisions allowing married women to own separate property and to share in the wealth and benefits gained during marriage. Shortly thereafter, Wisconsin lawmakers debated copying the Texas law or some combination of other states' laws. Supporters of these laws argued that they would protect a married woman from a husband's creditor, thus making her less likely to rely on public assistance or support. By the late antebellum period, all three states in this study adhered to constitutional precepts aimed at protecting the property rights of women. In particular, the states safeguarded the possessions that women brought into the marriage by treating them as separate property. When women appeared in court they were essentially, in the words of historian Victoria Bynum, appealing to other men (judges and juries) for assistance in the face of patriarchal abuses. As a result, the vulnerability of the women masked the potential challenges to the male-headed household contained in their complaints. After all, the divorce records sustained the idea that expanded conceptions of marital cruelty and intemperance allowed wives to claim increased rights to the fruits of their own labors.[22]

The "greater combativeness" of wives especially emerged if inebriate husbands attempted to seize their wages. Wisconsin women, in particular, mounted fervent defenses to maintain their individual earnings. Their insistence, perhaps, was born out of a culture in which women frequently worked outside the home to support their idle spouses, even in rural settings. Susan Hull, for example, tried to tell the court how frustrated she felt when her husband, a chronic inebriate, took the money she earned by working out in others' kitchens and spent it on liquor. It took her a significant amount of time to build up a successful business in the farming community of Eau Claire County. Another woman, Adelaide Klemo, eventually failed in her attempt to keep a Green County boarding house due to the cruel spending habits of her husband. Thomas Klemo would search out her secreted business profits, spending the monies on various vices. As a result, Adelaide could not continue to purchase the provisions required for operation. Marital cruelty, in this case, meant taking possession of the other spouse's property for purposes not beneficial to the couple overall. Women's complaints centered upon the failure of an anticipated labor partnership in marriage. They also argued that in those situations in which circumstances forced wives into outside labor, they alone should choose how to utilize the profits. According to this logic, inebriate and idle husbands behaved cruelly when they claimed the privileges of rule afforded to proper patriarchs even though they no longer belonged to that group.[23]

Even if a wife experienced all of the problems discussed above, it was still quite possible for her to lose her case if she did not at least attempt to reform her husband. As the touted moral vessels in marriage, wives keenly felt an obligation to uplift all members of their households. In situations of intemperance, society expected women to address the issue in-house before requesting outside assistance. If they did not, the law considered them guilty of cruelty as well. As such, the vast majority of wives who petitioned under cruelty and intemperance made sure to include at least a statement expressing their hope for their husband's reform. It was also common for women to assert that their husbands' multiple failed promises to change constituted cruelty as well. They would describe how they fell into a pattern of reconciling with a repentant spouse only to realize that all claims of rehabilitation were untrue. These attempts at reuniting proved particularly damaging if the inebriate used them as opportunities to seize additional monies and property.[24]

When we think of intoxication and marital conflict today, the image that instantly springs to mind is that of the battered wife cowering under the hand of the out-of-control inebriate husband. Physical violence, rightfully, dominates our understanding of the relationship between problem marriages and addiction. However, this has not always been the case. As the chapter argues, in the antebellum period, the wives of inebriates pursued divorces for intemperance and cruelty based on arenas of conflict that appear mundane on the surface. They described how intemperate husbands fostered distorted gender roles by failing to satisfy proper labor expectations. The cruel effects of such shifts in duty particularly affected the frontier wives of Wisconsin and Texas, who labored under already challenging conditions. Through their attacks on growing tavern culture and their emphasis on manly bodily control, antebellum women revealed the extent to which they expected marriages built upon mutually beneficial labor partnerships. While the rhetoric of companionate marriage provided additional protections to wives, this utilitarian view of relationships reflected recognition of survival needs in the face of changing market conditions.[25]

As the drinking patterns of men faced increasing scrutiny, the habits of the female inebriate remained cloaked in obscurity. In fact the intoxicated woman all but disappeared from the majority of reformist writings after the 1830s. The author of the early-nineteenth-century moral tract *The Drunkard's Looking Glass,* for instance, devoted the entire text to the problems caused by intoxicated men. After all, chronicling the accounts of the moral failings of woman drunkards failed to accord with a growing emphasis on woman's moral supremacy. Luckily for historians, divorce records from the period provide details that testify to the fact that a small percentage of women continued to imbibe, and communities, as a whole, talked about the actions of these deviants. Although this study does not undertake a statistical analysis of alcohol consumption patterns, it is clear that women faced drinking accusations far less frequently than their male counterparts. When female drinking was addressed, the comments made within divorce proceedings centered upon the ways in which intoxication prevented a wife from fulfilling her labor responsibilities within the home environment. The words of the plaintiffs, defendants, and deponents pointed to the importance of women's productivity, especially in frontier settings. A woman inebriate was deemed cruel when her failure to live up to role expectations, particularly in labor, resulted in family suffering. A husband's petition, therefore, focused attention on his wife's drinking patterns as well as the effects of her actions. Men pursuing divorces in this period needed to establish a solid link between intemperance and cruelty because, of the three states studied, only Wisconsin recognized female intemperance as a cause for separation.[26]

To receive a divorce an aggrieved husband needed to demonstrate that his wife imbibed as part of an established habit, beyond the occasional lapse in judgment. To do this he could point to the frequency of drinking, the type of alcohol consumed, and troubling physical and mental behaviors. Although there was no set definition for what constituted drunkenness in women, the failure of basic motor skills served as a chief indicator. With wives often attempting to hide their addictions from their husbands, a practice discussed later in this chapter, third party witnesses frequently provided the most detailed accounts of a woman's habit. Outsiders could go to great lengths to observe behaviors in order to verify their suspicions regarding a particular woman.

Fueled by curiosity and community policing motives, Philip Devolt of Wisconsin appeared in court and testified against a fellow boarder, a Mrs. Winterminte. He claimed that Mrs. Winterminte lived in a state of perpetual inebriation, which justified Mr. Winterminte in seeking a legal separation. Devolt related to the court how he meticulously gathered evidence of Mrs. Winterminte's behavior. First, he carefully listened to local rumors chronicling her habit of using liquor. Second, he engaged her in conversation and found her to be so intoxicated "that she could not talk distinctly." As Devolt's testimony illustrates, the antebellum divorce court was one arena in which discussion of a woman's body was not only sanctioned but encouraged, and witnesses seemed to relish the opportunity. One man even described how he secretly followed a local married woman home in order to observe her walking abilities and to verify his suspicions regarding her conduct. According to antebellum logic, spending nights out drinking or indulging in alcohol at all would deplete a woman's limited reserve of strength by fostering excitability. Following this line of reasoning, a wife would then approach her home life not only with an irritable temper but with an inability to complete the most basic of tasks.[27]

A chief complaint made in the record focused on wives leaving their families for extended periods of time on drinking binges and/ or acting uninterested in working while at home. Husbands across all three states expressed clear expectations that their wives at least participate in the preparation of meals and maintain a clean and orderly house in accordance with the family's level in society. Patrick Murphy, a Wisconsin husband, felt confident that his wife "neglected her household duties" by drinking liquor to excess and, as a result, not serving his supper or breakfast on time. He argued with her frequently on this account, but made little headway. In fact, he alleged that his wife grew violent when he questioned her behavior. During one confrontation, she took up an axe and threatened to "split his brains out" if he did not turn over three dollars for her to purchase liquor. At another time she threw a bottle at the back of his head, knocking him down and rendering him senseless for an undetermined number of hours. When he awoke he discovered that the fall had injured his face, making it impossible for him to labor for nearly two months. He claimed to the court that, not only did his wife fail to perform her own duties, she prevented him from completing his as well. Simply put, she was a liability and not an asset. This belief accords with a comment made by numerous husbands that a wife who neglected her household duties was less of a woman as a result. Her husband, therefore, owed her little to no protection or care.[28]

Community members and litigants reserved their most vehement criticisms for women who performed badly as mothers due to their attachment to alcohol. The late antebellum period still held to many of the ideals of republican motherhood. According to these precepts, mothers were to set proper examples for their offspring. They were to treat their children with the greatest of care, as society considered motherhood the most important office a woman could hold. Like many ideals, republican motherhood was much more attainable for women of the middling or upper-class ranks. They possessed the resources and time to devote to raising proper citizens. However, women situated in farming or frontier households also felt the allure of this set of ideals. And they still faced judgment from their peers and betters when, or if, they failed to properly live up to these standards. Therefore, women who perpetrated maternal abuses were castigated not only for committing injury against a child but also society as a whole. Consider, for example, the case of Louise Schaeffner. Louise's husband Edward filed for divorce, after over a decade of marriage, claiming that his wife developed an affinity for liquor that left her incapable of "discharging her duties." He could tolerate her abusive language and personal violence, but he drew the line when she began to corrupt their thirteen-year-old son. She would force the child to consume whiskey and, as a result, permanently compromised the boy's health. The testimony of the local tavern keeper further tarnished Louise's maternal credibility. He claimed that she came in two to four times a week and "drank every kind of stuff" available. Charles, the son in question, also provided an accounting of maternal neglect. He described how his mother kept her whiskey underneath the bed. She sometimes started drinking in the morning and did not rise up all day. He also recalled how his mother gave him whiskey "very often" and as a reward when he went to fetch some for her.[29]

The conversation and controversy surrounding Louise's maternal skills represented a textbook example of the criticisms leveled against mothers who partook of alcohol to excess. The concern was that these women set bad examples as they imbibed intoxicants and cruelly encouraged addiction within their households. By forcing their children to drink, they permanently damaged their offspring's health and future possibilities. Family members in a handful of cases even expressed the fear that a woman might kill her infant via the misapplication of rum for teething or other ailments. Concerned parties spoke on the belief that drinking suppressed a woman's natural maternal sensibilities, thus making horrors possible if not likely.

Cruelty on a woman's part then forced her husband to shoulder the heavy burden of child care. An unprepared father usually appeared in a favorable light when compared with a potentially dangerous mother. The neighbors of one conflict-ridden Virginia couple echoed this sentiment. The Higgs family watched as Martin and Elizabeth Fogle grew apart over time. Elizabeth began staying out nights, interacting with bad sorts of people, and openly drinking whatever she was offered. When Martin filed for divorce, the Higgs stepped forward to testify. According to their observations, Elizabeth could no longer act as a proper guardian for her young child because she "gets drunk and mistreats it she dont dress it well nor keep it clean." Generally, they argued, the woman can do better for a child "but in this case . . . the man can do better." Elizabeth's maternal failures paved the way for additional accusations that eventually led to her being divorced and losing custody of her sole child. For our purposes the Fogle case illustrates how a man could connect a woman's shortcomings in areas of maternal labor with alcohol abuse and thereby prove marital cruelty.[30]

In addition to the womanly duties of household upkeep and child care, wives often acted as the chief purchasers of goods consumed within the home. This responsibility involved determining which items in what amounts a household needed to function. On a less utilitarian front, women also acquired those nonessential items that transformed a house into a home. Because of her purchasing power, a woman's decisions could greatly impact a family's finances for good or ill. In the case record, many of the criticisms leveled against wives focused on their tendency to excess. Antebellum society anticipated a certain degree of "womanly" impulse spending, but consumerism crossed into cruelty when alcohol use impaired a woman's ability to make reasonably sound purchasing decisions. "Extravagant" was the typical descriptor used for such a woman. She lived her life in an immoderate and excessive fashion with no attempt at impulse control.[31]

A cruel extravagant woman might use all of her family's valuable resources to purchase selfish and wasteful items, such as liquor and tobacco. Robert Ingraham's wife, for instance, gave little thought to financial stability. Shortly after their marriage, Robert discovered his wife's hopeless addiction to intemperance. She spent any and all monies "in order to procure the means of intoxication." And when the funds dried up and she grew desperate, "she would sell whatever goods . . . she could lay her hands on." As a result, the majority of his personal items went missing "without his [prior] knowledge or consent." Robert filed for divorce, and won, because his wife made no scruples about ill using him. The choice of the phrase "ill usage" reveals the degree to which his wife's actions injured his masculinity and turned him into someone who felt used, as opposed to someone who exhibited mastery. After all, "ill usage" comments usually appeared in tandem with complaints relating to a man's mistreatment of a woman.[32]

Extravagant cruelty could also occur if alcohol removed all of a woman's inhibitions and led to her purchasing items beyond her station in life. In these scenarios, women who enjoyed lenient spending habits could transform into real dangers to the household upon the introduction of intoxicants. A handful of men in the records blamed themselves for allowing inordinate luxury to initially enter their relationships as part of the courtship process. However, according to these men, they expected their wives to rein in spending as the relationship progressed. They argued that cruel women not only ignored the duty of frugality but elevated expenditures with alcohol-fueled purchases.

In a typical petition of this sort, one man described how he spoiled his intended bride with a wide variety of items before their marriage with the expectation that she would make careful financial choices after their nuptials. He asked the court to imagine his surprise when he discovered that his new bride intended to liquidate his entire estate to fund her growing liquor habit. Unable to cope with her corruption of duty, he pursued a separation. Virginia husbands, in particular, complained about the ways in which existing systems of credit opened the door for abuse by opportunistic, alcoholic wives. Washington Chiles downplayed his own complicity in his wife's cruelties. He related to the court how a brief solo trip to the West spelled his financial ruin. Despite being well acquainted with the fact that his wife suffered from "disgusting excess" in drink and money, Chiles left her in their marital home with access to unlimited credit under his name. When he returned, "he heard from all quarters of the continued extravagance of his wife." He later learned that she had plunged him deep into debt. Even with the widespread existence of debt during this period, to be a debtor was still a blemish upon one's character. Husbands spoke with one voice when they proclaimed that only a cruel wife willingly shackled them to debt. In addition, many of the spouses in Texas and Wisconsin emphasized to the court how they migrated searching for financial prosperity. Under these circumstances a wife's capricious spending proved even more harmful, as it could render an entire move meaningless.[33]

As they brought their financial problems to court, husbands faced a series of difficult questions as to why they did not interfere earlier, take action to prevent a wife's drinking, and thereby ensure their household's stability. Within their answers the men in question presented the image of marriages characterized by secrecy instead of companionate transparency. They claimed that they possessed no prior knowledge of their wife's weakness for drink until it developed into a problematic habit. To make this point plausible and to sustain their reputation as patriarchs, they described various methods by which a woman might keep her affinity for alcohol a secret. One Wisconsin man recalled how his wife obtained liquor secretly while he worked away from the house as a blacksmith. The art of deception seemed particularly well-suited to housewives, as husbands traced how their partners used a woman's intimate knowledge of the household to hide items in places that others overlooked. Concealing alcohol from detection might simply involve emptying a bottle of one substance and refilling it with intoxicants. Unfortunately, this practice also increased the risk of household poisonings. This pattern of supposedly private, home-based indulgence in alcohol on the part of women is in accordance with historian Thomas Pegram's description of late 1850s saloon behavior. When women would patronize these public establishments they would avoid the social "male drinking culture," preferring instead to approach at the back door for beverages, i.e., bottles of booze, to go. All of these efforts at concealment revealed their hope that, by drinking within the boundaries of the home, they would minimize damage to their reputation. However, total privacy was a difficult thing to achieve. It was quite often only a matter of time before a woman's imbibing entered the realm of public knowledge.[34]

As such, husbands who sought divorces might convincingly claim that they first learned of the habits of their wives through the intervention of neighbors and community members. According to these narratives, a wife could successfully hide her addiction for a significant period of time before her spouse grew concerned. Suspicions, often focusing on a woman's diminished labor productivity, would then be confirmed in the form of local reports. Armed with what they considered reliable community knowledge, husbands would then feel qualified to act. For example, Jonathan and Margaret Bridges married in New Jersey and then moved to Wisconsin by the late 1850s. Jonathan believed that his family's new situation was ideal until his neighbors alerted him to a potential problem. They told Jonathan that Margaret was fond of drinking excessively in his absence. To test this information, Jonathan began coming home unexpectedly during the day and discovered, to his horror, that the community reports proved accurate. He frequently found his wife "so badly intoxicated that she scarcely knew anything." Whereas he previously believed that she was just a poor housekeeper, he now knew that her weakness for intoxicants made her unable to complete the most basic of household tasks. After a brief period of trying to persuade Margaret to cease in her negative behaviors, Jonathan gave up and approached the court, requesting a divorce on the grounds of drunkenness, cruelty, and neglect.[35]

Jonathan confronted a common dilemma faced by antebellum men in troubled marriages when he contemplated whether or not to attempt to reform his marital partner. The burden of reforming fallen drunkards usually fell to women, so men in this position ventured into uncharted territory. It was, therefore, not that surprising that husbands felt unsure as to how to proceed. As they described their actions to the court they stressed their lack of expertise in moral arenas, but related how they exerted great efforts to save their wives nonetheless. One Wisconsin man recalled how he destroyed gallons of liquor hidden by his wife, ordered the children and servants not to fetch any more for her, and did "everything in his power to reclaim" her from intemperance. It all failed, however, and she continued stockpiling alcohol in secret. Filing for divorce signified his final attempt to reach her. Other men adopted less physical measures and instead tried to counsel their wives back to temperance. As heads of household they were accustomed to having their voices heard and acknowledged, so they could only respond with shock when their wives "rejected & disregarded" their counsel.[36]

A handful of men attempted to implement a policy of containment when faced with inebriated wives who behaved cruelly. Containing a wife was a process by which husbands would isolate their partners out of a desire to minimize the damage caused by their drinking. The records most frequently mention men locking their spouses in particular rooms. If questions arose regarding this strategy, husbands proved ready with answers. They might comment that this practice kept a wife's drunken sprees from disturbing the neighbors. In the words of a Wisconsin husband, shutting up his wife in a room until "she should become sober & quiet" was not an ideal solution, but it did address her excessive noise level. Although the racket caused by a drunkard might appear minimal in retrospect, antebellum men and women provided evidence as to how such disturbances could even compromise a family's living arrangements. If boarding, they could get thrown out of the house. In these situations the wife's intoxicated actions proved costly because the family now had to pay a premium for lodging, especially in a small community. In addition, a husband might attempt to contain his wife if she had tried on prior occasions to disrupt or destroy his potential to earn a living. Numerous witnesses testified to the fact that having a drunken wife appear at one's workplace could easily get a man fired. In general, a woman's movements outside of the home could already prove problematic, but a wife who refused to recognize any boundaries was particularly threatening to family economic stability.[37]

While not as widespread a problem as the male alcoholic, the female drunk still served as the centerpiece of many heated divorce cases. Within these proceedings, community members and aggrieved spouses expressed their concerns about how a woman's affinity for alcohol might pose a threat to her family's financial stability and thereby constitute cruelty. In addition, female drinking proved problematic because it made plain the "artificiality of domesticity." It forced society to come to terms with the fact that not all women were capable of proper behavior. When women imbibed, they perverted gender roles by exercising what was seen as a masculine prerogative. And they behaved cruelly by no longer occupying a submissive marital stance characterized by continual devotion to household enterprise. A bodily rebellion of this nature was troubling even if it was not intentional.[38]

Paying close attention to gender and region, this chapter has chronicled the attempts by antebellum men and women to give shape to the amorphous social ills of intemperance and marital cruelty. It has argued that the performance of labor responsibilities served as the primary determining factor as to whether or not a spouse's intoxication shaded into cruelty. The inebriate husband could pose a threat to family stability in numerous ways. He might refuse to engage in any category of paid work, thus placing the burden of breadwinning on his spouse. Or, he could abdicate all responsibility for household upkeep, thereby exposing his marital partner to community censure and ridicule. The intoxicated wife, while appearing less frequently in the records, could prove equally dangerous to a family's survival. She might ignore her domestic duties, including those of a maternal nature, thus forcing her husband to engage in tasks typically labeled feminine. Or she could abuse her consumer prerogative by spending excessively, thereby indebting the household. Regardless of the gender of the person in question, frontier communities such as Wisconsin and Texas appeared to suffer inordinately from the intoxicated cruelties of residents. As witnesses to developing economies, men and women complained to the courts that struggling families paid the cost for thriving drinking cultures. An examination of intemperance and marital cruelty allows for an extended engagement with the ways in which understandings of marriage and the body intersected to redefine the nature of mutual spousal obligation.

CHAPTER 5

"I Did Not Come to Quarrel"

Community Responses to Perceived Abuses

T he Grinnins' small Wisconsin home could not contain their domestic troubles. Rumors and reports about the conflicted couple trickled out into the community at a consistent pace from the date of their marriage in June 1843 until the veritable floodgates of scandal opened four years later when Mary Grinnin filed for divorce. In the case file, Michael Grinnin, Mary's husband, comes across as an overbearing drunk who enjoyed tormenting his wife by burning her clothes and threatening her life at regular intervals. Further reading of the court documents reveals detailed testimonies provided by neighbors and relatives of the couple who corroborated Mary's account. Hannah Dooley, Mary's sister, who lived with the couple for "a while," described how Michael would "drive her [Mary] about as he would a dog." From Hannah's statement, we are presented with the image of one sister watching the other one being abused without intervening or offering immediate assistance.[1]

In an unexpected twist, it was a nearby neighbor who served as Mary's primary confidante and protector. Catharine Grogan, a local woman, tried to stay out of the Grinnins' marital troubles, but Mary's repeated requests for assistance pushed her into the fray. Their friendship began when Mary arrived at Catharine's house, ostensibly on a social visit. However, when her neighbor managed to stay all day and began to relate stories of spousal abuse and dissipation, Catharine realized that Mary's appearance at her doorstep was not mere happenstance. As night drew near, Catharine tried to convince her guest to return home, only to have the troubled woman refuse to leave until Catharine agreed to serve as her escort. When they arrived at the Grinnin household, Catharine stayed a while and witnessed as Michael arrived home and "immediately commenced abusing the said Mary," including attempting to pour scalding water on her from a coffee pot. He "would have succeeded" had Catharine not, with all her "energy, interfered and prevented him." When she believed that everyone had calmed down, she finally returned home, only to be followed shortly by Mary, who had been thrown out of the house. Mary continued to seek refuge with her neighbor-protector for years. For her part, Catharine grew increasingly aggressive in protecting the abused woman. In one instance when Michael attempted to hit his wife with a chair, Catharine "by force beat him off with a stick of wood." As such, when she learned of the impending divorce, Catharine could feel justified in breathing a veritable sigh of relief that her household would no longer feel the burden of the Grinnins' troubles.[2]

This chapter explores how third parties, such as Catharine, in communities and households across antebellum Virginia, Texas, and Wisconsin, reacted and responded when faced with possible situations of marital cruelty. Divorce records from this period again and again reveal outsiders who were forced to make a series of moral choices when confronted with marital discord. If we turn again to the Grinnin divorce case, we can trace the decisions made by third-party witnesses. Hannah determined whether or not to intervene when witnessing Michael abusing her sister. After listening to Mary's accusations, Catharine considered if she should let Mary stay the night on that initial visit or send her home. Her decision to mix activism with restraint would set the tone for her approach to similar moral dilemmas. In particular, she would later choose to meet Michael's use of violence with her own in order to protect Mary, whom she perceived as a victim. The level and type of third-party involvement in situations of marital discord was shaped by understandings of proper domestic relations as well as beliefs in domestic privacy. To begin with, men and women assessed whether or not they thought that cruelties actually occurred. Then, their perspective on public/private divides shaped whether or not they took any actions and in what manner they responded.[3]

Although they might engage in disparate approaches to intervention, the majority of third parties behaved conservatively. Citizens in all three states did not categorize their actions or intentions in terms of dismantling marriages or directly challenging accepted marital norms. Rather, the actions of third parties represented a general public desire to perfect the marriage script in a time of perceived national marital crisis. In addition, the moral choices faced by third parties witnessing cruelties sheds additional light on mid-nineteenth-century struggles to define the degree to which family and marriage relations belonged in the realm of private or public affairs. Historians have described how this period marked a "crucial transition" in the relationship of the family to the state and to the public sphere. According to the standard narrative, as traditional rights of chastisement waned, cruel husbands voiced their desire to maintain domestic spaces no longer policed by outsiders. At the same time, states across the country passed divorce laws that increasingly intervened within the home for the sake of community peace. Legal separations often resulted from complex, occasionally long, processes of social negotiations that traversed many understandings of the public/private divide. In view of all this, this chapter is organized to mimic the process of discovery and possible action that each outsider went through. It starts within the household itself by exploring how marital troubles could become an unfortunate fact of life for boarders. Then, it turns attention to the ways in which this information spread from the supposedly private home sphere out into public spaces, and how that process differed from state to state. Finally, the analysis delves into the variety of ways in which outsiders responded when faced with cruelties.[4]

Not surprisingly, the individuals who lived with a discordant couple were generally the first persons to notice something "off" in a relationship. Even when disputes took place behind closed doors, the presence of thin walls and poorly partitioned rooms virtually guaranteed other inhabitants access to all categories of supposedly private activity. Often treated as invisible by the warring parties and not labeled as guests, boarders did not benefit from the ideals of public restraint that might have prevented couples from placing them in the midst of uncomfortable situations of domestic conflict. A boarder received varying degrees of food and lodging in return for labor performed or monies paid. Society's basic needs drove these arrangements, providing an avenue through which to integrate solo individuals into family situations.

Ironically, boarders could be the ones to call for increased controls on the men and women who ran boarding houses. Long-term boarders provided the courts with the most useful and detailed accounts of conflict, but this information came at a cost. Forced to be conciliatory or lose their lodgings, boarders could be pressured to serve as a confidant for one or both of the marital partners. The story of James Bailey, a boarder of Virginia couple Frances and James Jones, illustrates the possible perils. Burdened by the knowledge that Mr. Jones contracted a venereal disease as a result of committing adultery, Bailey found himself in an uncomfortable position. Jones asked Bailey what he should do to cure the illness, bought medicines, and kept them in the boarder's room so as to avoid detection by his wife. This, of course, created an extremely awkward situation for Bailey, which culminated in his testifying for Mrs. Jones in the divorce hearing. His statement and those made by others led to severance of Frances's union. Instances such as this reminded boarders that they lived as members of the household without the connected rights to privacy. Other household inhabitants could invade a boarder's physical space and mental energies at a moment's notice. Refusing to listen to such information was always an option, albeit with the cost of potentially losing one's lodging. Given their tenuous circumstances, boarders felt little to no responsibility for keeping cruelties safely contained within the domestic sphere. A boarder's story could quickly circulate via the local rumor mill.[5]

Before this chapter heads into a discussion of the various tactics used by third parties to intervene in problem marriages, from mediation to charivaris, it is important to briefly examine another avenue through which men and women learned of situations of discord. Again, they had to become informed before they could choose to act. In a fashion like today's, the majority of spousal abuse victims chose to hide their marks and bruises by employing carefully placed clothing items or by isolating themselves throughout the healing process. A small Wisconsin boy told the court that his mother would "hide the marks" left on her throat from her father's choking attack by wearing "a handkerchief on her neck for several days after." However, in Virginia a phenomenon developed alongside the growth of local reporting networks, that of showing wounds and scars to community members. Women, in particular, displayed marks from cruelties sustained at the hands of their spouses. Informal, and often secretive, viewings took place as women or men crept off to what they deemed a private space to view the victim's body. A short while after James Fulford whipped his wife and dragged her from room to room, a witness and boarder, Mary Rayner, approached Rosina Fulford out of a desire to view her injuries. As Rayner describes, "I examined her the same night and found marks upon her person." Rayner concluded her testimony by stating, "I do not regard him [James Fulford] with respect." The type of bodily display made by Rosina Fulford has a long history within Virginia. In the colonial period, community members and local authorities investigating crimes such as infanticide would perform a "reading of the body" to determine the cause of death and other information. They would explore and record everything from bruises to blood patterns. In a way, Rayner conducted a live autopsy on Mary Fulford. She employed a macabre practice to examine the body in order to piece together a more complete picture of the entire marriage; the principal difference being, of course, that Mary was alive during the exam. But that, of course, could change if the cruelties continued, and both women knew this.[6]

Victimized women often made social calls with the express intention of displaying their injuries. When Anne Souther went over to the house of Patsey Wyatt, she showed Wyatt the welts that she had sustained from a whipping twelve days earlier. After Wyatt studied Souther's body, she came to the determination that the bruises "looked very dark indeed." Why did Souther go to the trouble of visiting Wyatt and displaying her body? It is possible that Souther approached the other woman because she wanted the community to be aware of her sufferings, to take note of them in the event of a divorce, and perhaps to render immediate assistance. In a way, Souther was making a case before the community court of report and opinion, and her body served as her evidence. A victim could get an immediate read on the perspective of the neighborhood based upon whether or not an outsider would even consent to the viewing procedure. If met with a positive reaction, sympathy, a victim would often put their injuries on display numerous times for different community members. Sarah Womack, for example, showed her bruises to Mary C. Carlton, William Webb, and others.[7]

This practice appears to fly in the face of accepted and proper body interactions, especially when we consider the fact that modesty and substantial clothing coverage signaled female gentility in southern society. Historian Charlene Boyer Lewis found in her work on Virginia's planter interactions at the natural springs that "the public discussion of one's body," normally a social taboo, was accepted at the springs because of the connections to health and well-being. In a similar fashion, nudity could even be seen as permissible if it took place as part of a community investigation into cruelties. The historical records contain information on women who bared all to make their cases in the court of public opinion. A Mecklenberg County, Virginia, wife took off all of her clothes and showed her neighbor the "great many marks of violence" on her person. In another county, two women enjoyed an evening together until the conversation turned to the constant beatings that one of the parties suffered at the hands of her husband. As the abused woman rose to leave, she pivoted in the yard and raised her dress up high to show all of her person, including the stripes and bruises across her flesh. From her position on the porch, the female companion and confidante noted the placement and depth of the lash marks. On the other hand, Texas and Wisconsin settlers rarely traveled to show others their bruises and scars. This problem fed itself. Men and women hesitated to show their injuries to others because they could not rely on established networks to pass along these scenes. At the same time, local systems of reporting could only be built with information provided, in part, by such displays.[8]

To that end, community members attempted to engage in mediation with problem couples. Mediators wanted to reconcile the parties to perform marriage in the proper manner, in accordance with local ideas of the peace. They would approach the spouses in question, usually in the couple's household. These interactions would often take the form of informal hearings, with both spouses stating their cases and then the outsider(s) offering suggestions for future peaceful living. Clearly, the mediators who appear within the divorce records met with frustration in their efforts, yet they relate stories describing firsthand the gradual destruction of antebellum marriages. One man recalled that he "frequently endeavored to reconcile" a troubled couple in his neighborhood, but all to no avail. In another case, Addison Turner described how he went over and sat between a husband and a wife as they fought. Then, they each got a chance to state their side of the story, at which point Addison told them to "live in peace and quiet." His deposition encapsulated a journey from hope to failure in a matter of sentences. On occasion an attempt at mediation might end in one partner admitting that they might "try to do better" in the future, although a more likely response was continued conflict. A.B. Adams tried, along with a group of neighbors, to stage a marital intervention with one Wisconsin couple, but the entire exercise failed miserably. The meeting ended when the wife triumphantly declared that she had put her husband's tools "in the privy and he might go there and get them if he wanted them." The neighbors retreated at this point and waited for the official dissolution of the marriage. The divorce was granted in December 1858.[9]

Society expected marital partners to live together, unless a husband's business responsibilities necessitated otherwise. So, mediation and reconciliation efforts often focused on reuniting the couple under one roof. Community members might seek out the absent spouse, if they were staying in the area, and request them to return home. These encounters were anything but quick and simple, as the mediator could be drawn into a spouse's long story of woe, placing the outsider in what can only be described as an awkward situation. Or, a husband or wife could convey their refusal to return in brief terms, referencing their inability to "live together agreeably." From the records it appears as if mediators enjoyed some fleeting successes in convincing wayward spouses to return home. When Eveline Evans fled from her husband after he inflicted stripes on her with an ox whip, she assumed the move would be permanent. But after Jackson Evans, her husband, apologized, she decided to return and live with him again. Her mother, Nancy Drake, would later write a letter to Eveline, applauding her decision and commenting that the couple could be truly happy: "If you and *Jack* will both try it is very easy for any person to make themselves miserable, and it is almost as easy to make themselves happy." In the end, the reconciliation did not work out, and Eveline filed for divorce only months after her mother's letter.[10]

Eveline was not alone in facing pressure to reconcile, since communities generally viewed women as the ones responsible for keeping marriages intact. As Anya Jabour found in her study of one companionate marriage, "Wives, with the most invested in marriage, were assigned the task of ensuring the couple's success." Therefore, it should be relatively unsurprising that much of the reconciliation efforts of community members focused on instructing women on the mechanics of setting aside their victimization in order to achieve the higher goal of marriage once again. While visiting a household in crisis, one Virginia man suggested to the wife that she should "be as kind as she could to her husband notwithstanding his bad treatment of her." So, even though her husband whipped her until the point at which her health collapsed, this outsider pushed for reconciliation, despite the possible cost to this woman's own body and person. Although shocking to our modern sensibilities, this man's advice conformed very much to the overall goals espoused by community marital mediators. Keeping a marriage intact was what mattered, unless the couple threatened to destroy the institution or societal hierarchies through their actions.[11]

As hinted at through the examples above, spouses did not always embrace the efforts of community mediators. In fact, many husbands and wives felt as if these individuals were, at best, meddlesome and, at worst, direct competitors for household authority. Although mediation remains one of the most innocuous approaches for addressing cruelties in marriage, couples could still bristle at attempts to fix the potentially unfixable. In the records, mediators described how they paired their advice with statements demonstrating their peaceful, and passive, intentions. A proclamation of "I did not come to quarrel," could signal to all parties that the outsider did not wish to participate in the fray, except as counsel. However, community members could not manage all levels of action, and at some point they had to admit that they were entering a sphere in which they possessed few immediate controls. Hoping to get a couple to commit to reconciliation might involve some sacrifice on the part of the outsider. When William Hays came over for dinner at the Risk household, he no doubt expected a pleasant evening with general conversation. Instead, the couple immediately began quarreling, which prompted Hays to counsel them on amicable living. To prove his point and to keep the peace, he slept that night between the feuding couple. Despite his best intentions, events quickly unfolded that were beyond his control as the husband, armed with a dirk and pistol while lying in bed, tried to reach over Hays to stab his wife but in the process thrust the weapon through Hays's finger. Needless to say, Hays no longer attempted to solve or even suppress this couple's marital problems. The court agreed that the union was hopeless and dissolved the match.[12]

If outsiders could not convince a couple to reconcile via peaceful negotiations, then they might alter their strategy and pursue a more aggressive approach focusing on verbal shaming and confrontation. Openly questioning the actions of the cruel spouse, they would apply pressure in order to force a change in behavior. These confrontations could range from relatively informal to ones involving the entire community, lasting for hours, and taking place in a courtroom-like setting. Embodying the spirit of court proceedings in that all parties adopted an adversarial stance, this strategy represented a moving away from the mutual understanding and peaceful tone that characterized mediation. After a Wisconsin man learned about the injuries that his sister sustained at the hands of her husband, he went over to the house and proceeded to engage his brother-in-law in a debate about the morality of wife abuse. At the end of their talk, the husband "promised that he would not do it again," a vow that he later violated. Many awkward conversations related by deponents ended in a statement of apology and a promise of reform by the offending party. For example, Peter Julien pledged numerous times to his mother-in-law that he would no longer bring home, and infect, her daughter with venereal diseases caught during his time out at sea. His continued violation of this promise is unsurprising, but the consequences proved fatal when his wife gave birth to a child who died due to venereal infection.[13]

At the most basic level, verbal interventions followed similar patterns across all three states studied, but the records reveal subtle differences in approaches and results. Antebellum Virginians generally believed that all members of society should play their part to uphold societal hierarchies and social order. According to precepts of honor, if a man practiced his mastery in an inept way, other members of society must intervene and correct him. As the possession of an honorable character depended very heavily on public performance and perception, one of the most effective tools in a community's arsenal against deviants was shaming rituals. These activities reveal a great deal about what antebellum Virginians believed regarding domestic privacy. Verbal confrontations contained within them an unstated threat that if the marital violations continued, the privacy violations would escalate in kind. In the words of one divorce plaintiff, if an individual chose to "become an outcast from society—acknowledging no legal or moral restraints," then any remnants of privacy were moved aside to accommodate public scrutiny.[14]

Of course, even when faced with verbal accusations, Virginia's cruel husbands rarely relinquished their domestic rights without a fight. Requests made by community members often fell on deaf ears as abusive men continued to behave as they wished. If, for instance, it was pointed out to a cruel husband that it was "two [*sic*] scandalous" for him to whip his wife, the man still might choose to do so, thereby escalating conflict with the community. Or he might argue that the treatment was justified because he "had had to cook his own victuals for a week." If the outsider pushed the issue, then a battle over household authority could erupt, even though the third party might have only verbally questioned the alleged abuser. The very questioning of authority was enough to make a Virginia household head feel the need to defend his authority in a violent way. A local man described how a neighbor purchased a pistol to use on another resident if he continued to interfere in his household management by pointing out that cowhiding was not proper chastisement for a wife. In the end, community members engaging in verbal interventions in Virginia proceeded carefully while also realizing that they possessed a long heritage of public scrutiny that informed, and supported, their activities.[15]

The practice of verbal shaming is almost absent within the Texas records; but when confrontations erupted, they held the potential for substantial violence. One example is instructive with regards to the culture of antebellum Texas. Joseph Dye, a boarder with a Texas couple, after overhearing the husband speak poorly of the character of the wife, decided to verbally intervene. He made a moral choice. Telling the husband that he "would have the last drop of your [the abusive husband's] heart's blood" if one of his own female relatives were abused in such a way, Dye then cautioned the man to provide witnesses before slandering others. Dye, like many Texans, acted in a spontaneous fashion and did not rely on an established network of social relations. And although husbands and wives might violently defend their rights to domestic privacy, they also operated within a culture that condoned interference, albeit in a haphazard fashion.[16]

In Wisconsin the efforts of outsiders to verbally confront and shame cruel spouses took an aggressive turn. As described in earlier chapters, cruel husbands and wives in this state repeatedly made claims to absolute domestic privacy and total body ownership of domestic partners. These assertions, and the dangerous nature of cruelties in the state, indicated that spouses felt as if the frontier environment bred uncertainties in marital roles that could only be countered by isolating the household and policing its inhabitants by using the most extreme measures. Therefore, the interest of third parties in the marriages of other community members was often seen by the spouses in question as adding to the external factors threatening to destroy the institution of marriage itself. To critics, these interlopers into the "private" realm of marriage symbolized all that was dysfunctional in early Wisconsin society. In a worst-case scenario, even broaching the subject of abnormal household relations could prompt the targeted husband or wife to commit retaliatory physical violence against the offending third party. When Bridget Galvin, a Wisconsin wife, took too long to rise out of bed due to injury, her husband jumped onto the bed, kicking and beating her. Witnessing this attack, Bridget's father "remonstrated" with his son-in-law to stop the attack, at which point the man turned his focus on the father and threatened to beat him for interfering. Verbal confrontations unfolded with a high level of stress, in part because cruel spouses felt as if they were not only battling and being judged by the single outsider, but the entire system of their society as well.[17]

Despite this threat of violence, Wisconsin's third parties continued to interfere in marriages, and they met with fewer overall successes than their counterparts in other states. Outsiders in Virginia and Texas could, at minimum, claim that they provided the impetus for temporary behavioral changes, even if the marriages in question ended in failure over the long term. Wisconsin community members could point to few such fleeting victories. Instead of apologetic crocodile tears, they encountered outright denials of cruelties. Or, if an admission was made, it would be accompanied by no promises of an amelioration of future treatment of the victimized spouse. Andreas Kupfer was "one of the most dirty & disgusting fellows imaginable," according to his wife Fredericke. He would force her to engage in sexual intercourse "seven or eight times in a single night." Worse still, his private parts were infested with "crabs or crab-lice," which he would then pick off and, using force, "compel her [his wife] to swallow them." Milwaukee policemen agreed that Andreas, a frequent visitor to the city's bawdy houses, was an exceptionally disturbed man. Finally, Fredericke's mother stepped in to put an end to Andreas's cruelties. She cornered him one day and pointed out the myriad ways in which he violated his marriage bonds, concluding, "You must use her like a man, and not like a beast." Note that she referenced the term *use* to reflect that wives could be "used," the issue being proper versus improper usage. Andreas responded to her concern by stating that if he could not have sexual intercourse in the ways in which he wished it at home, he would continue to go elsewhere. Intentionally or not, he missed the point, and the verbal intervention dissolved into nothingness, as the marriage would months later. As outsiders resorted to more aggressive patterns of verbal confrontations, they faced spouses very much wedded to ideals of domestic privacy and few limits to marital cruelties. These conversations took place on a plane in which violence was an ever-present possibility and a primary mode of communication, thus offering an indication that violent conflict was expected, not avoided, in the state of Wisconsin.[18]

Now, we will turn our attention to a form of intervention in which third parties had only moments to make a moral choice, the offering of shelter to a victim of marital cruelty. Because most outsiders would not take the initiative to offer shelter on their own, the injured party generally requested assistance, thereby thrusting the community member into a potentially dangerous position. Again, the practice of sheltering reflected local involvement in supposedly private situations. As this chapter argues, whether or not third parties offered a husband or wife shelter depended on their ideas regarding domestic privacy and their perception as to whether or not cruelty had occurred. The privacy question was lessened by the arrival of domestic conflict, in the form of a supplicant, on another's doorstep. However, third parties still tried to balance concerns over privacy with concerns over the person's, and their own, welfare. When they accepted a victim into their house, they were not hoping to speed along the dissolution of the other's marriage but rather desiring to provide a safety valve of sorts, a space to let off some steam.

Situations resulting in requests for outside shelter usually arose when a marital partner either escaped or was driven from his or her household. The great majority of spouses who left were women, although a handful of men appear within the records as well. Leaving the home was generally a traumatic affair that could serve as the culmination of years of problems or occur after a seemingly spontaneous violent conflict. An abused woman could create and execute an elaborate escape plan. Or a woman could leave without a moment's notice or preparation, as a Virginia woman did when she ran off in the rain and "did not even take any clothing with her." Similarly, cruel husbands gradually drove women away with tortures over time or by immediate threats of death. Of course, the more dramatic scenes received additional explanation within the divorce bills. A husband ordering a wife away while brandishing a pistol was simply more interesting than a man making a single declaration to his wife to leave the premises. Various patterns of flight can be discerned from a close reading of the documentary archive. To begin with, a woman was most likely to leave, whether by choice or by force, during nighttime hours. This timing coincides with the prevalence of night attacks within the records. Night was a particularly ripe period for discord in marriages. Few distractions were present, and the house space generally closed in on itself with temporary visitors leaving before nightfall. Of course, night escapes also contributed to the danger and drama found within petitioners' accounts. Leaving one's house under the cover of darkness allowed for a secret escape but also posed numerous challenges to personal safety. Making a decision to take along one's children presented another obstacle to a successful departure. The majority of women were simply not able to take along all of their small children on these frantic, often spontaneous trips. They would generally choose to save the youngest child, the one they deemed most in need of their particular maternal care. When Johannette Lange left her abusive husband August, she fled with only her one-and-a-half-year-old, leaving her four other children behind.[19]

The journey presented its own challenges. In some cases, a husband would chase after a wife, forcing the woman to travel with great haste at night and in treacherous territory. The ramifications of not moving quickly enough to evade capture could be great. One Texas woman fled in the middle of night hoping to reach "a place of safety." Unfortunately, her husband overtook her and "draged her about by the hair for the half a mile back home." Texas women, in particular, suffered the consequences of distance and relative isolation when they attempted to flee from situations of domestic cruelty. As stated earlier, households in early Texas could be spread out at great distances, making it difficult to reach other areas even in ideal conditions and in daylight. Joan Cashin, in her work on the Texas frontier, describes how "geographic isolation" presented a great problem for women hoping to rely upon outsider interventions for protection. I disagree with Cashin's argument that connections between family members collapsed under such conditions, but they were definitely strained by the frontier environment. For example, when Rebecca Harper ran from her Texas home in the dark, she traveled three miles on foot, in the rain, before arriving at her father's house. The trip broke her constitution, and she remained ill until the time she filed for divorce. Other women in sparsely populated farming communities complained that even after an arduous journey of escape, they could only reach the locations where "strangers" resided.[20]

We have established that women often left their homes in frantic ways. Now let us try to discern the image that might have met a person who opened his or her door to discover such a refugee. By candlelight, the person might observe that their neighbor was soaked from head to toe from the rain or even covered in bruises with their clothes partially ripped off. Or perhaps the woman would be missing a chunk of hair from her scalp. She might not be wearing shoes, even in snowy winter conditions. An outsider would take in all of this information quickly, as it was not proper to leave a person standing on the doorstep. After an initial survey of the supplicant, this third party then made a sequence of moral decisions that impacted the welfare of all involved. Of course, to begin with, a person might not have opened the door to prevent being placed in this position. For obvious reasons, individuals who "pretended not to be home" do not appear within the record. Those people who did open the door would first try to evaluate whether or not cruelties had actually occurred. They would quickly look over the woman's appearance to assess the degree of visible damages. The likelihood that shelter would be offered correlated with the perceived extent of injuries. If a woman was "very much bruised" or appeared unable to make the trek back home, then shelter was highly likely. However, by fleeing their homes the abused women were protesting marital cruelties through the bodily act of relocation, so privacy concerns weighed heavily in the decisions made by outsiders. Accepting a woman into one's home represented a willingness to involve oneself in the marital affairs of others. Therefore, some community members deflected responsibility by telling the woman to go back home or even by escorting her home themselves.[21]

What occurred after a neighbor or relative opened the door and allowed the injured woman to enter? In countless cases, many of which never made it into the record, nothing of particular note happened at all. The woman stayed the night or for a few hours and then returned home, with the pattern perhaps repeating itself again later. Not all sheltering situations proceeded in such placid ways. Whether a man kicked his wife out of doors or she fled on her own, a husband could still feel the need to track his wife down and demonstrate his mastery before a public audience. His ultimate goal was to regain possession of her body, which she had placed momentarily beyond his control, thereby reasserting his manhood. To allow a wife to become a dependent in another's household, even momentarily, commented negatively on a man's ability to manage his affairs. The records describe husbands arriving at the houses of the third parties determined to take back their wifely property. Once an angry husband arrived at the doorstep, the neighbor was faced, again, with a moral decision. Should they continue to provide shelter? At what point was the potential for danger just too great? Should they turn over the woman and hope for the best? Although it is difficult to believe, many community members allowed the husband to seize the wife, even if she was clearly in hiding. One such man, Jefferson Arthur, described how a feuding husband chased his injured wife up Arthur's stairs, picked her up, and left with the woman in tow. These events, while shocking, are not overly surprising. After all, images of husbands "hunting" wives abound within the divorce records. The natural conclusion of the hunt was to find the wife and bring her back to the marital home. These hunts, often occurring in areas where slavery was present, mirrored, to some degree, the search for escaped bondspeople. Husbands on these types of missions, with gun or knife in hand, held the potential to inflict violence on anyone they encountered.[22]

When faced with an irate husband, a third party could also refuse to allow the man to enter the dwelling. This decision was usually made in an effort to avoid conflict and to allow everyone to calm their nerves, but it often backfired. Left outside with nothing but his anger, a spurned husband could become even more dangerous and desperate to assert his dominance in the situation. In a Virginia domestic dispute, an intoxicated man followed his wife to her father's dwelling, where he was refused entry. He then proceeded to stumble around outside, yelling and threatening to storm the house and take her away by force. In other scenarios, a man might attempt to make his way inside the dwelling in question through the use of force. Wielding dangerous weapons and willing to risk serious injury to accomplish his goals, such a man proved difficult to subdue. Power struggles of this sort could take hours, as the residents of the shelter household maintained vigilance and the husband tested the limits of their guard. On the heels of a particularly brutal whipping, Hariet Mallory fled and was offered shelter by her sister Julia Hill. The arrangement worked out smoothly until Mr. Mallory arrived, with pistol in pocket, to "visit" his wife. When Julia would not allow him entry, he drew his pistol and attempted to break down the door. When that strategy proved unsuccessful, he waited on the porch for an opportunity when one of the women would step near a window, providing a clear shot. Thinking quickly, Julia managed to sneak a slave out to go and fetch the local lawmen, who removed Mr. Mallory. The above story supports, in part, what Nancy Tomes found to be true for mid-nineteenth-century London. Outsiders demonstrated a marked hesitance to become involved in domestic conflicts because they understood that "such intervention entailed serious risks, since the husband's rage was often turned on the person attempting to aid his wife." Extending shelter to a woman in need could carry with it potentially deadly consequences.[23]

On the surface it appears as if these conflicts were built upon quarrels between competing masculine authorities; however, the presence of women offering shelter complicates that interpretation. Victoria Bynum, Stephanie McCurry, and other noted historians have argued that fleeing women essentially "invoked the authority of one set of men" against their husbands by taking shelter under a new masculine roof. This category of power struggle played out most prominently in Virginia, as the majority of individuals who appeared in the records as offering shelter were men. This absence of women could reflect an inherent bias in the records, as women who openly challenged men may not have felt comfortable recalling their actions in court. Simply put, violating gender norms during a heated one-on-one interaction was quite different from declaring one's actions to the community at large. Women who offered assistance were not immune from facing violent penalties for their actions. A story from an antebellum Richmond newspaper provides a window into what could happen when women helped women in this way. The paper recounts how a man, Joseph Nelton, hit a woman because she was allegedly sheltering his wife and children after he had driven them from the house. Wisconsin women, in particular, appeared quite willing to engage in sheltering and to retaliate in physical ways if the thresholds of their households were breached by cruel men. When John Lewis pursued his wife into Mary Ulrich's home, she forced him from the premises and stated that she "did not want any fighting" in her house. Despite Lewis's threat that he would "knock" a hoe into Ulrich's head, she still won the day and he left sans wife. This is not to argue that Wisconsin women were naturally violent individuals but rather that the culture of the area allowed for interactions to take place on a violent plane. Keeping the peace of a household might require a woman to respond violently, just as sustaining the peace of the community necessitated aggressive action. Again, the community in Wisconsin made a claim that domestic privacy was a privilege, not a right.[24]

Much to the chagrin of well-wishers, a temporary extension of shelter to a desperate woman could eventually turn into a permanent living arrangement. A transition period usually took place, in which a woman would be induced to return to her marital home, only to suffer cruel treatment again and to repeat the process of fleeing. Because of the conservative impulse of the third parties to try to keep the marriage intact, victimized women were forced to engage in these maneuvers even if they truly only wished to establish a new permanent residence. After numerous attempts at physical reconciliation, a woman was most likely to settle in with relatives to begin the long-term healing process. Fathers, brothers, sons, sons-in-law, daughters, mothers, and even mothers-in-law could all provide alternative permanent living arrangements to a relative in need. Returning to a parent was a gendered remedy, available solely to wives, as injured husbands generally did not move into their father's household. Rejecting the shelter provided by a marital partner could prove costly in numerous ways for women. In particular, the economic consequences of their decision would weigh upon the community, as it now had another helpless dependent to support out of the group fodder. Complaints about these burdens most frequently surfaced in the records in those areas in which resources were scarcest and survival most difficult. For example, Wisconsin residents would relate how they wanted to help a victimized woman but could not do so due to financial concerns.[25]

As the above pages demonstrate, third parties could be forced into a moral dilemma due to a request for shelter, but they also could be drawn into conflict by what I refer to as "the noises of violence." I include within this phrase any and all audible emanations associated with marital discord. Of course, these vocalizations were not intentional in the majority of conflicts, but they still represented an active beckoning of third parties. The degree to which domestic strife is characterized by sound is a subject that has yet to be the focus of serious exploration by historians. However, as contemporary horror films demonstrate, incidents that are experienced without an accompanying visual script are often the most terrifying. It is possible to contend that to fully understand domestic violence, we must approach it from a variety of sensory perspectives. In some circumstances community members only had their hearing to determine whether or not, and how, to intervene in a conflict.

In what situations might a third party hear the noises of violence? The most obvious answer to this question is that those individuals who resided under the same roof possessed the highest likelihood of hearing conflicts. The information provided by children and boarders reflects the fact that some of the noises were practically inescapable within dwellings. Again, thin walls and shoddy construction in houses across all three states made the transmission of sound practically unavoidable. The witnesses would recall hearing general noises as well as specific terms and words. In some situations their recollections could even be quite humorous, in retrospect. One boarder recalled listening to a couple quarreling during the night. He heard the man step toward the woman and her scream at him not to shoot her. He then heard the man reply, "you damn fool I am only going to take a chew of tobacco." However, the majority of listeners who suffered from loss of sleep due to these loud conflicts found little to laugh about. Hearing a person getting kicked out of bed could wake a person up. Hearing "screaming and hallowing" could wake a person up. On these occasions even children would take action to restore the silence of the household, as a Wisconsin girl did when she went to her parents' bedroom "to quiet them." Other people suffered in silence listening to the noises of husbands and wives in turmoil. A Texas boarder recalled how "many a night I was very much annoyed" from the sounds of violence, "so much so that I could not sleep."[26]

Moreover, the noises of violence ranged beyond the confines of domestic spaces and could travel hundreds of feet to the ears of neighbors and community members passing by the households in question. Witnesses would relate how they heard the sounds of conflict while attending to their daily tasks. They would assert that they could not avoid listening to these noises no matter how much they tried to stay away from the location in question. A Virginia man recalled how he used water from the same spring as a troubled couple, and that he constantly overheard them arguing from across the stream. As described earlier, houses in rural Wisconsin were spaced at quite a distance from one another due to farming needs, therefore posing a challenge to travel. It could be assumed that this distance would prevent the spread of noises, but Wisconsin neighbors stated to the court that audible indications of violence could easily cross many yards of quiet countryside. Samuel Young would hear his neighbor "swear and scold" at his wife while everyone was in the fields. In another case, a Wisconsin man asserted that, although he lived "forty rods [six hundred feet] from the parties," he still "often heard" the noises associated with their feuds.[27]

If a third party was presented with audible or visible evidence of a marital conflict in progress, how did he or she decide whether or when to intervene? How did these moral choices play out? To begin with, as this chapter argues, questions of privacy were addressed, but these became less important if the witness viewed the cruelties firsthand. Wives and husbands across all three states tolerated a degree of cruelty, so the issue, again, was where to draw the line. After initially learning about a conflict, the witness usually tried to gather additional information with which to make their decision. If they were a neighbor "attracted by the cries" of a marital victim, they might head over to the location to see everything in person. If they were outside when the attack occurred, they might rush inside. Of course, it would be untrue to assert that all third parties chose to intervene after gathering more information. Some individuals remained on the sidelines during the conflict. For example, one Milwaukee woman watched from her doorstep in the Eighth Ward as her neighbor beat his wife over the head with a chair.[28]

As Christine Stansell describes, those community members who physically intervened restricted their actions to a "patterned series of moves and countermoves," a dance fully recognized by all involved. This, of course, is not to downplay individual agency, but third parties were very aware that their choices would be scrutinized in terms of local social mores. Divorce petitioners related countless stories of the miraculous outsider saving them from a brutal death at the hands of their spouses; however, the incidents related by the outsiders themselves are much more informative for our purposes. From their accounts it can be determined that third parties across all states believed that, at a minimum, a threat against a person's life permitted a community member to intervene in a physical way. The issue was determining exactly when a marital conflict had escalated to the point of being life-threatening for either spouse. That is one reason why outsiders were very willing to respond to cries of "murder," taking these proclamations to be serious indicators of a deadly struggle in progress. Across all three states in this analysis, wives mostly, and a few husbands, resorted to calls for assistance. "Murder" yells appear to have been particularly effective in Wisconsin, as they were mentioned frequently within the records, and they almost always prompted a neighbor to leave immediately to render aid to the afflicted. This could be the case because community members in this state were well aware of the level of violence found within homes and possessed ample evidence from their daily lives that domestic murders could, and did, take place. This type of violence was almost expected, if not condoned. In addition, the records indicate that, despite the prevalence of instances of aid from third parties in the archive, Wisconsin wives resorted to this measure strategically, perhaps attempting to resolve the problem on their own, maybe even in a physical way, before "calling in the cavalry," so to speak. The small daughter of Delia and Lyman Tubbs told the court that, "Mother does not hallow unless she is in great danger." Of course, a woman who cried wolf too often ran the risk of being ignored when she really required the assistance of others.[29]

Once a third party arrived at the scene of the conflict, the records indicate that a variety of factors continued to influence the manner of their intervention. In particular, the use of weapons by one spouse against another often led to a physical intervention due to the escalated risk of serious injury by the parties. The most common response was to prevent the cruel spouse from carrying out his or her intentions by grabbing or blocking the chosen weapon. Again, Wisconsin community members regularly engaged in these types of interventions. Both male and female observers would put their own bodies at risk to prevent the use of a weapon against a person whom they perceived to be a victim. Whether it was grabbing a chair from an irate husband or taking fire tongs from an angry wife, Wisconsin residents appeared to feel as if they were obligated to meet force with force. The descriptions of these interventions drip with physicality, with men and women springing to action. They even put their bodies at risk in the heat of the moment, blocking a thrown item prior to identifying it. However, spontaneous decisions could prove very injurious, even fatal, if the lobbed item was a butcher knife. Texas and Virginia community members, in contrast, appeared to have been less willing to resort to physical measures of intervention.[30]

This marked difference between the three states continues as the analysis shifts to include circumstances in which third parties grabbed and restrained the abuser. Wisconsin citizens engaged in all manner of preventive grappling, including seizing the arms, legs, or even the torso of the offending party. One guy and "two others" jumped on William Garrick as he pounded his wife with his fists. Many witnesses categorized their actions as interference when testifying in court, but they maintained their right to do so. When recounting his efforts to break up a feuding couple, George Smart recalled, "I then interfered and took him from her by force." Smart's account both celebrated his course of action and emphasized the necessity of using physical methods. In Texas, moments of physical confrontation generally unfolded in more seemingly random scenarios, such as when two travelers came into a house to stop a man from throwing household items at his wife. In this state the physical fragmentation of society combined with the push by cruel husbands to retain domestic privacy led to a community attitude less prone to physical prevention.[31]

The organization of this chapter has emphasized an escalating sense of urgency on the part of third parties as well as an increased sense of danger for all involved in marital conflicts. In this situation, after individual attempts at intervention and mediation failed, or if a couple's problems proved simply too offensive for toleration, the entire community could engage in general censure of the cruel husband or wife. Essentially, they would join together to target the person who was flaunting their supposed independence from societal restraints. Then the group would use a variety of shaming techniques to demonstrate the extent to which this person was indeed still very much under local control and could not hide, even behind the rhetoric of domestic privacy. It is important to note that these efforts were still preventive and not intentionally destructive of marriages. The community did not seek to destroy marriages but rather to "prevent negative behaviors" from gaining a permanent foothold and creating an environment of general social disruption. These negative behaviors were also extraordinary in nature and did not reflect the norm in any sense. However, these situations are important to study because participants in shaming rituals clearly communicated their understandings of acceptable marital behaviors.[32]

It is relatively unsurprising that Virginia emerges as the state in which, of the three studied, community actions appeared to play the most significant part in overall culture. The handful of historians who have studied these rituals of regulation have argued that extralegal measures sprung up as a partial response to an ineffective formal legal system. As this argument goes, individuals frustrated by or untrustful of the "law" would fashion their own law in order to address community problems. My disagreement with this interpretation lies in its oversimplification of local authority systems. In Virginia, as with other southern states, the local and formal law intertwined at their cores. Therefore, it is possible to contrast types of local authority, but it is impossible to extract local influence from southern legal practices. Virginians would not have seen community action or legal action as a choice between two radically different approaches. Other historians have argued that extralegal measures reflected the influence of southern honor as well as a regionally distinctive willingness to resort to violence to resolve conflicts. However, this study refutes these claims by showing how citizens in Texas, and Wisconsin in particular, demonstrated more of a reliance on violence as a means of communication.[33]

We will examine two categories of community censure: church-based and charivaris. It is an understatement of massive proportions to say that evangelical churches influenced the development of culture and society in the South. Churches were among the few institutions granted the power to peer behind closed doors and evaluate the private lives of parishioners. During disciplinary hearings, church members would be asked to recount their behaviors in front of a "court of their peers." As this study does not rely on evidence from church records, quite possibly a very rich source of information of marital conflicts, one example that was found within a personal papers collection will have to suffice. Robert Saunders, a Virginia resident, in a letter to his wife, recalled how Richmond was abuzz with rumors following the death of the wife of John Caskie, "formerly of Congress." The streets were "ringing with accounts of his brutal treatment," as she had died with "marks" on her body. Saunders did not attend the funeral, but he heard that the pastor made it quite clear that he "regarded the accounts as generally true." During the sermon the pastor said that "he would say no more of the departed than that no friend of hers should do otherwise than *rejoice* that she was gone . . . and that *he would not cover up or draw attention from the vices and wrongs of the living by a eulogy upon the dead.*" As this brief anecdote demonstrates, church members and pastors in the South could use their considerable influence to shape supposedly private behaviors.[34]

In addition, community intervention against cruel spouses could take the form of charivaris, or group-based shaming rituals. A charivari, also referred to as a skimmington or "rough music," occurred when a number of community members gathered together to humiliate or conduct violence against another person with the goal of pressuring the deviant in question to conform to societal ideals of behavior. The occurrence of charivaris has a long history, stretching back to the colonial period in the United States and far earlier in European nations. Historians have described how Quakers and Puritans policed their societies by relying, in part, on such rituals. Brenda Stevenson notes that among the Quakers, "Neighborhood leaders assessed the situation, decided on a course of action, and then carried it out." In the case of one man, "They dragged him out of bed, beat him severely, placed him in a shallow grave, and then proceeded to cover him up with wooden boards." He later escaped and filed a suit for kidnapping and assault, but unsurprisingly, no one appeared for him.[35]

The pattern of these attacks changed very little over the next century or two. In the antebellum period, a surprise assault was generally followed by the local people ordering the perpetrator to "leave town or else." Group action required that many individuals acquire a shared base of information that they believed was correct and actionable. This information also had to elicit an emotional response, enough to justify a reaction beyond mediation or shaming. Newspaper articles both announced the possibility of charivaris and also inspired them. For example, a small mention in the *Richmond Dispatch* that James Hamilton was convicted of beating his wife could have been enough to create a mob action had the Hamiltons not been free blacks. In 1858 the *Richmond Enquirer* related how a local man killed his wife via poisoned lemonade. The paper also commented that the community had been stirred to "great excitement" by the crime and that "Lynch law will be put in execution."[36]

Very few charivari victims left behind descriptions of the events in question. As such, the 1857 account of R. D. Addington is exceedingly rare. This text relates how a man could become the target of general community distaste. According to the work, Addington made an ill match when he wed Hannah Weed, the daughter of a local family in severe financial constraints. Shortly after the marriage, Addington believed that the Weed family had begun to create schemes to smear his character and swindle him out of his money. One of these schemes involved spreading a report that Addington had whipped his wife, forcing her to leave him and file for divorce. This information moved quickly throughout the community, and one night he returned to his office to find his door "daubed with gas-tar, and sprinkled with feathers." A crowd gathered to demand his attention, at which point, fearing for his life, he donned a bonnet and shawl and escaped out the back door. The local newspapers advertised that he should leave Richmond quickly or he would be wearing a suit of tar and feathers. Addington took refuge in Norfolk only to hear that a "storm is brewing" in the city to match the one in Richmond. Addington had to flee again. Charivari participants followed the same questioning process as those involved in individual action. The group determined whether or not a violation had occurred. Then, if enough people knew about the cruelties, the men and women involved would overrule any claims to privacy for the deviant in question and proceed as they desired. As such, Addington could not hide behind the claim of domestic privacy. The time for that passed when the newspapers became involved and transformed his marriage into a matter for public consumption. The local information networks ensured that Addington could not escape this stigma even by moving to another city. Although charivaris were rare, they symbolized the leverage of extreme force to counter what the community perceived as an extreme problem.[37]

Finally, if individual and group-based interventions failed to successfully integrate the problem couple back into the community, then legal remedies existed as a last resort. Legal authorities, such as magistrates or sheriffs, were not divorced from the earlier events described in this chapter. As individuals in communities, they were very much enmeshed in local systems of reporting and informal law. In fact, these same men might have attempted to mediate with the couple prior to being called to intervene as a representative of formal law. Magistrates often spent a fair amount of their time gathering evidence for peace warrants against troubled men and women in the community. A peace warrant required that a person give a bond, generally a monetary guarantee, that they would no longer disturb the peace. A wide variety of individuals could request a warrant, from the victimized spouse to a concerned neighbor. In addition, this legal restraint usually included a short period in the local jail for the abuser, depending on the perceived severity of cruelties. Although the warrant and the jail time were intended to provide a cooling down period for all involved, it could have the opposite effect of angering an already cruel spouse and then releasing them to the care of a surprised marital partner. Wives, in particular, complained that warrants proved ineffective in the long term, as cruel husbands violated the vows almost "right away."

Even if ineffectual, peace warrants served as a representation of the interconnectedness of domestic private peace and the public peace. As Laura Edwards contends, these warrants were attempts to limit the actions of husbands who had overstepped the proper boundaries of domestic authority, to the damage of society as a whole. Virginians, in particular, appeared to gravitate toward peace warrants as legal solutions to domestic disputes. This makes sense considering the well-documented distaste of southerners for anything touching on formal legal action. Peace warrants allowed southern communities to place the pressure of a formal legal system on an abuser while not acknowledging any outside control over local society itself.[38]

In contrast, when Wisconsin residents called on legal authorities, it was quite often out of an effort to press a criminal assault charge against a cruel wife or husband. As one newspaper put it, when a man or woman made themselves "a dangerous member of society," the onus was placed on their peers to curb the extent of the damage to social order. Therefore, unlike in southern communities, questions of honor were put aside and pragmatic concerns ruled the day. A justice of the peace for one county recalled how local citizens became so frustrated with a "notorious" wife beater that they seized him and turned him over to the "proper authority" to face criminal assault charges.[39] Although this study does not examine criminal assault records, these charges repeatedly appear in divorce proceedings, generally as precursors to divorce. Within the accounts related to assault charges, Wisconsin citizens would assert that they felt obligated to escalate their interventions from mediation to formal legal measures. For example, after Horace Baggs repeatedly kicked and hit his wife, many members of the community filed formal complaints. One such man, Samuel Dunbar, recalled, "I felt it my duty to make the complaint. I have no ill feeling against Baggs." To Samuel this was a matter of equal force for the sake of peace, and personality had nothing to do with it. From the records we can discern that settlers in the Midwest felt fewer qualms about turning to the limited local legal authorities in search of a solution to problem marriages in their communities. The citizens in Wisconsin tolerated nearly lethal levels of violence but drew the line at death, and this partially explains their willingness to charge cruel spouses with assault rather than pursuing peace warrants.[40]

Finally, when the avenues of community intervention outlined throughout this chapter failed to prove effective, an ultimate legal remedy appeared, the sundering of marriage ties as enacted through divorce. Men and women across all of the states within this study were hesitant to suggest divorce for others because they understood that it was an enormous social and legal undertaking. As one Virginia man stated, divorce amounted to "destroying the house." The house metaphor is apt, as divorce also rocked the very foundations of broader societal order. By the time that antebellum husbands and wives filed their petitions, they had advanced through a variety of interventions and arrived at the last possible option for a peaceable existence. Therefore, divorce records provide not only a window into the immediate events surrounding separation but a perspective on broader community understandings of marital breakdown and conflict.[41]

Going back to the opening story, what did Catharine do when faced with Mary's domestic crisis? By reaching out to this other woman, Mary plunged Catharine into a series of moral decisions that would peak with her eventually physically confronting the abuser in question. Placing Catharine in context alongside other community members reveals her actions as critical, but not singular, interventions into Mary's troubled marriage. The community stepped in numerous times to cajole, pressure, and eventually force, via divorce, the Grinnins to conform to proper, and peaceful, marital practices. This chapter contends that at every step of this process, the involvement of third parties in situations of marital cruelty was shaped by their understandings of proper domestic relations as well as their beliefs in domestic privacy. Outsiders first assessed whether or not cruelties were indeed taking place, a process fed by ideas of cruelty explored in earlier chapters. Then, they determined whether or not intervention was warranted and what form it needed to take.[42]

Employing a comparative approach and investigating the interrelationship of custom and intervention reveals that regional location affected the ways in which community members addressed the series of moral choices presented to them by situations of cruelty. In Virginia, well-established local reporting networks facilitated a belief that private matters were legitimate fodder for public discussion. Virginians then pursued intervention strategies tailored to result in domestic peace without the risk of physical harm to the outsider. Emphasizing consistency over aggressiveness, Virginia's third parties would attempt mediation and shaming, only resorting to physical action as a last resort when faced with the most egregious cruelties. This leads to the conclusion that southerners did not view violence as unavoidable but instead condoned only certain categories of violence, such as those practiced on slaves, while increasingly regulating others. In fact, as one studies the actions of community members, it becomes evident that they sought to prevent, and avoid, violence every step of the way. On the other hand, interventions in Texas were characterized more by spontaneity than by careful planning over the long term. Outsiders did not have the opportunity to gather information over time and instead acted on spur-of-the-moment emotion and evidence. Broad-based community action was almost nonexistent, with interventions taking place on an individual basis. The behaviors of Texans reflected life in a hybrid southern frontier society. They surely would have fallen into a pattern similar to Virginia's had they possessed the legal or community structures to do so. Texans were caught in a veritable limbo, wanting to mediate but instead looking to violent methods of intervention because they did not have the local support required to make nonaggressive approaches successful.

In contrast, individuals living in Wisconsin regularly engaged in aggressive policing of domestic disputes. Acting without the benefit of a well-established rumor network, Wisconsin citizens tended to attempt only limited mediation until the cruelties in question reached a level approaching lethality. When that threshold was reached, third parties of both genders used violence as a tool with which to reestablish local peace. Countering physical force with physical force, their actions betrayed the impossibility of looking to formal, or even local, legal cultures for assistance. These men and women went into domestic frays as individuals but hoped to construct communities based on protest against lethal violence in the process. It can be concluded, therefore, that the proximity to frontier conditions influenced the pattern of interference adopted by third parties. Men and women in long-established communities, such as Virginia, had numerous local resources to draw upon that, in turn, pushed them towards nonviolent solutions. In contrast, men and women on the frontier grappled with limited avenues for outside assistance and, as a result, emphasized violent solutions to violent problems.

Tracing community interventions in cruel marriages across three states significantly enhances our understandings of violence, region, and the family. In the South we learn that violence was increasingly only sanctioned against certain bodies, slaves, but elaborate protective processes were in place if conflict erupted in white marriages. In frontier areas, physical force ruled the day; however, citizens refused to treat cruelties as acceptable and struggled to establish new norms forged through violent responses. Furthermore, this study shows that the uncertainties regarding the public/private nature of marriage that plague modern-day efforts to intervene in situations of domestic violence possess a long history. Cruel partners across all three states repeatedly emphasized the sanctity of the domestic realm in order to prevent community action. Other men and women routinely put aside these warnings, intervened, and in the process constructed new marital ideals from the ashes of conflict.

Conclusion

Antebellum moralist Virginia Cary once mused, "Conjugal love is too delicate in its texture, not to undergo a thousand violences." After a study of over one thousand nineteenth-century divorce cases, this work has shown that Cary possibly underestimated the vast array of tensions that could creep into romantic relationships. Although the majority of men and women entered into unions with expectations of permanence, marital failure existed as an ever-present possibility. To put it simply, marriage was changing in the 1840s and 1850s. With coverture waning in influence, a new set of companionate ideals emerged to take its place. Through an examination of troubled relationships, this work contends that antebellum men and women described the ideal marriage as one in which both spouses worked together as a balanced, productive unit. While they surely desired love, duty was what mattered. Such a finding moves our discussion of nineteenth-century marriage away from supposed ideals and into the realm of day-to-day practices and beliefs.[1]

So, where did antebellum men and women draw the line between unacceptable and acceptable conjugal behaviors? The records show that cruelty was born out of those relationships in which one or both partners failed to live up to the precepts of marital productivity. Husbands and wives also employed cruelty and violence in an effort to push their spouses back into traditional gender roles. Across the three states, the presence of marital cruelty directly correlated with the degree of gender role confusion experienced by the citizens of the area. Simply put, when men and women were unsure about what exactly their domestic roles entailed, this uncertainty prompted anxieties that, in turn, led to escalated violence. For this reason, Wisconsin husbands and wives were the most likely to commit near-lethal cruelties in marriage. Without a guiding set of gender norms to cling to, midwestern husbands attempted to violently impose traditional understandings of marital roles upon their wives. Not to be outdone, Wisconsin women used cruelty to assert their bodily rights within unions. Southerners, too, understood marital cruelty to be connected with marital management. However, they were principally concerned with the relationships between abuse, chastisement, honor, and mastery. Virginians, in particular, sought to refine the practice of mastery so as to present the image of a benevolent South. Within a southern context, cruelty occurred if one spouse attempted to practice inappropriate mastery over the other. Virginians carefully regulated and policed the practice of violence, thus directly challenging the stereotype of southern bloodthirstiness.

This work has also highlighted local legal practices and the ways in which antebellum community courtrooms existed as forums for extended dramas that were not only reflective but constitutive in relation to the developments of higher courts. In original jurisdiction cases, local men and women served as judges, jurors, witnesses, litigants, and audience members. Characterized by broad-based community participation, these proceedings demonstrate the degree to which local and formal law were often one and the same. Moreover, divorce records from this period reveal that local consumers of the law were perfectly capable of articulating quite sophisticated definitions of where exactly to draw the line separating cruelty from insensitivity or abrasiveness, for example. They meted out community justice based on local knowledge, thus providing historians with detailed descriptions of commonly held values and beliefs.

Court records document the gradual erosion of domestic privacy in American society. The legal separation process made previously unmentionable subjects, such as the details of a woman's figure, not only sanctioned but encouraged topics of public conversation. Discussions of marital cruelty fed off of, and were shaped by, changing understandings of the human form. Male bodies appeared particularly susceptible to beastly emotions whereas female bodies bordered on the ridiculously fragile. As such, society admonished men to control their baser instincts and women to protect their limited productive potential. The rise of antebellum humanitarian reform movements focused additional attention on the body while encouraging an active dialogue on the role of pain. In a departure from earlier eras, by the mid-nineteenth century men and women began to differentiate between varying types of pain. Reformists directed their energies towards those individuals whom they viewed as practicing cruelty, otherwise known as "the needless and deliberate infliction of pain." Slaveholders, in particular, came under scrutiny for behaving cruelly and spreading "moral contamination." As a result, southern patriarchs began to actively regulate the practice of cruelty, and even chastisement, when directed towards certain bodies, i.e., white women. They needed these women to remain intact and to serve as clear symbols of southern benevolent mastery. It is important to note, however, that the cruelties directed at other southern bodies, i.e., enslaved men and women, remained relatively unchanged. Women's rights reformers also seized upon the idea of pain as a vehicle through which to push for expanded bodily rights for wives. They argued, with limited success, that a wide variety of harmful sexual practices constituted divorceable wrongs.

The story of marital cruelty is, necessarily, a tale emphasizing the extent of human depravity. In antebellum society, divorce was a failure and cruelty even more so. However, in the end, it is useful to remember that men and women pursued separations hoping to perfect, not destroy, the marital script.[2]

NOTE ON SOURCES AND METHODOLOGY

Original jurisdiction divorce court cases constitute the primary source base for this study. Cases were gathered by visiting local archives as well as contacting court clerks. The research net included all counties formed up until 1860 (and no counties that later composed West Virginia). Across all three states, only divorce proceedings in which cruelty was claimed were included within the study. In addition, only those marriages formed prior to 1860 were used, although the time of case filing was opened at 1840 and cut off at 1865. Out of this information, a records database was constructed that included all extant cruelty cases available to scholars at the time the research for this work was completed. In total, this database contains 1,541 total cases covering 145 counties across Virginia, Texas, and Wisconsin.

Local court documents have traditionally been underused by historians, and this work attempts to show the versatility and significance of these records. In a way similar to that used in Norma Basch's *Framing American Divorce,* this work chooses to highlight the practices of the courts of original jurisdiction, eschewing an analysis of higher court or appellate rulings. The cases in the database generally come from the district courts of Texas, the circuit and district courts of Wisconsin, and the circuit and chancery courts of Virginia. Legislative petitions from all three states are included in the database as well.[1]

While it is my contention that cruelty cases from the antebellum period exist as "potentially revealing cultural texts," they do limit one's ability to conduct class, racial, and ethnic analyses. When the records suggest an individual's class affiliation, either through a litigant's self-identification or as evident via attached property proceedings, this study uses that information. In the same fashion, this work explores ethnicity when the records provide an entry point into that conversation. Racial analysis, as well, represents an important component of this work. However, as slave marriage was not legally recognized in the South, this study is unable to explore the internal dynamics of those relationships.[2]

The appearance and completeness of the court records varies a great deal depending on the "nature of the case and the preservation status of the documents." At the conclusion of a case, the court clerk would generally roll up all of the related papers into a bundle and place it into a records cabinet. Within these bundles, the civil case papers are the most useful for modern researchers. They might contain petitions and bills, answers, depositions, and various administrative notices. In some, but not all, of the cases the conclusion or verdict was noted in a formal document, but a researcher is more likely to find a single line verdict scrawled on the exterior of the roll itself. Each proceeding varies in substance and range of commentary, with some only showing a single line of complaint while others take up hundreds of pages and are split into multiple rolls. As this study is more interested in the extended conversations found within the records, it makes only a minimal use of minute and judgment books because the commentaries contained therein are usually not substantive. Due to theft, time, and varying preservation practices, the records on the whole do not reflect a complete case catalogue. Therefore, this work chooses to refrain from attempting a statistical or quantitative analysis of cruelty or divorce, believing that the final product would not reflect an accurate portrayal of historical circumstances.[3]

Questions of accuracy have always plagued historians who work with legal documents. The reliability of divorce cases, in particular, has been the subject of intense questioning by scholars. This work, following in the path of Nancy Cott, Thomas Buckley, and others, acknowledges the framed nature of these documents while also asserting that the comments contained therein provide invaluable portrayals of antebellum life. After all, litigants needed to present believable accounts of events in order to receive favorable verdicts. While an individual could choose to waive the right to a jury trial, the majority of men and women counted upon the local knowledge of their peers to ensure a forthright proceeding. The voices of the plaintiffs and defendants come across most clearly in the bills and answers portions of the case records. Husbands and wives were often restricted from providing direct testimony aside from these formats.

This practice makes it even more critical, and useful, to examine the accounts provided by local witnesses.[4]

In addition to court cases, this study also references a variety of personal documents and public writings from the antebellum period. Because domestic violence was a generally hidden subject, these sources were gathered by visiting various scholarly repositories and surveying the available personal materials from the period. This research approach resulted in the discovery of a substantial number of documents chronicling abuse from nonlegal perspectives. Diaries, letters, memoirs, newspapers, and moral and religious tracts were drawn upon in the creation of this work. In the end, the hope is that these sources will, in the words of one prominent frontier historian, "provide systematic information about the behavioral regularities of daily life as well as insight into popular values and beliefs" in antebellum America.[5]

NOTES

INTRODUCTION

1. *Mary Jane Lansing v. Andrew Lansing* (1862), OSH-WC.

2. Hendrik Hartog, *Man and Wife in America: A History* (Cambridge: Harvard University Press, 2000), 11, 22; Norma Basch, *Framing American Divorce: From the Revolutionary Generation to the Victorians* (Berkeley: University of California Press, 1999), 8.

3. Nancy F. Cott, *Public Vows: A History of Marriage and the Nation* (Cambridge: Harvard University Press, 2001); Joel Prentiss Bishop, *New Commentaries on Marriage, Divorce, and Separation as to the Law, Evidence, Pleading, Practice, Forms, and the Evidence of Marriage in All Issues on a New System of Legal Exposition, Vol. 1* (Chicago, n.p., 1891), 632–633 (first and second quotes); Robert Griswold, "Law, Sex, Cruelty, and Divorce in Victorian America, 1840–1900," *American Quarterly* 38 (Winter 1986): 726 (third quote), 729; Robert Griswold, "The Evolution of the Doctrine of Mental Cruelty in Victorian American Divorce, 1790–1900," *Journal of Social History* 20 (Autumn 1986): 127–148; Hartog, *Man and Wife in America*, 90, 105, 116, 152.

4. Margaret Abruzzo, *Polemical Pain: Slavery, Cruelty, and the Rise of Humanitarianism* (Baltimore: Johns Hopkins University Press, 2011), 6 (quote); Myra C. Glenn, *Campaigns against Corporal Punishment: Prisoners, Sailors, Women, and Children in Antebellum America* (Albany: State University of New York Press, 1984); Martin S. Pernick, *A Calculus of Suffering: Pain, Professionalism, and Anesthesia in Nineteenth-Century America* (New York: Columbia University Press, 1985); Elizabeth B. Clark, "'The Sacred Rights of the Weak': Pain, Sympathy, and the Culture of Individual Rights in Antebellum America," *Journal of American History* 82 (September 1995): 463–493.

5. Anya Jabour, *Marriage in the Early Republic: Elizabeth and William Wirt and the Companionate Ideal* (Baltimore: Johns Hopkins University Press, 1998), 5 (quote), 9; Reva Siegel, "'The Rule of Love': Wife Beating as Prerogative and Privacy," *Yale Law Journal* 105 (June 1996): 2144–2145; Hendrik Hartog, "Lawyering, Husbands' Rights, and the 'Unwritten Law' in Nineteenth-Century America," *Journal of American History* 84 (June 1997): 67.

6. Michael Grossberg, *Governing the Hearth: Law and the Family in Nineteenth-Century America* (Chapel Hill: University of North Carolina Press, 1985), 7, 9, 19.

7. E. Anthony Rotundo, "Body and Soul: Changing Ideals of American Middle-Class Manhood, 1770–1920," *Journal of Social History* 16 (Summer 1983): 27; John Mack

Faragher, *Women and Men on the Overland Trail* (New Haven: Yale University Press, 1989), 147–148; Dawn Keetley, "From Anger to Jealousy: Explaining Domestic Homicide in Antebellum America," *Journal of Social History* 42 (Winter 2008): 269–297.

8. Elizabeth Pleck, *Domestic Tyranny: The Making of Social Policy Against Family Violence from Colonial Times to the Present* (New York: Oxford University Press, 1987); Linda Gordon, *Heroes of Their Own Lives: The Politics and History of Family Violence: Boston, 1880–1960* (Urbana: University of Illinois Press, 1988), 3 (quote); Griswold, "Evolution of the Doctrine"; Hartog, *Man and Wife in America;* Basch, *Framing American Divorce;* Cott, *Public Vows.*

9. David Peterson del Mar, *What Trouble I Have Seen: A History of Violence Against Wives* (Cambridge: Harvard University Press, 1996); Drew Gilpin Faust, *Mothers of Invention: Women of the Slaveholding South in the American Civil War* (Chapel Hill: University of North Carolina Press, 1996), 63 (quote).

10. W. J. Cash, *The Mind of the South* (New York: A. A. Knopf, 1957); Bertram Wyatt-Brown, *Southern Honor: Ethics and Behavior in the Old South* (New York: Oxford University Press, 1982); Dickson D. Bruce Jr., *Violence and Culture in the Antebellum South* (Austin: University of Texas Press, 1979); Richard Nisbett and Dov Cohen, *Culture of Honor: The Psychology of Violence in the South* (New York: Oxford University Press, 1996); Gilles Vandal, *Rethinking Southern Violence: Homicides in Post–Civil War Louisiana, 1866–1884* (Columbus: Ohio State University Press, 2000); Edward Ayers, *Vengeance and Justice: Crime and Punishment in the 19th-Century American South* (New York: Oxford University Press, 1984); Clayton E. Cramer, *Concealed Weapon Laws of the Early Republic: Dueling, Southern Violence, and Moral Reform* (Westport, CT: Praeger, 1999); and David T. Courtwright, *Violent Land: Single Men and Social Disorder from the Frontier to the Inner City* (Cambridge: Harvard University Press, 1996). Many of these theories are buttressed by historical statistics showing elevated murder rates for the South as compared with other regions. However, the usefulness and reliability of such numbers have yet to be definitively established by scholars.

11. Ariela J. Gross, *Double Character: Slavery and Mastery in the Antebellum Southern Courtroom* (Princeton: Princeton University Press, 2000), 47, 48 (first quote); Wyatt-Brown, *Southern Honor,* 281(second quote). The dominant interpretation of honor is a gendered one that asserts that women served as audience members only. The danger of such an argument is that it threatens to relegate southern women to the sidelines of history. The usage of character or credit as the female parallel of honor, and as employed by Laura Edwards, is a far more helpful, and I would argue accurate, way to approach the subject of power relations in southern culture. Laura F. Edwards, *The People and Their Peace: Legal Culture and the Transformation of Inequality in the Post-Revolutionary South* (Chapel Hill: University of North Carolina Press, 2009), 112–113; Jonathan Daniel Wells, *The Origins of the Southern Middle Class, 1800–1861* (Chapel Hill: University of North Carolina Press, 2004).

12. Rhys Isaac, *The Transformation of Virginia, 1740–1790* (Chapel Hill: University

of North Carolina Press, 1982); Steven M. Stowe, *Intimacy and Power in the Old South: Ritual in the Lives of Planters* (Baltimore: Johns Hopkins University Press, 1987); Peter Kolchin, *A Sphinx on the American Land: The Nineteenth-Century South in Comparative Perspective* (Baton Rouge: Louisiana State University Press, 2003), 4, 24, 39, 43; Vandal, *Rethinking Southern Violence,* 14 (quote). Finding divorce records for free black families also posed a problem. Historian David Silkenat, in his study of divorce and debt in North Carolina, suggests that the legal process may have been cost-prohibitive for free blacks. David Silkenat, *Moments of Despair: Suicide, Despair, & Debt in Civil War Era North Carolina* (Chapel Hill: University of North Carolina Press, 2011), 94.

13. Randolph Campbell, *Gone to Texas: A History of the Lone Star State* (New York: Oxford University Press, 2003), 110–111; Terry G. Jordan, "Population Origins in Texas, 1850," *Geographical Review* 59 (January 1969): 83–103.

14. Carroll, *Homesteads Ungovernable,* 77, 81; Joan Cashin, *A Family Venture: Men and Women on the Southern Frontier* (New York: Oxford University Press, 1991).

15. Ayers, *Vengeance and Justice,* 12 (quote); Mark Wyman, *The Wisconsin Frontier* (Bloomington: Indiana University Press, 1998); Alice E. Smith, *The History of Wisconsin: Volume 1, From Exploration to Statehood* (Madison: State Historical Society of Wisconsin, 1973); Robert C. Nesbit, *Wisconsin: A History,* 2nd rev. edition, ed. William F. Thompson (Madison: University of Wisconsin Press, 1989); Joseph A. Ranney, *Trusting Nothing to Providence: A History of Wisconsin's Legal System* (Madison: University of Wisconsin Law School, 1999).

16. Glenda Riley, "Legislative Divorce in Virginia, 1803–1850," *Journal of the Early Republic* 11 (Spring 1991): 66 (quote); Basch, *Framing American Divorce,* 48, 56; Thomas Jefferson Headlee Jr., *The Virginia State Court System* (Richmond: Virginia State Library, 1969); *Acts Passed at a General Assembly of the Commonwealth of Virginia [Acts of Virginia], 1826, 1840–1841, 1847–1848, 1852–1853.*

17. Lawrence M. Friedman, *A History of American Law* (New York: Simon and Schuster, 1973), 150 (quote); Edward Markham Jr., "The Reception of the Common Law of England and the Judicial Attitude Toward That Reception, 1850–1859," *Texas Law Review* 29 (1951); Joseph W. McKnight, "The Spanish Legacy to Texas Law," *American Journal of Legal History* 3 (1959): 222, 299; Francelle L. Blum, "When Marriages Fail" (PhD diss., Rice University, 2008); H. P. N. Gammel, comp., *Laws of Texas, 1822–1897; Texas Reports.*

18. Mark A. Stamp, "Wisconsin's Marriage and Divorce Laws: A Historical Perspective" (ML thesis, University of Wisconsin, 1982); Pleck, *Domestic Tyranny,* 55; Basch, *Framing American Divorce,* 48. An excellent treatment chronicling the development of Wisconsin's legal culture can be found within Ranney, *Trusting Nothing to Providence.* This liberal legal tradition continued when, in 1866, Wisconsin became the first state to permit no-fault divorce, dissolving marriages after a voluntary separation of five years.

19. Nancy F. Cott, "Eighteenth-Century Family and Social Life Revealed in Massachusetts Divorce Records," *Journal of Social History* 10 (Autumn 1976): 21; Edwards,

The People and Their Peace, 23; Hartog, *Man and Wife in America,* 317n4; Basch, *Framing American Divorce,* 194n8; Thomas E. Buckley, *The Great Catastrophe of My Life: Divorce in the Old Dominion* (Chapel Hill: University of North Carolina Press, 2002), 5–6.

20. For additional information on how the divorce records used in this study were gathered, see the Note on Sources and Methodology at the end of the work.

21. Roderick Phillips, *Putting Asunder: A History of Divorce in Western Society* (Cambridge: Cambridge University Press, 1988), 340 (first quote); Robin D. G. Kelley, *Race Rebels: Culture, Politics, and the Black Working Class* (New York: Free Press, 1994), 1 (second quote).

CHAPTER ONE

1. *Rebecca Harper v. Robert Harper* (1859), DCTX-FC.

2. Ibid.

3. Although "epithet" can simply refer to a word used for labeling, this chapter uses the definition of epithet as a term of derision. And the full phrase of the above quote is, a "reasonable apprehension of danger to life, limb, or health," as found within the Stowell opinion from the *Evans v. Evans* (1790) case. See Bishop, *New Commentaries, Vol. 1,* 632–633 (quote).

4. *Nogees v. Nogees,* 7 Tex. 538 (1852) (first quote); *Pinkard v. Pinkard,* 14 Tex. 356 (1855) (second quote); *Johnson v. Johnson,* 4 Wis. 135 (1855) (third quote). The question can be asked why a frontier man or woman would bother going to the trouble of obtaining a legal divorce. After all, it was quite common for unhappy spouses to simply abandon their partners. There is no simple answer to this question. It is possible that they wanted to be free to remarry in the same community or area. Or they felt the need to defend their reputation, or gain control of the marital property, or custody of any children. Regardless, even in frontier areas, the evidence shows a steady stream of spouses pursing legal separations in antebellum America.

5. *Nancy Nogues v. John Nogues* (1857), SHRL-OC.

6. Campbell, *Gone to Texas,* 232 (quote). When she asked if she could have some new clothing, one Texas wife was rebuffed by her husband, who "abused her, reproached her with being lazy and worthless and said he would get her no other clothing but the coarsest and meanest such as Negroes wear, that he would get her brogan shoes." See *Augustia Henson v. John Henson* (1858), DCTX-SC.

7. *Victoria Frederic v. Samuel Frederic* (1856), DCTX-GoC (all quotes); *Elizabeth Ann Pratt v. John Pratt* (1855), DCTX-GoC; *Nancy Nogues v. John Nogues* (1857), SHRL-OC.

8. *Rhoda Carlisle v. Henry Carlisle* (1859), DCTX-KC (first quote); *Thomas Dowling v. Harriett Dowling* (1858), PLAT-IC (second quote); *Mary Falvey v. Jeremiah Falvey* (1860), SHRL-JC; *Eveline Evans v. Jackson Evans* (1854), SHRL-JeC; *Malvina Barden v. Ahira Barden* (1861), SP-PC; *Mary Ann Avery v. James Avery* (1858), WW-RC; *Sarah*

Lewellin v. John Lewellin (1837), LVA-Ly; *Anne Souther v. Simeon Souther* (1843), LVA-H. Concubine was also represented within Wisconsin court documents; see *Sally Baggs v. Horace Baggs* (1854), WW-WC. In modern usage "bitch" can also refer to a griping or nagging woman, but in the antebellum period, I found no indication of these alternate meanings. In the nineteenth century, "bitch" carried with it certain connotations relating to female animal sexuality. On a related note, ethnic and religious epithets were most frequently found within Wisconsin's divorce records. Due to ongoing Catholic/Protestant conflicts, the label *Catholic,* for example, was used in a pejorative manner within some divorce cases. Ethnic epithets were another related form of verbal cruelty. Aside from calling his wife a "damned bitch" and indulging in "crazy fits" in which he would tear her garments, Harvey Luther also verbally harassed his Native American wife in front of others. John Brown, a visitor in the house, recalled one instance when Harvey Luther chased Mary Luther up the stairs calling her a "damn squaw." The reason for Harvey's outrage, according to John, was that "he wanted to learn her to keep her place." Therefore, calling her a "squaw" reminded his wife that she owed her social position to him and that, without him, she was nothing more than a member of one of the lowest social orders in Wisconsin. See *Mary Jane Luther v. Harvey Luther* (1863), EC-EC. For additional ethnic and religious epithets, see also *Mary Kirby v. Silas Kirby* (1861), STO-DC; *Mary West v. John West* (1861), EC-EC. Geoffrey Hughes in his study of swearing finds that "Racial or ethnic insults cover numerous categories, but have at their base some humorous, ironic, or malicious distortion of the target group's identity or 'otherness.'" Geoffrey Hughes, *Swearing: A Social History of Foul Language, Oaths, and Profanity in English* (New York: Blackwell, 1991), 124.

9. H. P. N. Gammel, comp., *Laws of Texas, 1822–1897* (Austin, 1898–1902), II, 483; *Pinkard v. Pinkard,* 14 Tex. 355 (1855) (first quote); *Lucas v. Lucas,* 2 Tex. 113 (1847) (second quote); Loren Schweninger, *Families in Crisis in the Old South: Divorce, Slavery, and the Law* (Chapel Hill: University of North Carolina Press, 2012), 8.

10. *Anne Souther v. Simeon Souther* (1843), LVA-H.

11. Ibid. (quote); Wyatt-Brown, *Southern Honor*; Edwards, *The People and Their Peace,* 112–130; Gross, *Double Character,* 47–49; *Sophia Rohde v. J. Rohde* (1860), DCTX-GC; *James Henderson v. Louisa Henderson* (1852), DCTX-LC; *Nancy Jane Cundiff v. Calvin Cundiff* (1859), DCTX-ColC; *Eunice Bascom v. Emerson Bascom* (1857), RF-SCC; Louisa *Ann Rollins (n.d.),* Van Buren Co.,WHS-WL; *Sarah Folly v. William Folly* (1847), LVA-Bo; *Mary Jane Ramey v. Isaac Ramey* (1853), LVA-F.

12. *Harriett Smith v. William Smith* (1847), LVA-Bo.

13. *Garland Mallory* (1850), Chesterfield Co., LVA-VL (all quotes); Rotundo, "Body and Soul," 27; Bruce *Violence and Culture,* 8–9; Hartog, "Lawyering, Husbands' Rights, and the 'Unwritten Law,'" 90, 93–94; Robert M. Ireland, "The Libertine Must Die: Sexual Dishonor and the Unwritten Law in the Nineteenth-Century United States," *Journal of Social History* 23 (Autumn 1989): 27–44.

14. *Rebecca Harper v. Robert Harper* (1859), DCTX-FC (first quote); *Caleb Creswell*

(n.d.), WHS-WL; *Rebecca Hughes v. Torrence Hughes* (1841), LVA-C (second and third quotes). Sally was accused by her husband of "incontinence with his own brother," which she vehemently denied; see *Sally Odineal v. Joel Odineal* (1857), LVA-Fr (fourth quote).

15. *Fredericka Nordhausen v. Charles Nordhausen* (1855), DCTX-FC. See also *Mary Hewitt v. James Hewitt* (1856), DCTX-GuC; *Mary Ann Avery v. James Avery* (1858), WW-RC; *Delia Tubbs v. Lyman Tubbs* (1862), OSH-WC. Husbands also made accusations questioning the paternity of children. See *Augusta Rhodius v. Christian Rhodius* (1861), DCTX-ComC; *Anna Rathaka v.* Meckeral *Rathaka* (1859), DCTX-WC; *Sophronia Vincent v. William Vincent* (1857), WW-RC; *Jane Bell v. John Bell* (1860), PLAT-GnC; Nancy F. Cott, "Passionlessness: An Interpretation of Victorian Sexual Ideology, 1790–1850," *Signs* 4 (Winter 1978): 219–236.

16. *Clarksville (Texas) Standard,* April 19, 1853 (quote); John Burnham, *Bad Habits: Drinking, Smoking, Taking Drugs, Gambling, Sexual Misbehavior, and Swearing in American History* (New York: New York University Press, 1993) 213; Rotundo, "Body and Soul," 27; Bruce Jr., *Violence and Culture,* 8–9.

17. *Elizabeth Ann Pratt v. John Pratt* (1855), DCTX-GoC (first, second, and third quotes); *Epharilla Fossett v. Lewis Fossett* (1845), LVA-R (fourth quote).

18. *Sally Baggs v. Horace Baggs* (1854), WW-WC.

19. *Joseph William Balthis v. Rebecca Ann Balthis* (1857), LVA-S (all quotes). Sarah Randall described how her abusive and profane husband "did not appear to exercise any control over his passions." *Sarah Randall v. Sydney Randall* (1855), WW-WC.

20. Hartog, "Lawyering, Husbands' Rights, and the 'Unwritten Law,'" 90, 93–94.

21. Terri Snyder, *Brabbling Women: Disorderly Speech and the Law in Early Virginia* (Ithaca, NY: Cornell University Press, 2003), 3 (quote); Kathleen M. Brown, *Good Wives, Nasty Wenches, and Anxious Patriarchs: Gender, Race, and Power in Colonial Virginia* (Chapel Hill: University of North Carolina Press, 1996); Victoria E. Bynum, *Unruly Women: The Politics of Social & Sexual Control in the Old South* (Chapel Hill: University of North Carolina Press, 1992), 14.

22. *Edward Luxton v. Christine Luxton* (1856), MIL-MC.

23. *John Miller v. Eliza Miller* (1858), DCTX-AC (first quote); Gross, *Double Character,* 47 (quote), 49; Karen Halttunen, *Confidence Men and Painted Women: A Study of Middle-Class Culture in America, 1830–1870* (New Haven: Yale University Press, 1982), 26, 48.

24. *Stephen Barzak v. Erva Barzak* (1860), DCTX-AuC (first quote); *Almira Brown v. Thomas Brown* (n.d.), WHS-DC (all other quotes).

25. *James Brewer v. Harriet Brewer* (1851), DCTX-NC.

26. *Elisha Lovell v. Mary Ellen Lovell* (1859), DPL-DC (first and second quotes); *John McElroy v. Elizabeth McElroy* (n.d.), DCTX-AC (third quote). Additionally, an accusation of incest could result in irreparable character damage. A widower with three children, Christian Streapa married Sophia in May 1850. She immediately focused her abuse on the children, driving them from the house. Not content with breaking up

his family, Sophia determined to break his spirit as well. She "filled with malice and vindictiveness" did "falsely & wantonly charge" her husband "with the foul & horrible crime of incest with his own daughter." See *Christian Streapa v. Sophia Streapa* (1856), DCTX-AuC.

27. *Simeon Barton v. Mary Barton* (1853), VRHC-JC (first quote); *Eveline Wade v. David Wade* (1854), DCTX-FC (second quote); *Thomas Dickinson v. Mary Dickinson* (1859), DPL-DC (third quote); *Elisha Lovell v. Mary Ellen Lovell* (1859), DPL-DC (fourth quote); Basch, *Framing American Divorce*, 124 (fifth quote).

28. *Albert Bowker v. Mereda Bowker* (1863), WHS-DC; Stephanie McCurry, *Masters of Small Worlds: Yeoman Households, Gender Relations, and the Political Culture of the Antebellum South Carolina Low Country* (New York: Oxford University Press, 1995), 72 (quote).

29. *Anna Catharine Strauss v. Julius Strauss* (1855), MIL-MC; Halttunen, *Confidence Men and Painted Women*, xvi, 48.

30. Jane Turner Censer, "Smiling Through Her Tears: Ante-Bellum Southern Women and Divorce" 25 *American Journal of Legal History* (January 1981), 35; Elizabeth Blair Clark, "The Inward Fire: A History of Marital Cruelty in the Northeastern United States, 1800–1860" (PhD diss., Harvard University, 2006), 71; Bishop, *New Commentaries,* 632–633.

31. Mary Poovey, "'Scenes of an Indelicate Character': The Medical 'Treatment' of Victorian Women," in *The Making of the Modern Body: Sexuality and Society in the Nineteenth Century,* ed. Catherine Gallagher and Thomas Laqueur (Berkeley: University of California Press, 1987), 146; *Charlotte Cowen v. James Cowen* (1846), PLAT-GnC (first quote); *Isabella Clark v. Matthew Clark* (1858), LVA-Wa (second quote); Carroll Smith-Rosenberg and Charles Rosenberg, "The Female Animal: Medical and Biological Views of Woman and Her Role in Nineteenth-Century America," *Journal of American History* 60 (September 1973): 335 (fourth quote). A Texas man's diary recalled how an Indian raid in central Texas sent "women crying and gathering their children together and seeking the safest retreat." Jonathan Hamilton Baker Papers, 1858–1932, CAH. A Wisconsin man's memoir described how his mother went gradually insane with her "chief hallucination . . . that the entire family was going to starve . . . she refused food, and for more than three months, was fed forcibly." Jacob and Jacob T. Foster Papers, 1847–1929, WHS. Microfilm.

32. Schweninger, *Families in Crisis,* 47; *Elizabeth Ann Pratt v. John Pratt* (1855), DCTX-GoC (first quote); *Ann Madden v. Peter Madden* (1857), PLAT-IC (second quote); *Nancy Hilburn v. John Hilburn* (1861), DCTX-EC (third quote); *Catharine Crandall v. John Crandall* (1859), WHS-DC (fourth quote); *Rosinah Westcott v. Russel Westcott* (1860), EC-EC; *Jane Filkins v. Henry Filkins* (1862), WHS-DC; *Margaret Gieseke v. Charles Gieseke* (1852), DCTX-ColC; *Milly Newsome v. Etard Newsome* (1859), DCTX-CC; *Milly Perdue v. Isaiah Perdue* (1855), LVA-Fr.

33. *Nancy Culbreath v. Greer Culbreath* (1851), LVA-Me (first quote); *Christy Mat-*

tison v. Evan Mattison (1861), PLAT-IC (second quote); *Catharine Gill v. William Gill* (1860), PLAT-LC (third quote); *John Henry v. Sarah Henry* (1846), WW-WC (fourth quote). Some cruel spouses even relied upon animalistic overtones to achieve the ultimate dramatic effect. According to the information provided by their spouses, both Chaney Luce, of Wisconsin, and Margaret Morris, of Texas, threatened to take the lives of their partners and to "drink his [and her] hearts blood." In a similar vein, Ella Bartlett's husband continued his course of tyrannical conduct by hitting her with fists and sticks, as well as threatening to cut her heart out. These images seem to connote that spouses were simply animals to be slaughtered at will. *Alexander Morris v. Margaret Morris* (1851), DCTX-CC; *Polly Luce v. Chaney Luce* (1851), WHS-DC; *Ella Bartlett v. Clark Bartlett* (1857), PLAT-GC.

34. *Ann Chick v. Littleton Chick* (1847), LVA-A (all quotes); *Harriett Smith v. William Smith* (1847), LVA-Bo; *Epharilla Fossett v. Lewis Fossett* (1845), LVA-R; *Eliza Hughes v. William Hughes* (1859), LVA-R; *Melzena Short v. M. Short* (1853), DCTX-GoC; *Lucinda Curliss v. John Curliss* (1860), MIL-MC; *Margaret Hand v. Jeremiah Hand* (1856), PLAT-GC; *Christiana Wadkins v. Samuel Wadkins* (1852), DCTX-WiC; *Celia Ann Bailey v. Thomas Bailey* (1859), OSH-WC; *Mary Corbett v. William Corbett* (1855), PLAT-IC; *Cornelia Ann Rossiter v. Charles Rossiter* (1849), MIL-MC; *Mary Moore v. Peter Moore* (1854), WW-WC; David Peterson, "Wife Beating: An American Tradition," *Journal of Interdisciplinary History* 23 (Summer 1992): 106; Clark, "Inward Fire," 51.

35. *Eliza Martin v. James Martin* (1858), LVA-He; Pamela Haag, "The 'Ill-Use of a Wife': Patterns of Working-Class Violence in Domestic and Public New York City, 1860–1880," *Journal of Social History* 25 (Spring 1992): 463 (quote).

36. *Elizabeth Kiley v. Thomas Kiley* (1852), SP-PC (first quote); *Elizabeth McCoy v. John McCoy* (1861), PLAT-LC (second quote); *Lucinda Benson v. Charles Benson* (1850), PLAT-LC (third and fourth quotes); *Josephine McKensie v. Allen William McKensie* (1862), GB-KC; *James Craton v. Susan Craton* (1850), PLAT-GnC; *Frederick Witte v. Wilhelmina Witte* (1864), EC-EC; *Clarenda Pitkin v. Oren Pitkin* (1846), WW-WC; *Cornelia Blodgett v. George Blodgett* (1860), MIL-MC.

37. *Daily Milwaukee News,* January 13, 1859 (first and second quotes); *John Fowler v. Eliza Fowler* (1858), SHRL-JeC (third and fourth quotes). A Virginia wife, Nancy Flinn, placed herself in the doorway of the house with a knife in hand and threatened to stab her husband if he entered. *Nancy Flinn v. James Flinn* (1844), LVA-F. One Texas wife grabbed "a certain fork (being a dangerous weapon)," which she threatened her husband's life with, and said she would "plunge it into his black heart." *Wallace v. Thomas Wallace* (1853), DCTX-GoC. Historian Jeffrey Adler describes how murderous wives of the early twentieth century were not social outcasts, but rather, "lived-and killed-within the boundaries of proper society." Jeffrey S. Adler, *First in Violence, Deepest in Dirt: Homicide in Chicago, 1875–1920* (Cambridge: Harvard University Press, 2006), 87.

38. *Dorcas Nelson v. Moses Nelson* (1856), LVA-Wa.

39. *Rebecca Hughes v. Torrence Hughes* (1840), LVA-C (first quote); *Mary Poe v. Andrew Poe* (1849), MIL-MC (second quote); *Jane Bonner v. Robert Bonner* (1858), DCTX-AuC; Cramer, *Concealed Weapon Laws*, 17–18, 35; Haag, "The 'Ill-Use of a Wife,'" 463.

40. *Garland Mallory* (1850), Chesterfield Co., LVA-VL; Spragins Family Papers, 1753–1881, VHS.

41. *Susan Menefee v. Banks Menefee* (1854), LVA-F (first quote); *Susannah Horner v. Ezra Horner* (1850), SP-PC (second quote); *Sarah Folly v. William Folly* (1847) LVA-Bo (third quote); *Caroline Hall v. Ira Hall* (1848), WHS-DC (fourth quote); *Almira Cooper v. John Cooper* (1856), MIL-MC (fifth quote); *Marg Leitenberg v. Anton Leitenberg* (1857), DCTX-FC (sixth quote). See also *Joset Idell v. Isaiah Idell* (1865), GB-OC; *Mary Hall v. John Hall* (1859), DCTX-HC; *Jane Prisk v. Samuel Prisk* (1854), PLAT-IC; *Josephena Caney v. John Caney* (1861), EC-EC; Barbara Welter, "The Cult of True Womanhood: 1820–1860," *American Quarterly* 18 (Summer 1966): 151–174.

42. *S. C. Miles v. E. Miles* (1850), LC-MC (first quote); *William Farnham* (1846), Rock Co., WHS-WL (second quote). For information on these southern anxieties see William A. Link, *Roots of Secession: Slavery and Politics in Antebellum Virginia* (Chapel Hill: University of North Carolina Press, 2003), 52–54; *Henry Eaton v. Jane Eaton* (1860), STO-DC; *John Tabor v. Maryette Tabor* (1851), WW-WC; *William Warren v. Melvina Warren* (1859), WHS-DC; *Mary Bauden v. Joseph Bauden* (1861), PLAT-LC; *Anna Catharine Strauss v. Julius Strauss* (1855), MIL-MC; *James Walkinshaw v. Delila Walkinshaw* (1852), SHRL-JC; *John Hayes v. Rebecca Hayes* (1859), SHRL-JC; *George Nixon v. Ellen Nixon* (1854), DCTX-AuC; *Charles Haswell v. E. Maria Haswell* (1857), DCTX-FC; *Susan Menefee v. Banks Menefee* (1854), LVA-F.).

43. *Betsey Carter v. Archibald Carter* (1863), EC-EC (first quote); *Mary Crowell v. Joseph Crowell* (1859), LVA-Wa (second quote); *Augustia Henson v. John Henson* (1858), DCTX-SC; *Elizabeth Fitzgerald v. Samuel Fitzgerald* (1860), LVA-Ly; *Horace Cashman v. Sarah Cashman* (1857), PLAT-GnC; Eastern State Hospital Patient Register, 1853–1854, LVA.

44. *Martha Crawford v. William Crawford* (1856), LVA-Sm (first quote); *Emmaline Craddock v. Hugh Craddock* (1862), LVA-Be; *Lucinda Latham v. Silas Latham* (1854), LVA-Be; *Margaret Bryant v. William Bryant* (1857), LVA-Roc. Richard Chused in his study of Maryland divorce found that at the turn of the nineteenth century, the legislature started to award women custody. Women were seen as the primary moral role models and caretakers. Richard H. Chused, *Private Acts in Public Places: A Social History of Divorce in the Formative Era of American Family Law* (Philadelphia: University of Pennsylvania Press, 1994), 68; Censer, "Smiling Through Her Tears," 43.

45. *Margaret Farrell v. Isaac Farrell* (1841), LVA-Fre (first quote); *Eliza Galbreath v. Samuel Galbreath* (1843), PLAT-GC (second quote).

46. *Sylvester Beverly v. Mary Beverly* (1857), LVA-Wi; *Polly Cox v. Jordan Cox* (1859), LVA-Ch; *George Mayhew v. Mary Mayhew* (1858), LVA-Be; *Ellender Arrington*

v. Arthur Arrington (1854), LVA-Fr; *Nancy Weatherford v. Henry Weatherford* (1843), LVA-Me; *Willard Minot v. Phebe Minot* (1856), PLAT-GC; *John Fritz v. Betsey Fritz* (1860), WHS-DC; *Eleanor Clover v. Thomas Clover* (n.d.), WHS-DC; *Horace Cashman v. Sarah Cashman* (1857), PLAT-GnC; *Matthew Hallas v. Elizabeth Hallas* (1858), WHS-DC; *Stephen Barzak v. Erva Barzak* (1860), DCTX-AuC; Wyatt-Brown, *Southern Honor,* 228; Snyder, *Brabbling Women,* 3, 10.

47. James O. Andrew, *Family Government, Or Treatise on Conjugal, Parental, Filial, and Other Duties* (Richmond, VA: John Early, 1848); Spragins Family Papers, 1753–1881 VHS; *Mary Yearout v. Charles Yearout* (1858), LVA-Fl; *Sally Dowell v. Richard Dowell* (1854), LVA-W; *John Allridge v. Charlotta Allridge* (1861), LVA-Wa. It was also discussed within the records that a woman's temper, and her inability to be controlled, was a sign of insanity. Ellen Crandall, admitted to the Mendota Mental Hospital in Wisconsin by her husband, was prone to want "to have her own way." Her husband lamented, "I cannot manage her at all." Admissions Records, 1860–1908, 1935–1968, Mendota Mental Health Institute, WHS. Margaret Hoss, also of Wisconsin, was "mentally deranged and . . . extremely bad tempered." *William Hoss v. Margaret Hoss* (1861), SP-PC.

48. *The Young Wife's Book: A Manual of Moral, Religious, and Domestic Duties* (Philadelphia: Carey, Lee, and Blanchard, 1838), 216. A Dallas newspaper, in an article entitled "Woman's Temper," cautioned wives, "Above all things . . . cultivate a sweet and amiable temper. It is this that makes home happy." *Dallas Herald,* June 15, 1859. A Matagorda, Texas, newspaper asserted that, "An ill-tempered, quarrelsome woman is a nuisance on the earth." *Matagorda Gazette,* February 5, 1859.

49. Robert Morris, *Courtship and Matrimony* (Philadelphia: T. B. Peterson, 1858), 333 (first quote); *Emily Berndt v. Louis Berndt* (1863), OSH-WC (second quote); *Sarah Randall v. Sydney Randall* (1855), WW-WC (third quote). See also *Ellen Campbell v. Sylvester Campbell* (1859), CCWI-RC; *Jane Filkins v. Henry Filkins* (1862), WHS-DC; *Amanda King v. Edward King* (1855), LVA-Me; *Joseph William Balthis v. Rebecca Ann Balthis* (1857), LVA-S.

CHAPTER TWO

1. *Albert Bowker v. Mereda Bowker* (1863), WHS-DC.

2. *Nogees v. Nogees,* 7 Tex. 538 (1852). As a point of reference, it is important to note that by 1840 all three states studied recognized physical cruelties that threatened life or limb as meeting the minimum requirements of legal cruelty, and therefore as legitimate grounds for divorce.

3. Edwards, *The People and Their Peace,* 171 (quote); *Polly Cox v. Jordan Cox* (1859), LVA-Ch; *Wilhemina Schmidt v. John Schmidt* (1854), DCTX-FC; *Harriet Boulieo v. Oliver Boulieo* (1843), MIL-MC.

4. *Lucy Burwell v. John Burwell* (1856), LVA-Me (first quote); *Sarah Mitchell v. J. Mitchell* (1846), SHRL-JeC (second quote); McCurry, *Masters of Small Worlds.*

5. *Matilda Bryant v. Robert Bryant* (1855), LVA-He (first quote); *Johanna Giese v. Frederick Giese* (1857), WHS-DC (second quote).

6. *Sarah Budd v. John Budd* (1863), OSH-WC (all quotes); Clark, "The Inward Fire," 48.

7. *Elizabeth Binns* (1840), Amelia Co., LVA-VL; *Zylpha Marmore v. William Marmore* (1854), DCTX-CoC (first and second quotes); Basch, *Framing American Divorce,* 117 (third quote). Rhoda French, originally from Massachusetts, complained that her husband changed in his demeanor upon the couple's arrival in Wisconsin. Aside from drinking to excess, he repeatedly expressed his desire to be alone. Kicking and beating her "black and blue," John French was determined to effect a separation of some sort and promised her that if she continued to live in the same house with him, he would "make the place so hot that I [his wife] couldnt stay in it." In the end, she was granted a divorce. See *Rhoda French v. John French* (1865), EC-EC.

8. Charlene M. Boyer Lewis, *Ladies and Gentlemen on Display: Planter Society at the Virginia Springs, 1790–1860* (Charlottesville: University Press of Virginia, 2001), 113; *Delia Tubbs v. Lyman Tubbs* (1862), OSH-WC (second quote). Another form of physical cruelty, pinching, was generally gendered male. At first glance, pinching appears relatively innocuous, but wives described how it could turn nasty quite quickly. A husband's pinching attack, as experienced by Sarah Hinton, could leave a wife with bruises on her face that "for many days and weeks were visible to all." See *Sarah Hinton v. Archibald Hinton* (1853), LVA-L.

9. *Mary Ann Mullens v. John Mullens* (1851), LVA-Ly (first and second quotes); *Elizabeth Graves v. John W. Graves* (1854), DCTX-AC (third quote); *Mary Dunn v. J. K. Dunn* (1858), DCTX-GuC (fourth quote). For instances of husbands knocking wives on the ground, see *Julia Childs v. Joseph Childs* (1860), SHRL-JeC; *Marg Leitenberg v. Anton Leitenberg* (1857), DCTX-FC; *Sarah Smith v. Archelas Smith* (1856), DCTX-BC; *Mary West v. John West* (1861), EC-EC. For examples of hair dragging, see *Elizabeth Herman v. Henry Herman* (1858), DCTX-ComC; *Elizabeth Behrens v. Johann Behrens* (1855), DCTX-GC; *Dorothea Mohr v. George Mohr* (1857), MIL-MC; *Maria Burrucker v. Friederick Burrucker* (1858), WHS-DC; *Martha Revely v. John Revely* (1853), LVA-Ly; *Patsey Slack v. Josiah Slack* (1852), LVA-No.

10. The *Baraboo Republic,* September 8, 1855 (all quotes); *Bridget Galvin v. Michael Galvin* (1856), PLAT-GC; *Sarah Ryan v. Patrick Ryan* (1865), OSH-WC; *Albertine Bribolz v. Fritz Bribolz* (1861), GB-MC. Another man, who possessed a self-proclaimed unmanageable temper, declared that he would kick his wife's "damned infernal head off" in the midst of one conflict. See *Ellen Campbell v. Sylvester Campbell* (1859), CCWI-RC.

11. *Caroline Hersey v. George Hersey* (1858), OSH-WC.

12. *E. A. Robinson v. Jesse Robinson* (1857), DCTX-LC (first quote); *Lucinda Curliss v. John Curliss* (1860), MIL-MC (second quote); *Ann Chick v. Littleton Chick* (1847), LVA-A; *Mary Dunn v. J. K. Dunn* (1858), DCTX-GuC; *Elizabeth McCoy v. John McCoy* (1861), PLAT-LC.

13. *Sarah Burdett v. Henry Burdett* (1844), DCTX-AuC (first quote); *Rachel Gardner*

v. Augustus Gardner (1859), WHS-DC (second quote). One of the articles that has garnered more recent, and widespread, attention is a study pointing to choking as a clear indicator of possible spousal murder. See Nancy Glass et al., "Non-Fatal Strangulation Is an Important Risk Factor for Homicide of Women," *Journal of Emergency Medicine* 35 (October 2008): 329–335.

14. *Elizabeth Waid v. William Waid* (1855), LVA-Fr (all quotes).

15. *Lucy Ann Baldwin v. Charles Baldwin* (1859), LVA-Pr.

16. *Margaret Compton v. John Compton* (1857), LVA-R (all quotes); Nancy Tomes, "A 'Torrent of Abuse': Crimes of Violence between Working-Class Men and Women in London, 1840–1875," *Journal of Social History* 11 (Spring 1978): 336.

17. Hartog, *Man and Wife in America,* 105 (quote), 116, 168. See also Pleck, *Domestic Tyranny,* 17–21; Clark, "The Inward Fire," 47, 51–55. This gradual disappearance of the rule of thumb coincided with the increase of companionate ideals and the gradual downplaying of the prerogative of chastisement. See Robert Griswold, *Family and Divorce in California, 1850–1890* (Albany: State University of New York Press, 1982), 176; David Peterson, "Wife Beating," 100, 105; Siegel, "'Rule of Love,'" 2144–2145.

18. Cott, *Public Vows,* 62–63; *Sally Dowell v. Richard Dowell* (1854), LVA-W (first quote); *Elizabeth Cole v. William Cole* (1860), DCTX-ColC; *Ann Rice Jeager v. John Jeager* (1859), DCTX-AuC; *Ernestine Martin v. James Martin* (1860), DCTX-GuC; *Catharine Goodall v. Samuel Goodall* (1856), DCTX-CC; *Patience Simons v. Charles Simons* (1857), VRHC-JC; *Elizabeth Adair v. Joseph Adair* (1838), VRHC-JC. Jane Earl tolerated the whippings by her husband "until endurance itself became no longer tolerable or patience a virtue." See *Jane Earl* (1837), Harrisburg Co., TSLAC-TL.

19. *Nancy Flinn v. James Flinn* (1845), LVA-F.

20. Elizabeth Fox-Genovese, "Family and Female Identity in the Antebellum South: Sarah Gayle and Her Family," in *In Joy and In Sorrow: Women, Family, and Marriage in the Victorian South, 1830–1900,* ed. Carol Bleser (New York: Oxford University Press, 1991), 19–20; Gross, *Double Character,* 114 (second quote). See also Siegel, "'Rule of Love,'" 2144–2145; Kristen E. Wood, "Making a Home in Public: Domesticity, Authority, and Family in the Old South's Public Houses," in *Family Values in the Old South,* ed. Craig Thompson Friend and Anya Jabour (Gainesville: University Press of Florida, 2010), 159; Bynum, *Unruly Women*; Brenda Stevenson, *Life in Black and White: Family and Community in the Slave South* (New York: Oxford University Press, 1996).

21. *Margaret Compton v. John Compton* (1851), LVA-R; *Polly Cox v. Jordan Cox* (1859), LVA-Ch.

22. *Marg. Leitenberg v. Anton Leitenberg* (1857), DCTX-FC (first and second quotes). For a discussion of Texas frontier conditions, see Angela Boswell, "The Social Acceptability of Nineteenth-Century Domestic Violence," in *The Southern Albatross: Race and Ethnicity in the American South,* ed. Philip D. Dillard and Randal Hall (Macon: Mercer University Press, 1999), 139–162; Campbell, *Gone to Texas,* 231–232; Mark M. Carroll, *Homesteads Ungovernable: Families, Sex, Race, and the Law in Frontier Texas,*

1823–1860 (Austin: University of Texas Press, 2001); Blum, "When Marriages Fail," 39–42; Cashin, *A Family Venture*. See also *Wilhelmina Schmidt v. John Schmidt* (1854), DCTX-FC; *Queen Elizabeth Nogues v. Jaques Nogues* (1847), SHRL-JeC; *Emeline Saunders v. James Saunders* (1858), DCTX-EC.

23. *Rosina Fulford v. James Fulford* (1859), LVA-No.

24. *Mary Clopton v. John Clopton* (1850), LVA-He (all quotes). Suzanne Lebsock, in her study of a murder in 1890s Virginia, described how one rope was shipped all over the South to be used in hangings. She continues, "After thirteen years of hangings, the rope had taken on an almost magical quality, bringing confidence to the executioner." See Suzanne Lebsock, *A Murder in Virginia: Southern Justice on Trial* (New York: W.W. Norton, 2003), 277. William Dunford would prepare "switches" in advance in case he chose to whip his wife. See *William Dunford v. Nancy Dunford* (1852), LVA-Cu.

25. *Sarah Womack* (1848), Halifax Co., LVA-VL (first quote); *Rosina Fulford v. James Fulford* (1859), LVA-No (second quote).

26. *Elizabeth Waid v. William Waid* (1862), LVA-Fr (first and second quotes); Gross, *Double Character*, 49 (third quote); Diana Paton, *No Bond but the Law: Punishment, Race, and Gender in Jamaican State Formation, 1780–1870* (Durham, NC: Duke University Press, 2004), 108–109.

27. *Anne Souther v. Simeon Souther* (1843), LVA-H (all quotes); William Alcott, *The Young Husband; or, Duties of Man in the Marriage Relation* (Boston: C. D. Strong, 1851), 263; *Jane Orndorff v. Henry Orndorff* (1848), LVA-Fr.

28. *Elizabeth Ann Pratt v. John Pratt* (1855), DCTX-GoC (quote); *Maria Betz v. Peter Betz* (1861), DCTX-GC; *Martha Barrett v. James Barrett* (1860), DCTX-KC; *Epharilla Fossett v. Lewis Fossett* (1845), LVA-R; *Rhoda Carlisle v. Henry Carlisle* (1859), DCTX-KC; *Johannette Lange v. August Lange* (1862), WHS-DC; *Susan Rollins* (1849), Spotsylvania Co., LVA-VL; *Nancy Lovell v. David Lovell* (1861), LVA-Fl; *Susan Bostic v. Sion Bostic* (1856), DCTX-ColC; *Rebecca Hanson v. Nicholi Hanson* (1853), DCTX-KC; *Caroline Westner v. Christian Westner* (1844), DCTX-FC.

29. *Maria Bryerton v. William Bryerton* (1862), WHS-DC (first quote); *Margaret Lewis v. Lewis Lewis* (1861), PLAT-IC (second quote); *Mary Burton v. Philo Burton* (1860), OSH-WC; *Celia Ann Bailey v. Thomas Bailey* (1859), OSH-WC; *Rebecca Gray v. F. Gray* (1860), RF-SCC; *Mary Grinnin v. Michael Grinnin* (1847), PLAT-GC. In his study of gender and crime in Victorian England, Martin Wiener found that "weapons use was readily seen as a marker of intent to kill." See Martin J. Wiener, *Men of Blood: Violence, Manliness, and Criminal Justice in Victorian England* (Cambridge: Cambridge University Press, 2004), 198.

30. *Daily Milwaukee News,* June 19, 1859 (all quotes); *Baraboo Republic,* June 23, 1859.

31. *Harriet Ann Davey v. Thomas Davey* (1851), SP-PC; *United States v. Thomas Davey* (1845), PLAT-IC; *Harriett Castle v. Horatio Castle* (1860), OSH-WC; *Daily Milwaukee News,* June 15, 1859.

32. Christine Stansell, *City of Women: Sex and Class in New York, 1789–1860* (Urbana: University of Illinois Press, 1987), 78 (first quote); *Harriett Castle v. Horatio Castle* (1860), OSH-WC (second quote). John Mack Faragher comments, "Indeed, nearly all the evidence that one can marshal concerning the relations of Midwestern men and women suggests that the notion of companionate marriage was foreign to the thoughts and feelings of ordinary farm folks." Faragher, *Women and Men on the Overland Trail,* 147–148; Wyman, *The Wisconsin Frontier*; Smith, *The History of Wisconsin: Volume 1*; Kathleen Neils Conzen, *Immigrant Milwaukee, 1836–1860* (Cambridge: Harvard University Press, 1976); Nesbit, *Wisconsin: A History.* See also references to Elizabeth Rieck's spilling a little bit of feed, which her husband saw, resulting in his beating her, in *Elizabeth Rieck v. Herman Rieck* (1861), WHS-DC; and to Ophelia Burlington's breaking a tea saucer and being beaten by her husband, in *Ophelia Burlington v. George Burlington* (1858), OSH-WC.

33. Peterson del Mar, *What Trouble I Have Seen,* 7 (quote); Bynum, *Unruly Women,* 3 (quote). The works of Laura Edwards stand as an important contrast to these interpretations; she argues that women and slaves, both dependents, challenged the authority of white males in the South, thereby demonstrating the limits of patriarchy. The women in Edwards's work are often aggressive and violent actors who used the law to assert a measure of independence. For texts that explore the possibilities of women's cruelty, see Edwards, *The People and Their Peace,* 79; Blum, "When Marriages Fail"; Jeffrey S. Adler, *First in Violence, 1875–1920* (Cambridge: Harvard University Press, 2006), 87. Adler argues, in part, that wives who committed murder were not "crazy" women but "lived—and killed—within the boundaries of proper society." For works that focus primarily on men or argue that women's cruelty was defensive or rare see David Peterson, "Eden Defiled: A History of Violence Against Wives in Oregon" (PhD diss., University of Oregon, 1993); Danelle Moon, "Marital Violence Revealed: California Divorce, 1850–1899" (Master's thesis, California State University, Fullerton, 1994); A. J. Hammerton, *Cruelty and Companionship: Conflict in Nineteenth-Century Married Life* (London: Routledge, 1992), 111–114. Importantly, Claire Renzetti has observed that "if women use violence in intimate relationships, we should not assume that they are 'acting like men.'" See Claire Renzetti, "The Challenge to Feminism Posed by Women's Use of Violence in Intimate Relationships," in *New Versions of Victims: Feminists Struggle with the Concept,* ed. Sharon Lamb (New York: New York University Press, 1999), 45.

34. *John Allridge v. Charlotta Allridge* (1859), LVA-Wa; *G.W. Tolley v. Elizabeth Tolley* (1855), LVA-Roc; *James Veasy v. Elizabeth Veasy* (1856), DCTX-AuC.

35. Hartog, *Man and Wife in America,* 150 (quote in text), 166 (quote below). Hartog continues, "The prospect of being a Prince Albert, a man ruled by his wife, was a terrifying one for many Americans." Bertram Wyatt-Brown states, "To permit a woman to hurt him physically would be a dire humiliation." See Wyatt-Brown, *Southern Honor,* 159.

36. *Margaret Kramer v. Adam Kramer* (1860), SP-MC (first quote); *Riley Pratt v. Elizabeth Pratt* (1857), DCTX-FC (second and third quotes); *G. W. Tolley v. Elizabeth*

Tolley (1855), LVA-Roc; *Phebe Foley v. James Foley* (1848), LVA-Roc; *G. M. Webb v. Margaret Webb* (1858), DCTX-FC.

37. *Mary Richmond v. Oliver Richmond* (1859), SP-PC (first quote); *Sarah Hinton v. Archibald Hinton* (1853), LVA-L (second and third quotes); *Thomas Russum v. L. Russum* (1856), DCTX-HC. It was rare to find a woman who choked her husband, but consult this case for an example: *Jane Patrick v. William Patrick* (1860), WHS-DC. Jane seized her husband by the throat with "great violence."

38. *Sally Vill v. Robert Vill* (1859), GB-OuC (first and second quotes); *Thadeus Pooler v. Jane Pooler* (1861), WHS-DC; *Sarah Hinton v. Archibald Hinton* (1853), LVA-L; *Alfred Council v. Susan Council* (1858), DCTX-HC (second and third quotes).

39. January 25, 1857, Entry, William Matthews Blackford Diaries, 1849–1864, UVA (all quotes); *Parlay Eaton* (1838), Iowa Co., WHS-WL; *James Veasy v. Elizabeth Veasy* (1856), DCTX-AuC; *State of Wisconsin v. Elizabeth Long* (1858), GB-MC.

40. Adler, *First in Violence,* 52; *Oliver Lee v. Sarah Lee* (1861), DCTX-CC (second and third quotes); *George Harris v. M. E. Harris* (1849), WHS-DC (first quote); *Mary Harris* (1851), Richmond Town/City, LVA-VL; *Lansing Roach v. Nancy Roach* (1857), WHS-DC; *Elizabeth Ann Pratt v. John Pratt* (1855), DCTX-GoC.

41. *Eveline Wade v. David Wade* (1854), DCTX-FC.

42. *John Allridge v. Charlotta Allridge* (1861), LVA-Wa (first and second quotes); *Inda Landreth v. William Landreth* (1858), LVA-Wi; *James Veasy v. Elizabeth Veasy* (1856), DCTX-AuC; Joshua Rothman, *Notorious in the Neighborhood: Sex and Families across the Color Line in Virginia, 1787–1861* (Chapel Hill: University of North Carolina Press, 2003).

43. *Benjamin Safford* (1848), Washington Co., WHS-WL (all quotes); *Robert Lawson v. Catharine Lawson* (1857), WW-WC; *Phebe Foley v. James Foley* (1848), LVA-Roc.

44. *Lucinda Smith v. Samuel Smith* (1854), WW-RC (all quotes); *Albert Bowker v. Mereda Bowker* (1863), WHS-DC; *Phebe Foley v. James Foley* (1848), LVA-Roc.

45. *Jane Patrick v. William Patrick* (1860), WHS-DC (all quotes); *Thomas Russum v. L. Russum* (1856), DCTX-HC. When Patrick Long ordered his wife to get breakfast, she told him that she would get it when she pleased and hit him "three times with the churn dash she then through the pail after him." See *State of Wisconsin v. Elizabeth Long* (1858), GB-MC.

46. *State of Wisconsin v. Brenig* (1866), GB-MC (all quotes); *Margaret Kramer v. Adam Kramer* (1860), SP-MC; *G. W. Tolley v. Elizabeth Tolley* (1855), LVA-Roc.

CHAPTER THREE

1. *Christiana Wadkins v. Samuel Wadkins* (1852), DCTX-WiC.

2. This chapter explores the creation of a new category of legal cruelty, sexual cruelty. Plaintiffs often chose to file under joint adultery and cruelty claims. Those cases where both causes were identified by name (or where cruelty was mentioned specifi-

cally) are used within this work. Those cases where adultery remained the focus (without a specific cruelty mention or discussion) are not examined. This decision reflects the choices made by the historical actors, who perhaps filtered complaints to target a particular category of causation.

3. *Johnson v. Johnson,* 4 Wis. 135 (1855) (first quote); *Sharman v. Sharman,* 18 Tex. 521 (1857) (second quote).

4. *Mary Dennis v. John Dennis* (1844), GB-BC (quote); John M. Biggs, *The Concept of Matrimonial Cruelty* (London: Athlone Press, 1962), 170. The Olneys moved from Missouri to Madison, Wisconsin, in order to "spare her the shame of a local divorce" on the grounds of "great bodily infirmity." See *William Olney v. Mary Ann Olney* (1855), WHS-DC. Another husband, John Rhodes, refused to discuss his wife's "infirmity" because "it would be improper." See *Mary Rhodes v. John Rhodes* (1851), LVA-A.

5. *Susan Moore* (1849), Loudoun Co., LVA-VL (all quotes); *Peter Moore* (1848), Fairfax Co., LVA-VL.

6. *John Hall v. Mary Hall* (1864), GB-KC; *Luzie Lohl v. Conrad Luhl* (1851), DCTX-ComC; *Nancy Rott v. Jacob Rott* (1851), SHRL-JeC; Gross, *Double Character.*

7. *Jacob Chancellor v. Mary Chancellor* (1850), DCTX-SC (first quote); *John Edgrine v. Joanna Edgrine* (1852), PLAT-LC (second quote); *Shepherd Adams v. Tabitha Adams* (1860), SHRL-OC (third quote); *Leonard Bailey* (1845), Wythe Co., LVA-VL (fourth quote).

8. Hartog, "Lawyering, Husbands' Rights, and 'The Unwritten Law,'" 67 (quote). For a sample list of rights violations see *Jacob Chancellor v. Mary Chancellor* (1850), DCTX-SC.

9. *Jacob Cool v. Rebecca Cool* (1858), LVA-Roc.

10. Anne Firor Scott, "Women's Perspective on the Patriarchy in the 1850s," in *Half Sisters of History: Southern Women and the American Past,* ed. Catherine Clinton (Durham, NC: Duke University Press, 1994), 79 (quote). For more information on pregnancy and childbirth in antebellum America, see Sally G. McMillen, *Motherhood in the Old South: Pregnancy, Childbirth, and Infant Rearing* (Baton Rouge: Louisiana State University Press, 1990); Judith Walzer Leavitt, *Brought to Bed: Childbearing in America, 1750 to 1950* (New York: Oxford University Press, 1986).

11. *Harriet Dow v. Cornelius Dow* (1861), PLAT-GnC; *George Hawley v. Mary Hawley* (1857), SHRL-JeC.

12. *S. C. Miles v. E. Miles* (1850), LC-MC. Lucinda Smith of Wisconsin supposedly threatened to "butcher" her husband in the event that she became pregnant again. *Lucinda Smith v. Samuel Smith* (1854), WW-RC.

13. *Elcana Blair v. Jane Blair* (1855), DCTX-GoC (all quotes); *Joanne Lamkin v. Silas Lamkin* (1856), VRHC-JC; *Albert Johnson v. Nancy Johnson* (1856), DCTX-HC; *Lewis Larham v. Lucinda Larham* (1858), SHRL-OC. Since not all wives felt confident in waging close attacks, they might instead choose to throw objects at their husbands. Lobbing a rock or other item at a man from a distance was viewed as a safer course of

action as opposed to engaging in any type of hand-to-hand combat. See *Charles Haswell v. E. Maria Haswell* (1857), DCTX-FC. See also Adler, *First in Violence,* 52.

14. Schweninger, *Families in Crisis,* 11.

15. *Eliza Wyman v. William Wyman* (1849), MIL-MC (all quotes). For information on the growing importance of emotional control see Rotundo, "Body and Soul," 27.

16. David Finkelhor and Kersti Yllo, *License to Rape: Sexual Abuse of Wives* (New York: Holt, Rinehart, and Winston, 1985), 2 (first quote); Warren Chase, *The Fugitive Wife: A Criticism on Marriage, Adultery, and Divorce* (Boston: Bela Marsh, 1866); Cott, *Public Vows,* 62–67; Merril D. Smith, "Introduction: Studying Rape in American History," in *Sex Without Consent: Rape and Sexual Coercion in America,* ed. Merril D. Smith (New York: New York University Press, 2001), 4; Pleck, *Domestic Tyranny,* 91, 94. I agree with Pleck that to look for an early history of marital rape, we must examine divorce suits as the precursors of what will later become descriptions of assaults.

17. *Harriet Hubbard v. Mortimer Hubbard* (1859), WHS-KC (quote); *Rachel Gardner v. Augustus Gardner* (1859), WHS-DC; *Edmund Stockwell v. Rachael Stockwell* (1857), OSH-WC.

18. Smith-Rosenberg and Rosenberg, "Female Animal," 334 (quote); *Christiana Wadkins v. Samuel Wadkins* (1852), DCTX-WiC; *Emily Gorton v. Laurentine Gorton* (1859), STO-PC.

19. Abruzzo, *Polemical Pain,* 70 (quote); Pernick, *A Calculus of Suffering,* 43, 65, 230.

20. *Elizabeth Bruss v. Frederick Bruss* (1858), MIL-MC (all quotes); Clark, "'The Sacred Rights of the Weak,'" 463–493. One problem facing spouses who presented sexual cruelty cases was that few individuals, aside from physicians, were willing to come before the courts and provide testimony. For example, in the Brusses' divorce proceeding, a bill and an answer were the only marital commentaries.

21. A solid overview of venereal disease history is found within Allan M. Brandt, *No Magic Bullet: A Social History of Venereal Disease in the United States Since 1880* (New York: Oxford University Press, 1985).

22. Clare A. Lyons, *Sex Among the Rabble: An Intimate History of Gender and Power in the Age of Revolution, Philadelphia, 1730–1830* (Durham: University of North Carolina Press, 2006), 253 (first quote); *Sallie Seymour v. Mansfield Seymour* (1857), LVA-Me (second and third quotes). When asked by the court, one man said that it was "commonly known" that his neighbor, John Paige, had the clap. See *S. A. Paige v. John Paige* (1859), DCTX-GuC.

23. *Mary Chiles v. Washington Chiles* (1860), LVA-A (quote); *Frances Jones v. James Jones* (1862), LVA-Ly; *Joanna Frederick v. John Frederick* (1861), WHS-DC; Lyons, *Sex Among the Rabble,* 253–255; Scott C. Martin, *Devil of the Domestic Sphere: Temperance, Gender, and Middle-Class Ideology, 1800–1860* (DeKalb: Northern Illinois University Press, 2008), 25, 32.

24. *Mary Pierce v. John Pierce* (1855), DCTX-FC (quote); *Henry Batten v. Lansany Batten* (1853), LVA-I.

25. *Eliza Julien v. Peter Julien* (1857), LVA-No (all quotes). For another example of the naval pattern of infection, see *Annie Tegetthoff v. Leopold Tegetthoff* (1859), LVA-No. In cases involving disease transmission, a court might also prohibit the infected partner from remarrying. This was an attempt to stop the further spread of infection. See *Margaret Norwood v. Nathaniel Norwood* (1853), LVA-Br.

CHAPTER FOUR

1. *Harriett Smith v. William Smith* (1847), LVA-Bo. Ardent spirits were various distilled liquors, including rum, gin, and whiskey.

2. Ibid.; Schweninger, *Families in Crisis,* 40, 42; Glenda Riley, *Divorce: An American Tradition* (New York: Oxford University Press, 1991), 47.

3. *Skinner v. Skinner,* 5 Wis. 449 (1856) (first and second quotes); *Camp v. Camp,* 18 Tex. 528 (1857) (third quotes). This work does not attempt a statistical analysis of rates of intoxication, as the haphazard current condition of the court case materials precludes such an effort. For information on divorce law, see *Acts Passed at a General Assembly of the Commonwealth of Virginia [Acts of Virginia], 1826, 1840–1841, 1847–1848, 1852–1853;* H. P. N. Gammel, comp., *Laws of Texas, 1822–1897; Statutes of the Territory of Wisconsin, 1838–1839, 1849.* One Virginia resident claimed that the state could not allow drunkenness as a sole cause for divorce because "it would hold out too strong a temptation to any man to become a drunkard who wanted to get rid of his wife." See *Garland Mallory* (1850), Chesterfield Co., LVA-VL.

4. *Elizabeth White* (1840), Isle of Wight Co., LVA-VL (quote); *Eliza Miller v. Daniel Miller* (1858), LVA-No. Intoxication at the time of marriage was also cited as an excuse for poor matrimonial choices.

5. *Catharine Chadwick* (1848), Dane Co., WHS-WL (second quote); *Augusta Rhodius v. Christian Rhodius* (1861), DCTX-ComC (first quote); *San Antonio Ledger,* October 27, 1853.

6. W. J. Rorabaugh, *The Alcoholic Republic: An American Tradition* (New York: Oxford University Press, 1979), 169 (quote); Matthew Warner Osborn, "A Detestable Shrine: Alcohol Abuse in Antebellum Philadelphia," *Journal of the Early Republic* 29 (Spring 2009): 101–132.

7. *Elizabeth Brooks v. Fletcher Brooks* (1853), WW-WC. The Washingtonians were a temperance movement founded in the early republic that focused on proselytizing to the working classes. One of their most common tactics was to engage reformed alcoholics on wide-ranging speaking tours.

8. Michael Frank Diaries, 1840–1889, 1916, 1945, WHS (all quotes); Elizabeth Gaspar Brown, "Poor Relief in a Wisconsin County, 1846–1866: Administration and Recipients," *American Journal of Legal History* 20 (April 1976): 79–117; Campbell, *Gone to Texas*; Wyman, *The Wisconsin Frontier.*

9. *Sarah Briley v. John Briley* (1848), MIL-MC; *William Smyth v. Martha Smyth* (1842), ETRC-SAC (all quotes); *Eliza Wade v. Micajah Wade* (1856), DCTX-GuC; Julie Roy Jeffrey, *Frontier Women: "Civilizing" the West? 1840–1880* (New York: Hill and Wang, 1998), 44, 68; Richard N. Current, *The History of Wisconsin: Volume II. The Civil War Era, 1848–1873* (Madison: State Historical Society of Wisconsin, 1976), 71.

10. *Sarah Dunford v. William Dunford* (1857), DCTX-ColC; *Jane Baxter v. Charles Baxter* (1853), SHRL-JeC (first quote); *Daily Milwaukee News,* July 31, 1857; Benjamin Rush, *An Inquiry into the Effects of Ardent Spirits on the Body and Mind . . .* (Brookfield, MA: E. Merriam, 1814), 12 (second quote); James Miller, *Alcohol and Tobacco: Its Place and Power* (Philadelphia: Lindsay & Blakiston, 1859); *Paulina Caspary v. John Caspary* (1848), DCTX-ComC; Maria Farnum to Elizabeth Fletcher, Fletcher Papers, 1848-1850, WMC (third and fourth quotes); *Samuel Hashberger v. Elizabeth Hashberger* (1855), LVC-Roc; *Amanda Hiles v. George Hiles* (1854), LC-MC; *Fidelia Amelia Blackburn v. James Blackburn* (1854), PLAT-IC; *Elisabeth Palmer v. Thomas Palmer* (1850), MIL-MC. After all, as Jane Marie Pederson argues, "Work defined life's purpose, measured character, and was the essence of one's identity." In a period in which individuals felt as if Jeffersonian labor ethics were under attack by an increasingly aggressive market structure, many continued to cling to traditional understandings of work and reward. See Jane Marie Pederson, *Between Memory and Reality: Family and Community in Rural Wisconsin, 1870–1970* (Madison: University of Wisconsin Press, 1992), 143. A Virginia woman, Elizabeth Spratt, kept trying to follow her drunkard husband to his place of employment to verify that he was indeed working. However, he would always give her the slip and she could never determine his exact destination. See *Elizabeth Spratt* (1850), Smyth Co., LVA-VL.

11. *Elizabeth Doyle*(1848), Milwaukee Co., WHS-WL (quote).

12. *Sarah Robinson v. Samuel Robinson* (1840), LVA-C (all quotes). For a discussion of the southern female body, see Smith-Rosenberg and Rosenberg, "The Female Animal," 334–335; Poovey, "'Scenes of Indelicate Character,'" 146; McCurry, *Masters of Small Worlds.*

13. Carroll, *Homesteads Ungovernable,* xix, 77, 82.

14. *Catharine Crandall v. John Crandall* (1859), WHS-DC (first and second quotes); *Daily Milwaukee News,* July 8, 1859 (third quotes).

15. *Susan Hull v. Friend Hull* (1865), EC-EC (first quote); *Ida Schmidmeyer v. Francis Schmidmeyer* (1861), EC-EC; *Mary Moore v. Peter Moore* (1854), WW-WC (second quote); *Thomas Dowling v. Harriett Dowling* (1858), PLAT-IC; *Louisa Burgess v. Andrew Burgess* (1858), WHS-DC; *Catharine Teas v. Frederick Teas* (1855), EC-EC; Nesbit, *Wisconsin: A History*; Wyman, *Wisconsin Frontier.* Another Wisconsin wife stated, "I was in the habit of knitting sewing and washing for other people to get provisions." See Fanny *Heatly v. Robert Heatly* (1861), OSH-WC.

16. *Sarah Ann Heath* (1848), Richmond (Town/City), LVA-VL (first quote); *Martha*

Howell v. John Howell (1860), SHRL-JeC (second quote); *Sarah Reed v. Charles Reed* (1855), MIL-MC (third quote); *Margaret Zimmerschitte v. Fred Zimmerschitte* (1848), DCTX-ColC (fourth quote).

17. Martin, *Devil of the Domestic Sphere,* 107; Thomas R. Pegram, *Battling Demon Rum: The Struggle for a Dry America, 1800-1933* (Chicago: Ivan R. Dee, 1998), 54; David J. Mollenhoff, *Madison: A History of the Formative Years* (Madison: University of Wisconsin Press, 2003), 49, 67; Ian R. Tyrrell, *Sobering Up: From Temperance to Prohibition in Antebellum America, 1800-1860* (Westport, CT: Greenwood, 1979), 21; Emily Huse Letter, 1847, WHS (quote). In addition, local hotels (not identified as saloons on the census) would include a wide variety of intoxicants on their menus. For example, the menu at Madison's Capital House Hotel included claret, brandy, smooth ale, sherry, and native wine. A young man traveling to Green Bay, Wisconsin, in 1854 sent a letter to his parents describing the pressures attendant on men to drink. He wrote: "The amount of liquor drunk in the traveling community is absolutely amazing. If you are introduced to a company of gentlemen you must take a drink if you get into conversation." See Letter, 1854, J.M. Smith to My Dear Parents, Elisha Morrow Correspondence, 1840–1943, GB.

18. *Milly Ann Newsome v. Etard Newsome* (1859), DCTX-CC (first quote). See also *Laura Burch v. William Burch* (1842), WHS-DC; *Mary Crowell v. Joseph Crowell* (1859), LVA-Wa; *Nancy McMills v. John McMills* (1857), DCTX-HC. The importance of the tavern as a social place is evidenced by the fact that many divorce cases were heard in saloons, even those in which the primary issue was alcohol abuse.

19. Caleb Coker, ed., *The News from Brownsville: Helen Chapman's Letters from the Texas Military Frontier* (Austin: Texas State Historical Association, 1992), 186 (first quote). The Temperance Society of Dryden Village, Wisconsin, described how "peace & good order are never secure" in their community. See Minutes of Meetings of the Temperance Society of Dryden Village, 1859, Moffat-Hughes Family Papers, 1807-1949, RF; Pegram, *Battling Demon Rum,* 56; *Cornelia Ann Rossiter v. Charles Rossiter* (1849), MIL-MC (second and third quotes). Temperance groups echoed the idea that the moral weakness of the individual created a susceptibility to numerous vices. Early temperance reformer Daniel Drake in *A Discourse on Intemperance* stated that vices "obey the universal law of association; and hence gaming, knavery, and drunkenness are, sooner or later, found united in the same individual." See Daniel Drake, *A Discourse on Intemperance: Delivered at Cincinnati, March 1, 1828* (Cincinnati: Looker & Reynolds Printers, 1828), 30.

20. *Maria Bryerton v. William Bryerton* (1862), WHS-DC (all quotes); *Thomas Dowling v. Harriett Dowling* (1858), PLAT-IC.

21. *Elizabeth Waid v. William Waid* (1862), LVA-Fr; *Sarah Roper* (1847), Milwaukee Co., WHS-WL (all quotes). In her study of divorce notices in early national New England, Mary Beth Sievens finds women claiming possession of "personal items" such as "household furnishings and utensils" in the home. This partially resulted from women

bringing these items into marriage. See Mary Beth Sievens, *Stray Wives: Marital Conflict in Early National New England* (New York: New York University Press, 2005), 58.

22. *Pamelia Hatch v. Sylvania Hatch* (1838), VRHC-JC (quote); *Elizabeth Behrens v. Johann Behrens* (1855), DCTX-GC; *Jane Powell v. James Powell* (1851), LVA-G; *Magdalen Carter v. John Carter* (1853), LVA-Be; Bynum, *Unruly Women*, 77; Ranney, *Trusting Nothing to Providence;* Carroll, *Homesteads Ungovernable;* Marylynn Salmon, *Women and the Law of Property in Early America* (Chapel Hill: University of North Carolina Press, 1986); Suzanne Lebsock, *The Free Women of Petersburg: Status and Culture in a Southern Town, 1784–1860* (New York: W. W. Norton, 1984); Catherine B. Cleary, "Married Women's Property Rights in Wisconsin, 1846–1872," *Wisconsin Magazine of History* 78 (Winter 1994–1995): 110–137.

23. *Susan Hull v. Friend Hull* (1865), EC-EC; *Adelaide Klemo v. Thomas Klemo* (1862), PLAT-GnC; A. J. Hammerton, *Cruelty and Companionship*, 88, 114 (quote).

24. *Rebecca Hughes v. Torrence Hughes* (1840), LVA-C; *Mary Yearout v. Charles Yearout* (1857), LVA-Fl; *Cynthia Brown v. Johnathan Brown* (1863), DCTX-HC; *Dorothea Neeb v. Ludwig Neeb* (1861), DCTX-ComC; *Magdalene Theis v. Frederick Theis* (1853), WHS-DC; Jabour, *Marriage in the Early Republic*, 139.

25. This is not to say that brutal and violent incidents did not appear in the records when, in fact, they did. However, the wives in question presented these incidents most frequently as evidence in connection with a larger point about domestic labor disturbances.

26. M. L. Weems, *The Drunkard's Looking Glass, Reflecting A Faithful Likeness of the Drunkard . . .* (1818); Scott C. Martin, "Violence, Gender, and Intemperance in Early National Connecticut," *Journal of Social History* 34 (Winter 2000): 318–319; Marian Sandmaier, *The Invisible Alcoholics: Women and Alcohol Abuse in America* (St. Louis: McGraw-Hill, 1980), xv; Martin, *Devil of the Domestic Sphere*, 11; *Statutes of the Territory of Wisconsin, 1838–1839, 1849*. Mirroring the antebellum silences, only a small handful of historians have discussed female drinking at any length. The great majority of these treatments have taken place within examinations of reformist movements. As a result, their source materials have not allowed for an analysis of the relationship between alcohol and women at the individual level. This chapter addresses this gap in the historiography by exploring antebellum perceptions of the cruel female drunk. Scott Martin is an exception to the above statement in that, within his work on antebellum temperance ideology, he devotes an entire chapter to the female drunk. Admitting that intoxication existed in the female community was difficult because it hinted at the potential for immorality within women because, as Julie Roy Jeffery states, "The roots of drunkenness, it was supposed, lay in the moral weakness of the individual drinker." Jeffrey, *Frontier Women*, 222.

27. *Sandford Winterminte v. Esther Winterminte* (1853), WW-WC (first quote); *Elizabeth Jackson v. John F. Jackson* (1848), LVA-F; David G. Pugh, *Sons of Liberty: The*

Masculine Mind in Nineteenth-Century America (Westport, CT: Greenwood, 1983), 73; Poovey, "'Scenes of Indelicate Character,'" 146; Smith-Rosenberg, "The Female Animal," 334; Diane Price Herndl, *Invalid Women: Figuring Feminine Illness in American Fiction and Culture, 1840–1940* (Chapel Hill: University of North Carolina Press, 1993).

28. *Patrick Murphy v. Sarah Murphy* (1856), WHS-DC (all quotes). As documented by historian John Mack Faragher, only a few folk songs from this period praised the hardworking woman, while many lamented the lazy wife. One proclaimed, "But since my wife got married, Quite worthless she's become. An' all that I can say of her She will not stay at home." See Faragher, *Women and Men on the Overland Trail,* 63.

29. *Edward Schaeffner v. Louise Schaeffner* (1856), MIL-MC (all quotes); Stephan, *Redeeming the Southern Family,* 135; Scott C. Martin, *Devil of the Domestic Sphere: Temperance, Gender, and Middle-Class Ideology, 1800–1860* (DeKalb: Northern Illinois University Press, 2008), 22.

30. *Martin Fogle v. Elizabeth Fogle* (1856), LVA-Roc (all quotes). Some women in the case records even threatened to kill their offspring while under the influence of alcohol. One Texas wife "repeatedly threatened to drown herself & them." See *James Latimer v. Louisa Latimer* (1855), VRHC-JC.

31. *Mary Hewitt v. James Hewitt* (1856), DCTX-GuC; Jeffrey, *Frontier Women,* 14.

32. *Robert Ingraham* (1842), Harris Co., TSLAC-TL (all quotes); *Mary Chiles v. Washington Chiles* (1860), LVA-A; *Mary Hewitt v. James Hewitt* (1856), DCTX-GuC. Alcohol exacerbated differences in spending habits that were already present in marriages. As historian Mary Beth Sievens has noted in her study of marital conflict, "What wives believed were necessary purchases husbands often labeled unreasonable and unjustifiable." Sievens, *Stray Wives,* 37.

33. *Mary Chiles v. Washington Chiles* (1860), LVA-A (all quotes); *William Jones v. Caroline Jones* (1848), DCTX-ComC; *Elizabeth Jackson v. John F. Jackson* (1846), LVA-F; Conzen, *Immigrant Milwaukee,* 33; David Silkenat, *Moments of Despair*; Cashin, *Family Venture,* 18.

34. Pegram, *Battling Demon Rum,* 11, 54 (quote), 56; *Lucinda Hooper* (1848), Dodge Co., WHS-WL. Although the case records shed very little light on this practice, historians have described how antebellum women might hide addictions that stemmed from an initial medical treatment. See Pernick, *A Calculus of Suffering,* 65.

35. *Jonathan Bridges v. Margaret Bridges* (1864), WHS-DC (quote); *Ellender Arrington v. Arthur Arrington* (1853), LVA-Fr.

36. *Peter Yates v. Mary A. Yates* (1856), MIL-MC (first quote); *William Jones v. Caroline Jones* (1847), DCTX-GuC (second quote); Martin, *Devil of the Domestic Sphere,* 50–53.

37. *Ann McGivern v. John McGivern* (1860), PLAT-LC; *Robert Wilkins v. Elizabeth Wilkins* (1854), LVA-Ly; *Margaret Kramer v. Adam Kramer* (1860), SP-MC (quote); *William Fahey v. Margaret Fahey* (1855), MIL-MC.

38. Martin, *Devil of the Domestic Sphere,* 11 (quote).

CHAPTER FIVE

1. *Mary Grinnin v. Michael Grinnin* (1847), PLAT-GC.

2. Ibid.

3. My approach in this chapter is inspired by Melton McLaurin's analysis of the trial of a slave woman for the murder of her master in late antebellum Missouri. See Melton McLaurin, *Celia, A Slave* (Athens: University of Georgia Press, 1991). For purposes of narrative fluidity I use the terms "outsiders" or "third parties" to refer to individuals outside of the marriage in question. These terms are not meant to refer to an individual's status within a community.

4. Cott, *Public Vows*, 52; Grossberg, *Governing the Hearth*, 6 (first quote). See also Siegel, "'The Rule of Love,'" 2117–2207; Ruth Bloch, "The American Revolution, Wife Beating, and the Emergent Value of Privacy," *Early American Studies* 5 (Fall 2007): 223–251.

5. *Frances Jones v. James Jones* (1861), LVA-Ly; *Sallie Seymour v. Mansfield Seymour* (1857), LVA-Me; Kathleen Neils Conzen, *Immigrant Milwaukee, 1836–1860* (Cambridge: Harvard University Press, 1976), 56. For example, one couple decided to stay temporarily in a boarding house in Racine, Wisconsin, while they set up housekeeping nearby. They almost immediately disliked the boarding establishment and its owners, a Norwegian couple. Aside from complaints regarding cleanliness, the behavior of the Norwegian wife finally drove her boarders to flee in search of more pleasant living quarters. Looking back on their departure, the visitor recalled, "the wrath of the woman grew warmer & warmer untill it was too hot for us. . . . I never saw just such a woman in my life." As the couple was only staying briefly, they could censure the boardinghouse owners and even leave without encountering major difficulties. See Joel Howd Diary, 1855, WHS.

6. *Rosina Fulford v. James Fulford* (1859), LVA-No (second and third quotes); *Rachel Gardner v. Augustus Gardner* (1859), WHS-DC (first quote). In another case, the sister of a victim described how her sister would "always, if possible, hide & conceal anything of that kind from me and I only heard & saw it [meaning abuse] at times when he would break out in my presence and curse her and whip her." See *Elizabeth Ann Pratt v. John Pratt* (1855), DCTX-GoC. Scotty Brown, a Virginia wife, opened her divorce petition with the claim that she had "endured" her husband's ill treatment long enough and had "never made his conduct public." See *Scotty C. Brown* (1848), Shenandoah Co., LVA -VL. Of course, victims would try to keep cruelties secret in order to protect themselves from additional bodily harm. If information about poor treatment began to circulate in the public sphere, then a brutal spouse might take retaliation against the original victim. When Mark Finneman thought that his wife had told the neighbors about "his abuse" he threatened to kill her and gave her "a violent push with his hand" so that she fell over as a result. See *Harriet Finneman v. Mark Finneman* (1861), PLAT-GC.

7. *Anne Souther v. Simeon Souther* (1843), LVA-H (all quotes); *Sarah Womack* (1848), Halifax Co., LVA-VL.

8. Lewis, *Ladies and Gentlemen on Display*, 113 (first quote); *Amanda King v. Edward King* (1855), LVA-Me (second quote); *Elizabeth Waid v. William Waid* (1862), LVA-Fr. For two examples of the ways in which injuries were commented on, see *Wallace v. Thomas Wallace* (1853), DCTX-GoC; *Maria Jackson v. Alexander Jackson* (1855), SP-PC.

9. Cornelia Hughes Dayton, *Women before the Bar: Gender, Law, and Society in Connecticut, 1639–1789* (Chapel Hill: University of North Carolina Press, 1995), 130; *Sarah Kindrick v. Preston Kindrick* (1857), LVA-Wa (first quote); *Margaret Compton v. John Compton* (1851), LVA-R (second quote); *Jane Patrick v. William Patrick* (1860), WHS-DC (third quote); *Edmund Stockwell v. Rachael Stockwell* (1857), OSH-WC (fourth quote). On occasion, one partner would seek out the assistance of neighbors to create a mediation scenario. William Smith wrote in a letter that "you nighbors must try and make peace for us," thus placing his burden on others. See *Harriett Smith v. William Smith* (1847), LVA-Bo.

10. *John Curtiss* (1848), Rock Co., WHS-WL (first quote); *Eveline Evans v. Jackson Evans* (1854), SHRL-JeC (second quote).

11. Jabour, *Marriage in the Early Republic*, 139 (first quote); *Polly Cox v. Jordan Cox* (1859), LVA-Ch (second quote).

12. *Eunice Bascom v. Emerson Bascom* (1857), RF-SCC (quote); *Jane Risk v. James Risk* (1844), LVA-Ro.

13. *Harriet Budlong v. William Budlong* (1856), WW-RC (quote); *Eliza Ann Julien v. Peter Julien* (1857), LVA-No.

14. *Elizabeth Fitzgerald v. Samuel Fitzgerald* (1857), LVA-Ly (quote).

15. *Anne Souther v. Simeon Souther* (1843), LVA-H (first and second quotes); *Hariet Mallory* (1850), Richmond (Town/City) LVA-VL; *Robert Wilkins v. Elizabeth Wilkins* (1854), LVA-Ly; Snyder, *Brabbling Women*.

16. *Elizabeth Bryan v. James Bryan* (1853), DPL-DC (quote).

17. *Bridget Galvin v. Michael Galvin* (1856), PLAT-GC.

18. *Frederike Kupfer v. Andreas Kupfer* (1860), MIL-MC. See also *Emile Ellis v. D. R. Ellis* (1854), PLAT-IC; *Mary Ann Lawson v. Robert Lawson* (1856), WW-WC; *Mary Carpenter v. Horace Carpenter* (1864), EC-EC; *Margaret Lewis v. Lewis Lewis* (1861), PLAT-IC; Haag, "The 'Ill-Use of a Wife,'" 447–477.

19. *Octavia Richards v. Edward Richards* (1841), LVA-F; *Elizabeth Waid v. William Waid* (1862), LVA-Fr (quote). See also *Emeline Collins v. Josiah Collins* (1853), WHS-DC; *Elizabeth Kiley v. Thomas Kiley* (1852), SP-PC; *Mary Falvey v. Jeremiah Falvey* (1860), SHRL-JC; *William Donaho v. Mary Donaho* (1859), DCTX-CC; *Mary Byas v. William Byas* (1857), DCTX-WC; *Johannette Lange v. August Lange* (1862), WHS-DC; *Margaret Compton v. John Compton* (1851), LVA-R; *John Allridge v. Charlotta Allridge* (1859), LVA-Wa; *Susan Menefee v. Banks Menefee* (1854), LVA-F; *Isham*

Finch v. Marietta Finch (1855), DCTX-GoC; *Smith Elkins v. America Elkins* (1851), DPL-DC.

20. *Mary Dunn v. J. K. Dunn* (1858), DCTX-GuC (quotes); *Elizabeth Petteway v. Macaijah Petteway* (1851), DCTX-HC. Travel difficulties were also faced by Wisconsin wives. See Wyman, *The Wisconsin Frontier*, 182; Cashin, *A Family Venture*, 97 (quote); *Rebecca Harper v. Robert Harper* (1859), DCTX-FC. For a mention of strangers, see *Elizabeth Adair v. Joseph Adair* (1838), VRHC-JC; *Polly Reels v. Patrick Reels* (1843), DCTX-ColC.

21. *Sarah Womack* (1848), Halifax Co., LVA-VL (quote). See also *Wallace v. Thomas Wallace* (1853), DCTX-GoC; *Mary Daly v. Bernard Daly* (1846), MIL-MC; Stephanie M. H. Camp, *Closer to Freedom: Enslaved Women & Everyday Resistance in the Plantation South* (Chapel Hill: University of North Carolina Press, 2004).

22. Camp, *Closer to Freedom; Milly Perdue v. Isaiah Perdue* (1855), LVA-Fr; *A. Hall v. George Hall* (1864), LC-MC.

23. Tomes, "A 'Torrent of Abuse,'" 335 (quote). See also *Magdalen Carter v. John D. Carter* (1853), LVA-Be; *Hariet Mallory* (1850), Richmond (Town/City), LVA-VL; *Sarah Budd v. John Budd* (1863), OSH-WC; *Margaret Thompson v. George Thompson* (1862), WHS-DC; *Victoria Clement v. James Clement* (1860), LVA-Fr. The domestic threshold and sheltering could relate to a boarder offering to hide a woman within his or her separate room. These scenarios played out in ways remarkably similar to those in conflicts within separate abodes. One man, a boarder and the wife's brother, allowed the woman to stay in his room after her husband tried to choke her to death. When the husband learned she was inside, he grabbed a chair and tried to "smash" down the brother in order to gain entry, but he failed. However, the conflict continued as "he kept trying to get her out of the bedroom all night." See *Elisabeth Aldrich v. Andrew Aldrich* (1854), WW-RC.

24. McCurry, *Masters of Small Worlds*, 89–90, 193 (first quote); Bynum, *Unruly Women*, 77; *Richmond Dispatch,* January 26, 1858; *Mary John v. Lewis John* (1862), OSH-WC (second and third quotes); *James Brewer v. Harriet Ann Brewer* (1851), DCTX-NC.

25. For patterns of women leaving and returning, see *Bertha Sandberg v. Louis Sandberg* (1860), WW-WC; *Mary Elizabeth Andrews v. Edwin Andrews* (1859), PLAT-IC. Situations in which relatives provided shelter are too numerous to list, but for a few cases, note *Lucinda Hughes* (1846), Marion Co., LVA-VL; *Sarah Jane Bowen v. Richard Bowen* (1857), DCTX-CoC; *John Hays* (1848), Waukesha Co., WHS-WL; *Eliza McKee v. Steward McKee* (1848), PLAT-GC. For examples of economic complaints, see *William Warren v. Melvina Warren* (1859), WHS-DC; *Sally Palmer v. George Palmer* (n.d.), WW-WC.

26. *Lucinda Latham v. Silas Latham* (1854), LVA-Be (first quote); *Mary West v. John West* (1861), EC-EC (second quote); *Rhoda French v. John French* (1865), EC-EC (third quote); *Elizabeth Bryan v. James Bryan* (1853), DPL-DC (fourth quote).

27. Stansell, *City of Women*, 58; *James B. Harrison* (1849), King William Co., LVA-VL; *Hannah English v. Samuel English* (1841), MIL-MC (first quote); *Hannah Rankins v. Daniel Rankins* (1858), STO-PC (second and third quotes).

28. *Elizabeth Waid v. William Waid* (1855), LVA-Fr.

29. Stansell, *City of Women*, 81 (quote); Tomes, "'A Torrent of Abuse,'" 336 (quote); *Delia Tubbs v. Lyman Tubbs* (1862), OSH-WC; *Rebecca Abbott v. Quartus Abbott* (1849), PLAT-LC; *Lucy Ann Hewett v. Phipps Malcom Hewett* (1860), MIL-MC.

30. *Margaret Kramer v. Adam Kramer* (1860), SP-MC; *Polly Luce v. Chaney Luce* (1851), WHS-DC; *Ann McGivern v. John McGivern* (1860), PLAT-LC; *Robert Lawson v. Catharine Lawson* (1857), WW-WC; *Celia Ann Bailey v. Thomas Bailey* (1859), OSH-WC; *Elizabeth Kirby v. John Kirby* (1842), MIL-MC.

31. *Margaret Garrick v. William Garrick* (1858), OSH-WC (first quote); *Janett McDonald v. Charles McDonald* (1860), MIL-MC (second quote); *Rebecca Hanson v. Nicholi Hanson* (1853), DCTX-KC (third quote).

32. Cott, *Public Vows,* 37 (quote).

33. For studies that examine legal beliefs, see Michael Stephen Hindus, *Prison and Plantation: Crime, Justice, and Authority in Massachusetts and South Carolina, 1767–1878* (Chapel Hill: University of North Carolina Press, 1980). See also Edwards, *The People and Their Peace;* Wyatt-Brown, *Southern Honor.*

34. McCurry, *Masters of Small Worlds,* 193 (quotes). For information on the influence of Texas evangelical churches in this period, see Nick Malavis, "Equality under the Lord's Law: The Disciplinary Process in Texas Baptist Churches, 1833–1870," *East Texas Historical Quarterly* 31 (1993): 3–23; Robert Saunders Letters, 1829–1867, WMC. The emphasis/underlining appears as it is found within the text. Church discipline was rarely mentioned in the court records examined for this study. This silence has proved rather unexpected and perhaps reflects a desire on the part of the plaintiffs to avoid pointing out the church's prior failures to achieve marital harmony.

35. Stevenson, *Life in Black and White*, 31–32 (all quotes).

36. *Richmond Dispatch,* March 18, 1858; *Richmond Enquirer,* June 22, 1858 (all quotes).

37. R. D. Addington, *History of the Courtship and Marriage and Subsequent Married Life of Dr. R.D. Addington and Miss Hannah E. Weed . . .* (Richmond: Printed for the Author, 1857), 77 (quote).

38. *Emmaline Craddock v. Hugh Craddock* (1862), LVA-Be (quote); Laura F. Edwards, "Law, Domestic Violence, and the Limits of Patriarchal Authority in the Antebellum South," *Journal of Southern History* 65 (November 1999): 750–751; *Amanda Crow v. Samuel Crow* (1840), LVA-C; *Eliza Minnietree v. Archibald Minnietree* (1856), LVA-Ly.

39. *Wisconsin Free Democrat,* March 5, 1851 (first quote); *Mary Smith* (1858), Lafayette Co., WHS-WL (second and third quotes); Boswell, "The Social Acceptability of Nineteenth-Century Domestic Violence," 158.

40. *Sally Baggs v. Horace Baggs* (1854), WW-WC (quote).

41. *Elizabeth Jackson v. John Jackson* (1848), LVA-F (quote). Community members could support a husband's or wife's petition for divorce by creating a memorial relating the couples' inability to cohabit peacefully. Examples include *Seth Marquisee* (1845), Racine Co., WHS-WL; *Olympia Blood* (1841), King William Co., LVA-VL; Basch, *Framing American Divorce*.

42. *Mary Grinnin v. Michael Grinnin* (1847), PLAT-GC.

CONCLUSION

1. For the Cary quote, see Stowe, *Intimacy and Power in the Old South*, 128 (quote).

2. Abruzzo, *Polemical Pain*, 6 (first quote), 92 (second quote); Clark, "'The Sacred Rights of the Weak,'" 463–493. It can be astutely argued that the "discovery" of domestic violence in America occurred in the 1850s, not the 1960s.

NOTE ON SOURCES AND METHODOLOGY

1. Basch, *Framing American Divorce*, 194n8; James W. Ely Jr. and David Bodenhamer, "Regionalism and the Legal History of the South," in *Ambivalent Legacy: A Legal History of the South,* ed. David Bodenhamer and James W. Ely Jr. (Jackson: University Press of Mississippi, 1984), 3–29.

2. Wiener, *Men of Blood*, 7 (quote).

3. Blum, "When Marriages Fail," 205 (quote). When discussing antebellum North and South Carolina divorce cases, Laura Edwards states that the incompleteness of the records makes "quantitative analyses of the remaining material pointless." According to Edwards, "volume is crucial" when working with legal materials. She continues, "With thousands of cases . . . the information accumulates and forms patterns." See Edwards, *The People and Their Peace*, 23–24. See also Bloch, "The Emergent Value of Privacy," 229.

4. Nancy F. Cott, "Eighteenth-Century Family and Social Life," 20–43; Buckley, *The Great Catastrophe of My Life*; Peterson del Mar, *What Trouble I Have Seen*, 2; Gross, *Double Character*, 40. Many of the litigants discussed in this work employed lawyers to frame and present their cases to the court. Lawyers would shape their clients' accounts to best meet the local legal rules and boundaries. However, at the core, lawyers still relied upon the details of specific misconduct provided by the parties.

5. Faragher, *Women and Men on the Overland Trail*, 3 (quote).

BIBLIOGRAPHY

ARCHIVAL LEGAL SOURCES

Texas

Archives and Information Services Division. Texas State Library and Ar
chives Commission. Austin, Texas.
Texas Legislature, Memorials and Petitions. (TSLAC-TL)

Dallas Public Library. Dallas, Texas.
District Court Civil Case Papers, Dallas County. Microfilm. (DPL-DC)

East Texas Research Center. Ralph W. Steen Library. Stephen F. Austin Uni
versity. Nacogdoches, Texas.
District Court Civil Case Papers, San Augustine County. (ETRC-SAC)

Office of the District Clerk. Anderson County Courthouse. Palestine,
Texas. District Court Civil Case Papers, Anderson County. Microfilm.
(DCTX-AC)

Office of the District Clerk. Austin County Courthouse. La Grange, Texas.
District Court Civil Case Papers, Austin County. Microfilm. (DCTX-AuC)

Office of the District Clerk. Bell County Courthouse. Belton, Texas.
District Court Civil Case Papers, Bell County. Microfilm. (DCTX-BC)

Office of the District Clerk. Caldwell County Courthouse. Lockhart, Texas.
District Court Civil Case Papers, Caldwell County. Microfilm. (DCTX-CC)

Office of the District Clerk. Collin County Courthouse. McKinney, Texas.
District Court Civil Case Papers, Collin County. Microfilm. (DCTX-CoC)

Office of the District Clerk. Colorado County Courthouse. Columbus, Texas.
District Court Civil Case Papers, Colorado County. Microfilm. (DCTX-
ColC)

Office of the District Clerk. Comal County Courthouse. New Braunfels, Texas. District Court Civil Case Papers, Comal County. Microfilm. (DCTX-ComC)

Office of the District Clerk. Ellis County Courthouse. Waxahachie, Texas. District Court Civil Case Papers, Ellis County. Microfilm. (DCTX-EC)

Office of the District Clerk. Fayette County Courthouse. La Grange, Texas. District Court Civil Case Papers, Fayette County. Microfilm. (DCTX-FC)

Office of the District Clerk. Gillespie County Courthouse. Fredericksburg, Texas.
District Court Civil Case Papers, Gillespie County. Microfilm. (DCTX-GC)

Office of the District Clerk. Gonzales County Courthouse. Gonzales, Texas. District Court Civil Case Papers, Gonzales County. Microfilm. (DCTX-GoC)

Office of the District Clerk. Guadalupe County Courthouse. Seguin, Texas. District Court Civil Case Papers, Guadalupe County. Microfilm. (DCTX-GuC)

Office of the District Clerk. Harrison County Courthouse. Marshall, Texas. District Court Civil Case Papers, Harrison County. Microfilm. (DCTX-HC)

Office of the District Clerk. Kaufman County Courthouse. Kaufman, Texas. District Court Civil Case Papers, Kaufman County. Microfilm. (DCTX-KC)

Office of the District Clerk. Lavaca County Courthouse. Hallettsville, Texas. District Court Civil Case Papers, Lavaca County. (DCTX-LC)

Office of the District Clerk. Nacogdoches County Courthouse. Nacogdoches, Texas.
District Court Civil Case Papers, Nacogdoches County. (DCTX-NC)

Office of the District Clerk. Smith County Courthouse. Tyler, Texas. District Court Civil Case Papers, Smith County. Microfilm. (DCTX-SC)

Office of the District Clerk. Washington County Courthouse. Brenham, Texas.
   District Court Civil Case Papers, Washington County. Microfilm.
   (DCTX-WC)

Office of the District Clerk. Williamson County Courthouse. Georgetown,
   Texas.
   District Court Civil Case Papers, Williamson County. Microfilm.
   (DCTX-WiC)

Sam Houston Regional Library & Research Center. Liberty, Texas.
   District Court Civil Case Papers, Jasper County. (SHRL-JC)
   District Court Civil Case Papers, Jefferson County. (SHRL-JeC)
   District Court Civil Case Papers, Orange County. (SHRL-OC)

Victoria Regional History Center. Victoria College/University of Hous-
   ton-Victoria. Victoria, Texas.
   District Court Civil Case Papers, Jackson County. (VRHC-JC)

Virginia

Library of Virginia, Richmond, Virginia

   Chancery Causes, Albemarle County. (LVA-A)
   Chancery Causes, Bedford County. (LVA-Be)
   Chancery Causes, Botetourt County. (LVA-Bo)
   Chancery Causes, Brunswick County. (LVA-Br)
   Chancery Causes, Campbell County. (LVA-C)
   Chancery Causes, Chesterfield County. (LVA-Ch)
   Chancery Causes, Cumberland County. (LVA-Cu)
   Chancery Causes, Fauquier County. (LVA-F)
   Chancery Causes, Floyd County. (LVA-Fl)
   Chancery Causes, Franklin County. (LVA-Fr)
   Chancery Causes, Frederick County. (LVA-Fre)
   Chancery Causes, Greene County. (LVA-G)
   Chancery Causes, Hanover County. (LVA-H)
   Chancery Causes, Henry County. (LVA-He)
   Chancery Causes, Isle of Wight County. (LVA-I)
   Chancery Causes, Lancaster County. (LVA-L)
   Chancery Causes, Lynchburg City. (LVA-Ly)

Chancery Causes, Mecklenburg County. (LVA-Me)
Chancery Causes, Norfolk County. (LVA-No)
Chancery Causes, Prince Edward County. (LVA-Pr)
Chancery Causes, Rappahannock County. (LVA-R)
Chancery Causes, Rockbridge County. (LVA-Ro)
Chancery Causes, Rockingham County. (LVA-Roc)
Chancery Causes, Shenandoah County. (LVA-S)
Chancery Causes, Smyth County. (LVA-Sm)
Chancery Causes, Warren County. (LVA-W)
Chancery Causes, Washington County. (LVA-Wa)
Chancery Causes, Wise County. (LVA-Wi)
Legislative Petitions, Virginia Legislature. Microfilm. (LVA-VL)

Wisconsin

Archives and Area Research Center. Forrest R. Polk Library. University of
Wisconsin-Oshkosh. Oshkosh, Wisconsin.
    Circuit Court Case Files, Winnebago County. (OSH-WC)

Area Research Center and Southwest Wisconsin Room. Karrmann Library.
University of Wisconsin-Platteville. Platteville, Wisconsin.
    Circuit Court and County Court Case Files, Iowa County. (PLAT-IC)
    Circuit Court Case Files, Lafayette County. (PLAT-LC)
    Circuit Court Civil Case Files, Grant County. (PLAT-GC)
    Civil and Criminal Case Files, Green County. (PLAT-GnC)

Area Research Center. Chalmer Davee Library. University of Wisconsin-River Falls. River Falls, Wisconsin.
    Circuit Court Criminal and Civil Case Files, Saint Croix County. (RF-
    SCC)

Area Research Center. Harold Anderson Library. University of Wiscon-
sin-Whitewater. Whitewater, Wisconsin.
    Circuit Court Case Files, Walworth County. (WW-WC)
    Circuit Court Civil Case Files, Rock County. (WW-RC)

Area Research Center. Library Learning Center. University of Wiscon-
sin-Stout. Menomonie, Wisconsin.
    Circuit Court Case Files, Dunn County. (STO-DC)
    Circuit Court Civil and Criminal Case Files, Pepin County. (STO-PC)

Harry H. Anderson Research Library. Milwaukee County Historical Society. Milwaukee, Wisconsin.
   Circuit Court Civil Case Papers, Milwaukee County. (MIL-MC)

Library-Archive. Wisconsin Historical Society. Madison, Wisconsin.
   Circuit Court Case Files, Kenosha County. (WHS-KC)
   Circuit Court Civil Case Files, Dane County. Microfilm. (WHS-DC)
   Memorials and Petitions, Wisconsin Legislature. (WHS-WL)

Office of the Circuit Court Clerk. Richland County Courthouse. Richland, Wisconsin.
   Circuit Court Civil Case Papers, Richland County. (CCWI-RC)

Special Collections and Area Research Center. Cofrin Library. University of Wisconsin-Green Bay. Green Bay, Wisconsin.
   Circuit Court Case Files, Brown County. (GB-BC)
   Circuit Court Civil and Criminal Case Files, Manitowoc County. (GB-MC)
   Circuit Court Civil and Criminal Case Files, Oconto County. (GB-OC)
   Circuit Court Civil Case Files, Kewaunee County. (GB-KC)
   Circuit Court Civil Case Files, Outagamie County. (GB-OuC)

Special Collections and Area Research Center. Murphy Library Resource Center. University of Wisconsin-La Crosse. La Crosse, Wisconsin.
   Circuit Court Civil Case Files, Monroe County. (LC-MC)

Special Collections and Area Research Center. William D. McIntyre Library. University of Wisconsin-Eau Claire. Eau Claire, Wisconsin.
   Circuit Court Case Files, Eau Claire County. (EC-EC)

University Archives and Area Research Center. James H. Albertson Library. University of Wisconsin-Stevens Point. Stevens Point, Wisconsin.
   Circuit Court Case Files, Marathon County. (SP-MC)
   Circuit Court Civil Case Files, Portage County. (SP-PC)

ARCHIVAL MANUSCRIPT SOURCES

Albert H. Small Special Collections Library. University of Virginia. Charlottesville, Virginia. (UVA)
   William Matthews Blackford Diaries, 1849–1864.

Area Research Center. Chalmer Davee Library. University of Wisconsin-River Falls. River Falls, Wisconsin. (RF)
  Moffat-Hughes Family Papers, 1807–1949.

Dolph Briscoe Center for American History. University of Texas at Austin. Austin, Texas. (CAH)
  Jonathan Hamilton Baker Papers, 1858–1932.

Earl Gregg Swem Library. College of William and Mary. Williamsburg, Virginia. (WMC)
  Fletcher Papers, 1848–1850.
  Robert Saunders Letters, 1829–1867.

Library-Archive. Wisconsin Historical Society. Madison, Wisconsin. (WHS)
  Admissions Records, 1860–1908, 1935–1968, Mendota Mental Health Institute.
  Emily Huse Letter, 1847.
  Jacob and Jacob T. Foster Papers, 1847–1929.
  Joel Howd Diary, 1855.
  Michael Frank Diaries, 1840–1889, 1916, 1945.

Library and Archives. Virginia Historical Society. Richmond, Virginia. (VHS)
  Spragins Family Papers, 1753–1881.

Library of Virginia. Richmond, Virginia. (LVA)
  Eastern State Hospital Patient Register, 1853–1854.

Special Collections and Area Research Center. Cofrin Library. University of Wisconsin-Green Bay. Green Bay, Wisconsin. (GB)
  Elisha Morrow Correspondence, 1840–1943.

PERIODICALS

Clarksville (Texas) Standard
Daily Milwaukee News
Dallas Herald
Matagorda Gazette
Richmond Dispatch
Richmond Enquirer
Wisconsin Free Democrat

PUBLISHED PRIMARY SOURCES

Acts Passed at a General Assembly of the Commonwealth of Virginia [Acts of
   Virginia], 1826, 1840–1841, 1847–1848, 1852–1853.

Addington, R. D. *History of the Courtship and Marriage and Subsequent Married Life of Dr. R. D. Addington and Miss Hannah E. Weed* . . . Richmond:
   Printed for the Author, 1857.

Alcott, William. *The Young Husband; or, Duties of Man in the Marriage Relation*. Boston: C. D. Strong, 1851.

Andrew, James O. *Family Government, Or Treatise on Conjugal, Parental, Filial, and Other Duties*. Richmond, VA: John Early, 1848.

Bishop, Joel Prentiss. *New Commentaries on Marriage, Divorce, and Separation as to the Law, Evidence, Pleading, Practice, Forms, and the Evidence of Marriage in All Issues on a New System of Legal Exposition, Vol. 1*. Chicago: n.p., 1891.

Chase, Warren. *The Fugitive Wife: A Criticism on Marriage, Adultery, and Divorce*. Boston: Bela Marsh, 1866.

Coker, Caleb, ed. *The News from Brownsville: Helen Chapman's Letters from the Texas Military Frontier*. Austin: Texas State Historical Association, 1992.

Drake, Daniel. *A Discourse on Intemperance: Delivered at Cincinnati, March 1, 1828*. Cincinnati: Looker & Reynolds Printers, 1828.

Gammel, H. P. N., comp., *Laws of Texas, 1822–1897.* 10 vols. Austin, 1898–1902.

Miller, James. *Alcohol and Tobacco: Its Place and Power*. Philadelphia: Lindsay & Blakiston, 1859.

Morris, Robert. *Courtship and Matrimony*. Philadelphia: T. B. Peterson, 1858.

Rush, Benjamin. *An Inquiry into the Effects of Ardent Spirits upon the Human Body and Mind, With an Account of the Means of Preventing, and of the Remedies for Curing Them*. Brookfield, MA: E. Merriam, 1814.

Statutes of the Territory of Wisconsin, 1838–1839, 1849.

Texas Reports

Weems, M. L. *The Drunkard's Looking Glass, Reflecting A Faithful Likeness of the Drunkard*. . . . 1818.

Wisconsin Reports

The Young Wife's Book: A Manual of Moral, Religious, and Domestic Duties. Philadelphia: Carey, Lee, and Blanchard, 1838.

SECONDARY SOURCES

Abruzzo, Margaret. *Polemical Pain: Slavery, Cruelty, and the Rise of Humanitarianism*. Baltimore: Johns Hopkins University Press, 2011.

Adler, Jeffrey S. *First in Violence, Deepest in Dirt: Homicide in Chicago, 1875–1920.* Cambridge: Harvard University Press, 2006.

Anderson, Lars, and Peter Trudgill. *Bad Language.* Cambridge: Basil Blackwell, 1990.

Ayers, Edward. *Vengeance and Justice: Crime and Punishment in the 19th-Century American South.* New York: Oxford University Press, 1984.

Bardaglio, Peter. *Reconstructing the Household: Families, Sex, and the Law in the Nineteenth-Century South.* Chapel Hill: University of North Carolina Press, 1995.

Basch, Norma. *Framing American Divorce: From the Revolutionary Generation to the Victorians.* Berkeley: University of California Press, 1999.

Biggs, John M. *The Concept of Matrimonial Cruelty.* London: Athlone Press, 1962.

Bloch, Ruth. "The American Revolution, Wife Beating, and the Emergent Value of Privacy." *Early American Studies* 5 (Fall 2007): 223–251.

Blum, Francelle L. "When Marriages Fail: Divorce in Nineteenth-Century Texas." PhD diss., Rice University, 2008.

Boswell, Angela. *Her Act and Deed: Women's Lives in a Rural Southern County, 1837–1873.* College Station: Texas A&M University Press, 2001.

———. "The Social Acceptability of Nineteenth-Century Domestic Violence." In *The Southern Albatross: Race and Ethnicity in the American South,* edited by Philip D. Dillard and Randal Hall, 139–162. Macon: Mercer University Press, 1999.

Brandt, Allan M. *No Magic Bullet: A Social History of Venereal Disease in the United States Since 1880.* New York: Oxford University Press, 1985.

Brown, Elizabeth Gaspar. "Poor Relief in a Wisconsin County, 1846–1866: Administration and Recipients." *American Journal of Legal History* 20 (April 1976): 79–117.

Brown, Kathleen M. *Good Wives, Nasty Wenches, and Anxious Patriarchs: Gender, Race, and Power in Colonial Virginia.* Chapel Hill: University of North Carolina Press, 1996.

Bruce, Dickson D. Jr. *Violence and Culture in the Antebellum South.* Austin: University of Texas Press, 1979.

Buckley, Thomas E. *The Great Catastrophe of My Life: Divorce in the Old Dominion.* Chapel Hill: University of North Carolina Press, 2002.

Burnham, John. *Bad Habits: Drinking, Smoking, Taking Drugs, Gambling, Sexual Misbehavior, and Swearing in American History.* New York: New York University Press, 1993.

Bynum, Victoria E. *Unruly Women: The Politics of Social & Sexual Control in the Old South.* Chapel Hill: University of North Carolina Press, 1992.

Camp, Stephanie M. H. *Closer to Freedom: Enslaved Women & Everyday*

Resistance in the Plantation South. Chapel Hill: University of North Carolina Press, 2004.

Campbell, Randolph. *Gone to Texas: A History of the Lone Star State*. New York: Oxford University Press, 2003.

Carroll, Mark M. *Homesteads Ungovernable: Families, Sex, Race, and the Law in Frontier Texas, 1823–1860*. Austin: University of Texas Press, 2001.

Cash, W. J. *The Mind of the South*. New York: A. A. Knopf, 1957.

Cashin, Joan. *A Family Venture: Men and Women on the Southern Frontier*. New York: Oxford University Press, 1991.

Censer, Jane Turner. "'Smiling Through Her Tears': Ante-Bellum Southern Women and Divorce." *American Journal of Legal History* 25 (January 1981): 24–47.

Chused, Richard H. *Private Acts in Public Places: A Social History of Divorce in the Formative Era of American Family Law*. Philadelphia: University of Pennsylvania Press, 1994.

Clark, Elizabeth B. "'The Sacred Rights of the Weak': Pain, Sympathy, and the Culture of Individual Rights in Antebellum America." *Journal of American History* 82 (September 1995): 463–493.

Clark, Elizabeth Blair. "The Inward Fire: A History of Martial Cruelty in the Northeastern United States, 1800–1860." PhD diss., Harvard University, 2006.

Cleary, Catherine B. "Married Women's Property Rights in Wisconsin, 1846–1872." *Wisconsin Magazine of History* 78 (Winter 1994–1995): 110–137.

Conzen, Kathleen Neils. *Immigrant Milwaukee, 1836–1860*. Cambridge: Harvard University Press, 1976.

Cott, Nancy F. "Eighteenth-Century Family and Social Life Revealed in Massachusetts Divorce Records." *Journal of Social History* 10 (Autumn 1976): 20–43.

———. "Passionlessness: An Interpretation of Victorian Sexual Ideology, 1790–1850." *Signs* 4 (Winter 1978): 219–236.

———. *Public Vows: A History of Marriage and the Nation*. Cambridge: Harvard University Press, 2001.

Courtwright, David T. *Violent Land: Single Men and Social Disorder from the Frontier to the Inner City*. Cambridge: Harvard University Press, 1996.

Cramer, Clayton E. *Concealed Weapon Laws of the Early Republic: Dueling, Southern Violence, and Moral Reform*. Westport, CT: Praeger, 1999.

Current, Richard N. *The History of Wisconsin: Volume II. The Civil War Era, 1848–1873*. Madison: State Historical Society of Wisconsin, 1976.

Dayton, Cornelia Hughes. *Women before the Bar: Gender, Law, and Society in Connecticut, 1639–1789*. Chapel Hill: University of North Carolina Press, 1995.

Degler, Carl N. *At Odds: Women and the Family in America from the Revolution to the Present.* New York: Oxford University Press, 1980.

Edwards, Laura F. "Law, Domestic Violence, and the Limits of Patriarchal Authority in the Antebellum South." In *Gender and the Southern Body Politic,* edited by Nancy Bercaw, 63–94. Jackson: University Press of Mississippi, 2000.

———. "Law, Domestic Violence, and the Limits of Patriarchal Authority in the Antebellum South." *Journal of Southern History* 65 (November 1999): 733–770.

———. *The People and Their Peace: Legal Culture and the Transformation of Inequality in the Post-Revolutionary South.* Chapel Hill: University of North Carolina Press, 2009.

Ely, James W. Jr., and David Bodenhamer. "Regionalism and the Legal History of the South." In *Ambivalent Legacy: A Legal History of the South,* edited by David Bodenhamer and James W. Ely Jr., 3–29. Jackson: University Press of Mississippi, 1984.

Faragher, John Mack. *Women and Men on the Overland Trail.* New Haven: Yale University Press, 1979.

Faust, Drew Gilpin. *Mothers of Invention: Women of the Slaveholding South in the American Civil War.* Chapel Hill: University of North Carolina Press, 1996.

Finkelhor, David, and Kersti Yllo. *License to Rape: Sexual Abuse of Wives.* New York: Holt, Rinehart, and Winston, 1985.

Fox-Genovese, Elizabeth. "Family and Female Identity in the Antebellum South: Sarah Gayle and Her Family." In *In Joy and In Sorrow: Women, Family, and Marriage in the Victorian South, 1830–1900,* edited by Carol Bleser, 15–31. New York: Oxford University Press, 1991.

Friedman, Lawrence M. *A History of American Law.* New York: Simon and Schuster, 1973.

Friend, Craig Thompson, and Anya Jabour. "Introduction: Families, Values, and Southern History." In *Family Values in the Old South,* edited by Craig Thompson Friend and Anya Jabour, 1–15. Gainesville: University Press of Florida, 2010.

Glass, Nancy, et al. "Non-Fatal Strangulation Is an Important Risk Factor for Homicide of Women." *Journal of Emergency Medicine* 35 (October 2008): 329–335.

Glenn, Myra C. *Campaigns against Corporal Punishment: Prisoners, Sailors, Women, and Children in Antebellum America.* Albany: State University of New York Press, 1984.

Gordon, Linda. *Heroes of Their Own Lives: The Politics and History of Family Violence: Boston 1880–1960.* Urbana: University of Illinois Press, 1988.

Griswold, Robert. "The Evolution of the Doctrine of Mental Cruelty in Victorian American Divorce, 1790–1900." *Journal of Social History* 20 (Autumn 1986): 127–148.

———. *Family and Divorce in California, 1850–1890.* Albany: State University of New York Press, 1982.

———. "Law, Sex, Cruelty, and Divorce in Victorian America, 1840–1900." *American Quarterly* 38 (Winter 1986): 721–745.

Gross, Ariela J. *Double Character: Slavery and Mastery in the Antebellum Southern Courtroom.* Princeton: Princeton University Press, 2000.

Grossberg, Michael. *Governing the Hearth: Law and Family in Nineteenth-Century America.* Chapel Hill: University of North Carolina Press, 1985.

Haag, Pamela. "The 'Ill-Use of a Wife': Patterns of Working-Class Violence in Domestic and Public New York City, 1860–1880." *Journal of Social History* 25 (Spring 1992): 447–477.

Halttunen, Karen. *Confidence Men and Painted Women: A Study of Middle-Class Culture in America, 1830–1870.* New Haven: Yale University Press, 1982.

Hammerton, A. J. *Cruelty and Companionship: Conflict in Nineteenth-Century Married Life.* London: Routledge, 1992.

Hartog, Hendrik. "Lawyering, Husbands' Rights, and the 'Unwritten Law' in Nineteenth-Century America." *Journal of American History* 84 (June 1997): 67–96.

———. *Man and Wife in America: A History.* Cambridge: Harvard University Press, 2000.

Headlee, Thomas Jefferson Jr. *The Virginia State Court System.* Richmond: Virginia State Library, 1969.

Herndl, Diane Price. *Invalid Women: Figuring Feminine Illness in American Fiction and Culture, 1840–1940.* Chapel Hill: University of North Carolina Press, 1993.

Hindus, Michael Stephen. *Prison and Plantation: Crime, Justice, and Authority in Massachusetts and South Carolina, 1767–1878.* Chapel Hill: University of North Carolina Press, 1980.

Hughes, Geoffrey. *Swearing: A Social History of Foul Language, Oaths, and Profanity in English.* New York: Blackwell, 1991.

Ireland, Robert M. "The Libertine Must Die: Sexual Dishonor and the Unwritten Law in the Nineteenth-Century United States." *Journal of Social History* 23 (Autumn 1989): 27–44.

Isaac, Rhys. *The Transformation of Virginia, 1740–1790.* Chapel Hill: University of North Carolina Press, 1982.

Jabour, Anya. *Marriage in the Early Republic: Elizabeth and William Wirt and the Companionate Ideal.* Baltimore: Johns Hopkins University Press, 1998.

Jeffrey, Julie Roy. *Frontier Women: "Civilizing" the West? 1840–1880.* New York: Hill and Wang, 1998.

Jordan, Terry G. "Population Origins in Texas, 1850." *Geographical Review* 59 (January 1969): 83–103.

Keetley, Dawn. "From Anger to Jealousy: Explaining Domestic Homicide in Antebellum America." *Journal of Social History* 42 (Winter 2008): 269–297.

Kelley, Robin D. G. *Race Rebels: Culture, Politics, and the Black Working Class.* New York: Free Press, 1994.

Kolchin, Peter. *A Sphinx on the American Land: The Nineteenth-Century South in Comparative Perspective.* Baton Rouge: Louisiana State University Press, 2003.

Leavitt, Judith Walzer. *Brought to Bed: Childbearing in America, 1750 to 1950.* New York: Oxford University Press, 1986.

Lebsock, Suzanne. *The Free Women of Petersburg: Status and Culture in a Southern Town, 1784–1860.* New York: W. W. Norton, 1984.

———. *A Murder in Virginia: Southern Justice on Trial.* New York: W. W. Norton, 2003.

Lewis, Charlene M. Boyer. *Ladies and Gentlemen on Display: Planter Society at the Virginia Springs, 1790–1860.* Charlottesville: University Press of Virginia, 2001.

Link, William A. *Roots of Secession: Slavery and Politics in Antebellum Virginia.* Chapel Hill: University of North Carolina Press, 2003.

Lyons, Clare A. *Sex Among the Rabble: An Intimate History of Gender and Power in the Age of Revolution, Philadelphia, 1730–1830.* Chapel Hill: University of North Carolina Press, 2006.

Malavis, Nick. "Equality under the Lord's Law: The Disciplinary Process in Texas Baptist Churches, 1833–1870." *East Texas Historical Quarterly* 31 (1993): 3–23.

Markham, Edward Jr. "The Reception of the Common Law of England and the Judicial Attitude Toward That Reception, 1850–1859." *Texas Law Review* 29 (1951).

Martin, Scott C. *Devil of the Domestic Sphere: Temperance, Gender, and Middle-Class Ideology, 1800–1860.* DeKalb: Northern Illinois University Press, 2008.

———. "Violence, Gender, and Intemperance in Early National Connecticut." *Journal of Social History* 34 (Winter 2000): 309–325.

McCurry, Stephanie. *Masters of Small Worlds: Yeoman Households, Gender*

Relations, and the Political Culture of the Antebellum South Carolina Low Country. New York: Oxford University Press, 1995.

McKnight, Joseph W. "The Spanish Legacy to Texas Law." American Journal of Legal History 3 (1959): 222–241.

McLaurin, Melton. Celia, A Slave. Athens: University of Georgia Press, 1991.

McMillen, Sally G. Motherhood in the Old South: Pregnancy, Childbirth, and Infant Rearing. Baton Rouge: Louisiana State University Press, 1990.

Mollenhoff, David J. Madison: A History of the Formative Years. Madison: University of Wisconsin Press, 2003.

Moon, Danelle. "Marital Violence Revealed: California Divorce, 1850–1899." Master's thesis, California State University, Fullerton, 1994.

Nesbit, Robert C. Wisconsin: A History. 2nd rev. ed., edited by William F. Thompson. Madison: University of Wisconsin Press, 1989.

Nisbett, Richard, and Dov Cohen. Culture of Honor: The Psychology of Violence in the South. New York: Oxford University Press, 1996.

Osborn, Matthew Warner. "A Detestable Shrine: Alcohol Abuse in Antebellum Philadelphia." Journal of the Early Republic 29 (Spring 2009): 101–132.

Paton, Diana. No Bond but the Law: Punishment, Race, and Gender in Jamaican State Formation, 1780–1870. Durham, NC: Duke University Press, 2004.

Pederson, Jane Marie. Between Memory and Reality: Family and Community in Rural Wisconsin, 1870–1970. Madison: University of Wisconsin Press, 1992.

Pegram, Thomas R. Battling Demon Rum: The Struggle for a Dry America, 1800–1933. Chicago: Ivan R. Dee, 1998.

Pernick, Martin S. A Calculus of Suffering: Pain, Professionalism, and Anesthesia in Nineteenth-Century America. New York: Columbia University Press, 1985.

Peterson, David. "Eden Defiled: A History of Violence Against Wives in Oregon." PhD diss., University of Oregon, 1993.

———. "Wife Beating: An American Tradition." Journal of Interdisciplinary History 23 (Summer 1992): 97–118.

Peterson del Mar, David. What Trouble I Have Seen: A History of Violence Against Wives. Cambridge: Harvard University Press, 1996.

Phillips, Roderick. Putting Asunder: A History of Divorce in Western Society. Cambridge: Cambridge University Press, 1988.

Pleck, Elizabeth. Domestic Tyranny: The Making of Social Policy Against Family Violence from Colonial Times to the Present. New York: Oxford University Press, 1987.

Poovey, Mary. "'Scenes of an Indelicate Character': The Medical 'Treatment' of Victorian Women." In The Making of the Modern Body: Sexuality *and Society in the Nineteenth Century,* edited by Catherine Gallagher and Thomas Laqueur, 137–168. Berkeley: University of California Press, 1987.

Pugh, David G. *Sons of Liberty: The Masculine Mind in Nineteenth-Century America.* Westport, CT: Greenwood, 1983.

Ranney, Joseph A. *Trusting Nothing to Providence: A History of Wisconsin's Legal System.* Madison: University of Wisconsin Law School, 1999.

Renzetti, Claire. "The Challenge to Feminism Posed by Women's Use of Violence in Intimate Relationships." In *New Versions of Victims: Feminists Struggle with the Concept,* edited by Sharon Lamb, 42–56. New York: New York University Press, 1999.

Riley, Glenda. *Divorce: An American Tradition.* New York: Oxford University Press, 1991.

———."Legislative Divorce in Virginia, 1803–1850." *Journal of the Early Republic* 11 (Spring 1991): 51–67.

Rorabaugh, W. J. *The Alcoholic Republic: An American Tradition.* New York: Oxford University Press, 1979.

Rothman, Joshua. *Notorious in the Neighborhood: Sex and Families across the Color Line in Virginia, 1787–1861.* Chapel Hill: University of North Carolina Press, 2003.

Rotundo, E. Anthony. "Body and Soul: Changing Ideals of American Middle-Class Manhood, 1770–1920." *Journal of Social History* 16 (Summer 1983): 23–38.

Salmon, Marylynn. *Women and the Law of Property in Early America.* Chapel Hill: University of North Carolina Press, 1986.

Sandmaier, Marian. *The Invisible Alcoholics: Women and Alcohol Abuse in America.* St. Louis: McGraw-Hill, 1980.

Schweninger, Loren. *Families in Crisis in the Old South: Divorce, Slavery, and the Law.* Chapel Hill: University of North Carolina Press, 2012.

Scott, Anne Firor. "Women's Perspective on the Patriarchy in the 1850s." In *Half Sisters of History: Southern Women and the American Past,* edited by Catherine Clinton, 76–92. Durham, NC: Duke University Press, 1994.

Siegel, Reva. "'The Rule of Love': Wife Beating as Prerogative and Privacy." *Yale Law Journal* 105 (June 1996): 2117–2207.

Sievens, Mary Beth. *Stray Wives: Marital Conflict in Early National New England.* New York: New York University Press, 2005.

Silkenat, David. *Moments of Despair: Suicide, Despair, & Debt in Civil War Era North Carolina.* Chapel Hill: University of North Carolina Press, 2011.

Smith, Alice E. *The History of Wisconsin: Volume 1, From Exploration to Statehood.* Madison: State Historical Society of Wisconsin, 1973.

Smith, Merril D. "Introduction: Studying Rape in American History." In *Sex*

Without Consent: Rape and Sexual Coercion in America, edited by Merril D. Smith, 1–9. New York: New York University Press, 2001.

Smith-Rosenberg, Carroll, and Charles Rosenberg. "The Female Animal: Medical and Biological Views of Woman and Her Role in Nineteenth-Century America." *Journal of American History* 60 (September 1973): 332–356.

Snyder, Terri. *Brabbling Women: Disorderly Speech and the Law in Early Virginia.* Ithaca, NY: Cornell University Press, 2003.

Stamp, Mark A. "Wisconsin's Marriage and Divorce Laws: A Historical Perspective." Master's thesis, University of Wisconsin, 1982.

Stansell, Christine. *City of Women: Sex and Class in New York, 1789–1860.* Urbana: University of Illinois Press, 1987.

Stephan, Scott. *Redeeming the Southern Family: Evangelical Women and Domestic Devotion in the Antebellum South.* Athens: University of Georgia Press, 2008.

Stevenson, Brenda. *Life in Black and White: Family and Community in the Slave South.* New York: Oxford University Press, 1996.

Stowe, Steven M. *Intimacy and Power in the Old South: Ritual in the Lives of Planters.* Baltimore: Johns Hopkins University Press, 1987.

Tomes, Nancy. "A 'Torrent of Abuse': Crimes of Violence between Working-Class Men and Women in London, 1840–1875." *Journal of Social History* 11 (Spring 1978): 328–345.

Tyrrell, Ian R. *Sobering Up: From Temperance to Prohibition in Antebellum America, 1800–1860.* Westport, CT: Greenwood, 1979.

Vandal, Gilles. *Rethinking Southern Violence: Homicides in Post–Civil War Louisiana, 1866–1884.* Columbus: Ohio State University Press, 2000.

Wells, Jonathan Daniel. *The Origins of the Southern Middle Class, 1800–1861.* Chapel Hill: University of North Carolina Press, 2004.

Welter, Barbara. "The Cult of True Womanhood: 1820–1860." *American Quarterly* 18 (Summer 1966): 151–174.

Wiener, Martin J. *Men of Blood: Violence, Manliness, and Criminal Justice in Victorian England.* Cambridge: Cambridge University Press, 2004.

Wood, Kristen E. "Making a Home in Public: Domesticity, Authority, and Family in the Old South's Public Houses," in *Family Values in the Old South,* edited by Craig Thompson Friend and Anya Jabour, 158–185. Gainesville: University Press of Florida, 2010.

Wyatt-Brown, Bertram. *The Shaping of Southern Culture: Honor, Grace, and War, 1760s–1880s.* Chapel Hill: University of North Carolina Press, 2001.

———. *Southern Honor: Ethics and Behavior in the Old South.* New York: Oxford University Press, 1982.

Wyman, Mark. *The Wisconsin Frontier.* Bloomington: Indiana University Press, 1998.

NOTES

Durrell, M. A., 24

duty: in frontier society, 8–9; traditional understandings of, 4, 11

duty. *See also* marital duties

Dye, Joseph, 118

Earl, Jane, 156n18

Edgrine, John, 68

Edwards, Laura, 17–18, 40, 133, 146n11, 158n33, 171n3

emotional distress, and verbal cruelty, 14, 16, 21, 25, 27, 30, 31, 32–33, 34, 35, 37

emotional distress. *See also* anxiety

emotions and feelings: channeling into productive processes, 4–5; in divorce records, 11; heightened recognition of, 4; mastery of, 22, 37, 150n19; morality sections of newspapers instructing on emotional control, 20; physical cruelty of husbands as expression of uncontrollable emotions, 40, 55–56; physical cruelty of wives as expression of uncontrollable emotions, 58; physical violence as expression of uncontrollable emotions, 39; sexual cruelty of husbands as expression of uncontrollable emotions, 73; verbal cruelty of husbands as expression of uncontrollable emotions, 18–19, 36–37; verbal cruelty of wives as expression of uncontrollable emotions, 25, 35–36, 154n47

emotions and feelings. *See also* emotional distress; tempers

enslaved dependents: criticisms of treatment of, 7, 140; gossip of, 59; lack of legal recognition of unions, 7; physical cruelty as challenge to authority, 158n33; sexual assault of enslaved women, 76; and variable

nature of cruelty, 4; whipping as form of punishment for, 48, 50, 52

enslaved dependents. *See also* slavery

epithets: and cursing or swearing, 16, 21, 22, 26, 149n8; ethnic epithets, 12, 149n8; public name-calling, 15–16, 18–19, 21; religious epithets, 149n8; and sexual morality, 16, 18, 19, 24, 26, 27; as term of derision, 148n3; as verbal cruelty, 12, 14, 15–16, 23, 27, 37, 61, 148n6

Evans, Eveline, 115

Evans, Jackson, 115

Evans v. Evans (1790), 3, 148n3

excesses, cruel treatment, or outrages: as reason for divorce, 10, 65, 66, 83; verbal cruelty included in, 14

Fairchild, Elvira, 21

Faragher, John Mack, 158n32, 166n28

Farrell, Isaac, 35

Faust, Drew Gilpin, 5

Finneman, Mark, 167n6

Flinn, James, 49, 50

Flinn, Nancy, 152n37

Florida, 82

Fogle, Elizabeth, 102–103

Fogle, Martin, 102–103

Fowler, Eliza, 31

Fowler, John, 31

Frank, Michael, 87

Frederic, Samuel, 16

Frederic, Victoria, 16

free blacks, 132, 147n12

French, John, 155n7

French, Rhoda, 155n7

frontier society: de facto divorces in, 42; difficulties of daily life in, 63, 83, 99; divorce records of, 7–8; epithets as verbal cruelty in, 15, 23; food preparation duties in, 60–61; and gender